# Uncoverings

## 2017

Volume 38 of the Research Papers
of the American Quilt Study Group

Edited by Lynne Zacek Bassett

D1262215

Presented at Manchester, New Hampshire
October 18–22, 2017

Copyright © 2017 by the American Quilt Study Group
All rights reserved

Copyright note: This is a collective work. AQSG holds the
copyright to this volume and any reproduction of it in whole.
Right to the individual articles are held by the authors.
Requests for permission to quote or reproduce material from
any article should be addressed to the author.

Published by the American Quilt Study Group
1610 L Street
Lincoln, NE 68508

Manufactured in the United States

*Uncoverings* is indexed in:
America: History and Life
ARTbibliographies
BHA (Bibliography of the History of Art)
Clothing and Textile Arts Index
Feminist Periodicals
Historical Abstracts
MLA International Bibliography
Sociological Abstracts

ISBN 10 digit 1-877859-33-8
ISBN 13 digit 978-1-877859-33-5
ISSN 0277-0628
Library of Congress catalog number: 81-649486

Cover image: Acadian format quilt of household fabrics,
c. 1970, 62 x 46 inches, Acadian Museum, Erath, Louisiana.
Photograph by Dale Drake.

# Table of Contents

# Foreword

NEW ENGLAND HAS A DEEP HISTORY of quilt ownership and quilt-making. The thirty-eighth annual Seminar of the American Quilt Study Group, held in Manchester, New Hampshire, offered attendees an especially rich opportunity to see and study eighteenth- and nineteenth-century quilts from the region. Coincidentally, the papers presented at the Seminar and published in this volume of *Uncoverings* also focused on the history of American quiltmaking prior to the twentieth century.

Dana Fobes Bowne has made the exciting discovery of a quilt with a history of ownership in Connecticut in the seventeenth century. Her exploration of the quilt's origins, ownership, and peregrination exemplifies the process of untangling fact from fiction, with tantalizing results. Could this Bengali quilt be the earliest quilt with a documented history of use in America? Remarkably, it was found in a regional arts and culture museum across the country—in Spokane, Washington—documenting not only the westward movement of many Americans in the nineteenth and early twentieth centuries, but how you never know what treasures of American history you will find in any collection, large or small.

The migration of quilts with their owners in the nineteenth century is a topic examined by Kathy Moore in her paper identifying a distinctive regional pattern, which she has dubbed the "Harlequin Star." Using resources that have developed over the past twenty years, including state quilt documentation books, The Quilt Index, and online genealogical databases, Moore has developed a material culture study of "taste and design aesthetics" originating in the southeastern corner of Tennessee and the northwestern corner of Georgia in the second half of the nineteenth century.

The skill of the quiltmakers in piecing tiny diamond-shaped bits of fabric to create the remarkable Harlequin Star quilts is perhaps matched only by the skill of the makers of the masterpiece Baltimore Album quilts examined by Deborah Cooney and Ronda McAllen. The research of

Cooney and McAllen has uncovered new information about possible designers and motivations for the making of these other regional quilts. Shifting cultural ideals for women in the 1840s stimulated in part by the Second Great Awakening are manifested in these great American quilts.

While some populations adapted to changing economies, technology, and environments, others remained steadfast in their cultural traditions. Dale Drake explores the weaving heritage of the Louisiana Acadians as seen in their quilts. Generations of Acadians over the course of several hundred years practiced particular textile traditions, including the weaving of *cotonnade* fabrics for use in clothing and in the household. Drake points out that while quilting is not a long-held practice among Acadians, an analysis of their quilts of the late nineteenth and twentieth centuries reveals much about their weaving traditions and their cultural values of self-sufficiency, frugality, and family.

The tale of a family discovered by Linda Welters and Rachel May through their interdisciplinary research, spurred by three unfinished quilts in the costume and textile collection of the University of Rhode Island, provides important documentation of antebellum American society and the early-twentieth-century Colonial Revival. Ties of friendship, family, and business between North and South—and the North's complicity in the slave trade prior to the Civil War—are revealed in the bits of paper used as templates in the hexagonal patches of the quilt tops. The later generation who picked up the project imprinted their own cultural values on the quilt tops.

Appliqué and whitework quilts, along with embroidered and looped-weft woven bed covers often feature motifs of baskets of flowers, and border designs of swags gathered up under bowknots. Such designs are so common that perhaps we take them for granted and do not think to consider their origins—but this is the inquiry made by Anita Loscalzo in her essay, "Whence Garlands, Swags, Bowknots, and Baskets?" Loscalzo traces their path from ancient Egyptian and Greco-Roman carvings to sixteenth-century architecture, to eighteenth-century manuals for artists and craftsmen, to American architecture, furniture, and other decorative arts, and—finally—to the quilted, embroidered, stenciled, and woven bed covers with which we are all so familiar.

—Lynne Zacek Bassett

# "Old Quilt Brought to America"

Dana Fobes Bowne

*The textile collection of the Northwest Museum of Arts and Culture in Spokane, Washington, includes an unusual embroidered quilt. A handwritten note in its file suggests that it was made in sixteenth-century England. However, the quilt's motifs indicate that it is more likely a seventeenth-century Bengali quilt. This paper describes the process to determine when and where the quilt was actually made and how it came to Spokane. Research methods included examining the quilt, fiber identification, comparison with photographs of other textiles, consultations with curators, and genealogical research. The results support a seventeenth-century Bengali provenance and suggest that the quilt was probably brought to colonial Massachusetts by ancestors of the donor. It was apparently kept in the family and handed down through generations, making it likely one of the oldest surviving quilts in the United States.*

## The Quilt

Since 1937, an extraordinary quilt has been in the collection of the Northwest Museum of Arts and Culture in Spokane, Washington. Its motifs—exquisitely embroidered—are not commonly found on American quilts. They suggest Persian design. However, a handwritten note in the quilt's accession file suggests a different provenance (fig. 1). It states:

> *Old quilt brought to America by the Willoughby family of Norwich, Connecticut in 1693.*
>
> *Said to have been embroidered by some of Queen Elizabeth's Maids of Honor.*

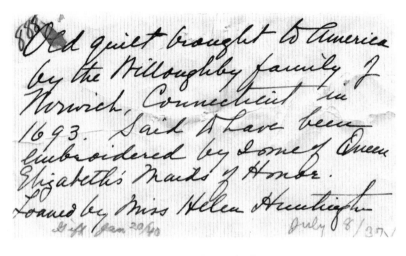

Fig. 1. Provenance note. Northwest Museum of Arts and Culture, 888.1

What is this piece? How did it get to Spokane? Is there any truth in the handwritten note? In support of the ultimate conclusion that this quilt is a rare surviving seventeenth-century Bengali quilt, this paper discusses early Bengali quilts and their historical context, offers a plausible explanation of how this particular quilt traveled halfway around the world, and examines the veracity of the handwritten note. Researching an early quilt can be like trying to assemble a complex jigsaw puzzle. But, in this case, surprisingly, the pieces fit together.

The monochromatic quilt, identified in the museum's database as accession number 888.1, has a face consisting of four panels of cream-colored plain weave cotton cloth. The backing is made of five light tan panels of plain weave cotton cloth (the color of both facing and backing panels may have changed with time). The panels are of varying widths, with the narrowest measuring just under eleven inches and the widest measuring just under twenty-seven inches. Examination of a tiny hole in the facing fabric with a magnifying lens revealed that there is an inner layer of coarsely woven fabric, a fiber of which was removed and identified as cotton.

Botanical motifs cover the quilt, embroidered with silk. Measurements taken at several different locations revealed that the stitching, which holds the layers together, was worked at fifteen to sixteen stitches to the inch (fig. 2). Because of their small size and consistency, some previous

Fig. 2. Detail: stitches on the face of the quilt. Northwest Museum of Arts and Culture, 888.1.
Photo by Brooke Shelman Wagner.

examiners thought the stitches might be machine work.[1] However, upon viewing the back of the quilt through a 10x magnification lens, the stitching was clearly identified as backstitching accomplished by hand.

The overall design, seen more clearly on the back of the quilt, is medallion-style (fig. 3). The central medallion has a diameter of forty-three inches, which is almost half the width of the quilt. It consists of a circle, nearly sixteen inches in diameter, surrounded by five rings of varying widths (figs. 4, 5). Above and below this are medallions and smaller motifs of stylized flowers and leaves (figs. 6, 7). The rest of the

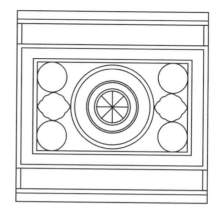

Fig. 3. Outline drawing showing overall design. Northwest Museum of Arts and Culture, 888.1. Drawing by Valerie Wahl and Jose Angel.

Fig. 4. Detail: Central medallion as seen on the quilt backing. Northwest Museum of Arts and Culture, 888.1. Photo by Brooke Shelman Wagner.

Fig. 5. Detail: One-quarter of the central medallion with five concentric rings. Northwest Museum of Arts and Culture, 888.1. Photo by Brooke Shelman Wagner.

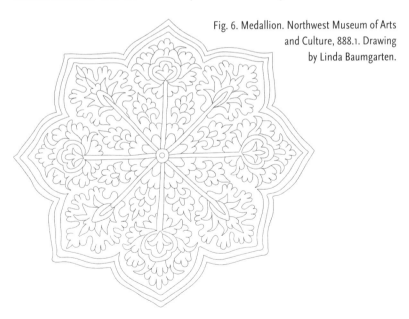

Fig. 6. Medallion. Northwest Museum of Arts and Culture, 888.1. Drawing by Linda Baumgarten.

Fig. 7. Medallion and smaller motifs. Northwest Museum of Arts and Culture, 888.1. Drawing by Linda Baumgarten.

quilt consists of borders and motifs in straight rows (fig. 8). The quilt's design and motifs were puzzling until Lisa Evans, an American quilt historian, viewed photographs and noted that the quilt's "foliate motifs" and "concentric rings," along with the silk thread, are "typical of Bengali trade quilts."[2]

Fig. 8. Detail: Border as seen on the quilt backing. Northwest Museum of Arts and Culture, 888.1. Photo by Brooke Shelman Wagner.

Bengali Quilts

Beginning around AD 1532, a "rare group of embroidered quilts" was made in Bengal for export to Europe by the Portuguese.[3] (Bengal refers to the region surrounding the Ganges River Delta, which today includes the Indian state of West Bengal, the country of Bangladesh, and parts of other states in northeast India). These quilts have been grouped together and attributed to Bengal based on the following generally shared common characteristics:[4]

1. The fabric is white cotton, embroidered with naturally colored wild silk. Typically, the silk is golden yellow.[5]

2. The embroidery is usually worked in chain stitch. Backstitch or running stitches were more commonly used in earlier pieces.[6]

3. The pieces are generally large, often roughly nine by eleven feet.[7]

4. Typical overall designs include concentric bands around a central medallion or rectangular panel.[8]

5. The motifs are usually figurative designs, as well as geometric motifs and medallions. The figures often represent European hunters, soldiers, and sailors; animals; stories from the Old Testament; Greco-Roman legends; and Hindu themes.[9]

These quilts are referred to as Bengali quilts, Bengalla quilts, Satgaon quilts, *colchas*, or Indo-Portuguese quilts in the literature. They are generally attributed to Satgaon (Modern *Saptagram* in the state of West Bengal), where the Portuguese established a "factory" around 1536, or the nearby city of Hooghly *(Hoogli* or *Hugli)*, which later replaced Satgaon as the principal port of Bengal.[10] As Portuguese trade from India declined, the production of Bengali quilts for export to Europe continued under Dutch and English patronage, at least through the mid-seventeenth century.[11]

### Early Indian Textiles

The trade in Bengali textiles did not begin with the arrival of Europeans. Bengal was a commercial center long before the sixteenth century and early written records indicate that embroidered quilts were made there before the arrival of the Portuguese.[12] India itself has a long history of producing and exporting sophisticated textiles; evidence suggests that cotton textiles were exported from the Indus River Valley (historically India) to Mesopotamia (Iraq) and Egypt at least three thousand years ago.[13] By the first century AD, there was an extensive overland trading network in India through which textiles were brought from inland areas to Indian ports and then shipped to ports on the Persian Gulf and the Red Sea, leading to Mediterranean markets.[14] After the collapse of the Roman Empire in AD 476, Arab and Gujarati traders began to control the regional sea trade, and Indian textiles enjoyed a wide distribution throughout the Arab world.[15] Arab and Gujarati traders also played an important role in the exportation of Indian textiles to Southeast Asia, where they were exchanged for pepper, cloves, nutmeg, and mace from eastern Indonesia, which could then be sold for high prices in India, West Asia, China, and Europe.[16]

India dominated the world's cotton textile markets for centuries, and the quality of its cotton was legendary.[17] In the thirteenth century, Marco Polo described the cloth of the Coromandel Coast as "the finest and most beautiful cottons that are to be found in any part of the world."[18] The Portuguese took control of the lucrative trade in Indian textiles and spices by the middle of the sixteenth century and they established fortified trading centers along India's coastline where goods, especially textiles, could be made to order for export to Europe.[19] Bengal was already well-established as a center of international trade. (A European traveler who journeyed there in 1503 noted that fifty ships "laden with silk and cotton goods" sailed from Bengal each year to "Persia, Egypt, Arabia and Ethiopia.")[20] This commercial activity continued under European patronage, as Nick Robins, a financial analyst who trained as a historian, describes: "Known throughout the East as a 'Paradise on Earth' for its wealth and prosperity, Bengal attracted waves of European merchants for the quality of its textiles."[21] Robins explains that the Portuguese were replaced in Bengal by the Dutch, who were themselves followed by the English, and adds that by the 1720s, over half of English imports from Asia originated in Bengal, "most of this coming via Calcutta."[22] According to Harvard historian Sven Beckert, textiles from Bengal played an important role in an increasingly global trade that had far-reaching consequences. He writes, "…African rulers and merchants almost always demanded cotton cloth in exchange for slaves… cotton from India, slaves from Africa, and sugar from the Caribbean moved across the planet in a complex commercial dance. The huge demand for slaves in the Americas created pressure to secure more cotton cloth from India. Not surprisingly, Francis Baring of the East India Company, concluded in 1793 that from Bengal an 'astonishing Mass of Wealth has flowed . . . into the Lap of Great Britain."[23]

## Is it a Bengali Quilt?

Many aspects of the quilt are consistent with the general characteristics of a Bengali quilt:

1.  The following fibers from the quilt were identified as cotton: The face fabric warp and weft, the backing warp and weft, and a fiber from the coarse inner layer (whether weft or warp is uncertain).[24] The embroidery thread is silk.[25]

2.  It is a large piece (93 1/2 by 95 1/4 inches).

3.  Its overall layout is consistent with those of Bengali quilts.

4.  The quilt's motifs suggest a Bengali origin.

When compared to photographs and descriptions of early quilts from other regions of India, this quilt appears to have features the most in common with Bengali quilts.[26] Two of its motifs are strikingly similar to

Fig. 9. Border motif and small motif. Northwest Museum of Arts and Culture, 888.1. Drawing by Linda Baumgarten.

ones in a late sixteenth-century Bengali quilt in Hardwick Hall in England, which is considered to be an early example of this type of quilt (fig. 9).[27] Rosemary Crill, Senior Curator of South and South East Asian textiles at the Victoria and Albert Museum in London, viewed photographs of the Spokane quilt and discussed them with colleagues. She wrote, "We think that as far as one can tell without looking at the piece itself that it appears to be Bengali, and I would think it dates from the 17th century."[28]

Some of the quilt's motifs appear in images of textiles, ceramics, and architecture from various places throughout the Middle East.[29] This fact does not weaken the argument for a Bengali provenance; rather, it reflects the widespread and long-lasting influence of Persian art and culture in the region.[30] Iran, along with most of Asia, was under Mongol control during during the Ilkhanid Period (1256–1353). During this time, ". . . the Iranian world [became] the undisputed center of artistic and cultural innovation in the Islamic world," according to Sheila S. Blair and Jonathan M. Bloom.[31] Suzan Yalman explains that the political situation "created an environment of tremendous cultural exchange . . . East Asian elements absorbed into the existing Perso-Islamic repertoire created a new artistic vocabulary, one that was emulated from Anatolia to India, profoundly affecting artistic production."[32] This influence continued during the Timurid Dynasty (1370–1506) and the Safavid Empire (1501–1732) when, as Aimée E. Froom writes, "The design traditions of fifteenth-century Iran and Central Asia, in particular vine scrolls, arabesques, and Chinese-inspired motifs, were passed on to the three great early modern Islamic empires: the Safavids of Iran, the Ottomans, and the Mughals of India."[33]

The wealthiest of these empires was the Mughal Empire (1526–1858), and by the 1570s, Bengal was under its control.[34] The Mughals were heavily influenced by Persian culture and Persian became the official language of the Empire.[35] Under the Mughal emperor Akbar "the Great" (r.1556–1605), Indian artisans were encouraged to collaborate with skilled immigrant Iranian artisans.[36] This collaboration between Iranian and Indian artists is reflected in Mughal architecture and decorative arts, including surviving examples of Mughal embroidery. John Irwin noted that the earliest Mughal works appear very similar to Persian embroidered work. "But," he wrote, "a distinctive Mughal style soon appears" with both Indian and Persian influences.[37] This "complex intermingling of very different traditions" continued under Akbar's successors.[38]

However, although the quilt's design suggests that it was made in Bengal during the Mughal period, there are two problems with this assumption:

1. The embroidery thread is not the golden or light yellow silk that is typical of Bengali quilts. Several types of silk were used in India, however, and by the seventeenth century, Bengal was a major source of Indian mulberry silk, a lustrous, white silk that is produced by the domesticated *Bombyx mori* silk moth.[39] Regardless, the author does not know what type of silk was used in this quilt.

2. Human and animal motifs generally appear in photographs and written descriptions of Bengali quilts, but there are no images of humans or animals in this quilt. However, Bengali quilts apparently did not always include such designs: In describing the embroidered quilts of Bengal from this time period, Rosemary Crill writes that they "often" mixed Indian design with "scenes of European soldiers and galleons" and "often" showed images from European myths or the Bible.[40] Perhaps this quilt is one of the few that did not.

Possibly, the quilt was actually made outside of Bengal, but it is also possible that it was made in Bengal, but originally intended for domestic use. Patrick J. Finn observes that, "The Indo-Portuguese quilts were produced for a select, upper-class clientele in India and abroad although most of the extant quilts are those that were traded to Europe."[41] European "factories" were not the only source of Mughal textiles; there were also imperial workshops *(kar-khanehs* or *Kharkhanas),* "of which there were nearly a hundred by the 1590s."[42] During the sixteenth and seventeenth centuries, textiles, furnishings, carpets, coins, illustrated books, and other items were produced in these workshops, and in workshops established by wealthy patrons.[43] Perhaps the quilt was made in an imperial workshop and originally intended for a wealthy Indian client who did not want figures of European hunters, soldiers, and sailors, or Old Testament stories. Future research may shed more light, but, for now, seventeenth-century Bengal remains the most likely provenance.

### How Did the Quilt Get to Spokane?

Miss Helen Huntington (1897–1970) of Spokane loaned the quilt to the Northwest Museum of Arts and Culture in 1937, but the actual donor was her aunt, Miss Gertrude Lea Huntington (1873–1963), the sister of Helen's deceased father, David Lynde Huntington (1870–1929). (Appendix A) In 1942, Gertrude indicated in writing that the quilt was now a gift to the museum.[44] The quilt was most likely an heirloom passed down through the Huntington family: Helen was not yet married when she signed the loan agreement, and Gertrude never married, so the quilt did not come from a spouse's family. Furthermore, Helen's mother, Helen Longacre Huntington (1871?–1946, the widow of David Lynde Huntington), was still alive in 1942. If the quilt was passed down through the Longacre family, then Helen Longacre Huntington would have been the one to officially present it, rather than her sister-in-law, Gertrude Huntington.

David Lynde Huntington moved from Philadelphia to Spokane in 1894 to work for the Washington Water Power Company, where he played an important role in the development of hydro-electric energy in the Inland Northwest. His parents and younger sister Gertrude apparently followed him to Spokane sometime after that.[45] Research suggests that the quilt was originally acquired by an ancestor of David and Gertrude Huntington and brought to Massachusetts during the seventeenth century. At this time, the earliest known surviving bed quilts from Massachusetts date from the second quarter of the eighteenth century.[46] Plausibly, this quilt may be an even earlier survivor.

Appendix A: Selective Lynde/Huntington Family Tree

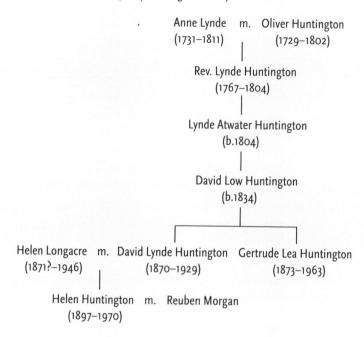

Anne Lynde  m.  Oliver Huntington
(1731–1811)         (1729–1802)

Rev. Lynde Huntington
(1767–1804)

Lynde Atwater Huntington
(b.1804)

David Low Huntington
(b.1834)

Helen Longacre  m.  David Lynde Huntington  Gertrude Lea Huntington
(1871?–1946)              (1870–1929)                (1873–1963)

Helen Huntington  m.  Reuben Morgan
(1897–1970)

## The Seventeenth Century

If the quilt dates to seventeenth-century India, the logical assumption is that it was first brought to England by the English East India Company (EIC), which was established in 1600. The EIC's trade in Indian textiles grew rapidly. According to Sven Beckert, "The East India Company as early as 1621 imported an estimated fifty thousand pieces of cotton goods into Britain. Forty years later, this number had increased by a factor of five."[47] Another reasonable assumption is that the quilt was first brought to the Netherlands by the Dutch United East India Company (De Veering Ooost-Indische Compagnie or VOC). The VOC, established in 1602, also imported large quantities of textiles from India during the seventeenth and eighteenth centuries.[48] The quilt would have then been brought to America.

Quilts were present in seventeenth-century America, but written evidence suggests that they were rare, costly, and often owned by those with connections to commercial trade. Proof of their existence comes primarily from occasional references in inventories, especially those taken upon the death of an individual.[49] The earliest known reference to a quilt in New England is the listing of an English quilt in the inventory of Samuel Fuller of Plymouth in 1633.[50] The earliest reference in Virginia is an "East Indyan Quilte" listed in the 1655 inventory of Major Peter Walker of Northampton County.[51]

Compared to other types of textiles, bed quilts were uncommon. In her study of early colonial quilts, Sally Garoutte examined the probate inventories of Providence, Rhode Island, from 1670 to 1726; the probate inventories of Plymouth Colony from 1631 to 1687; the wills of New Hampshire from 1659 to 1717; and the wills and a few inventories of the Hartford District of Connecticut from 1640 to 1749. When considering only the strictly seventeenth-century records, Garoutte found just three quilts listed, and the total number of quilts from all four sources was only ten, representing slightly over one percent of the total bedding items listed.[52]

George Francis Dow's survey of inventories from Essex County, Massachusetts (Salem area), between 1635 and 1674 also found that quilts were mentioned only rarely in comparison with "coverlets" and "ruggs."[53] The total number of quilt owners identified in the Dow and Garoutte studies combined was twelve, but only six of them were in the seventeenth century, and all but one of them owned only one or two quilts.[54] Even the very wealthy apparently did not own a large number of quilts. When Captain William Kidd married in 1691, his bride, Sarah Bradley Cox Oort, was "the wealthiest widow in New York City."[55] Their 1692 household inventory included three quilts.[56]

Boston was the economic center of the region during this time, and the textile trade played an important role in its commercial activity. However, quilts were uncommon even there: Linda Baumgarten examined 485 household inventories from Boston covering three different five-year periods: 1650 to 1655, 1670 to 1675, and 1690 to 1695. She found only thirteen quilts listed. In comparison, the inventories listed 151 bed rugs, twenty-six coverlets, and ten counterpanes.[57]

Sally Garoutte concluded that, "Quilts in the colonial period were few and far between. They were the most expensive bedding item inventoried. They were found in the households of well-to-do people, usually merchant-importers."[58] Indeed, of the twelve individuals who were identified as early American quilt owners by Garoutte and Dow, five were described as "merchants" and a sixth was described as a "mariner."[59]

By the middle of the seventeenth century, a pattern of transatlantic trade was established between New England, the West Indies, and Europe.[60] Ownership of quilts by individuals with connections to this maritime commerce reflects the economic power of the emerging—and increasingly wealthy—merchant class. A hierarchy developed among those associated with trade: "In a roughly ascending scale, itinerant and market peddlers were found at the very bottom ranks, superseded by traders, shopkeepers, seamen, sea captains, and finally by merchants."[61] In Massachusetts, most merchants, naturally, lived in the port cities of Boston, Charlestown, and Salem.[62] While international trade was their main occupation, many also engaged in shipbuilding, banking, and the construction of wharves and warehouses."[63] Lorinda B. R. Goodwin, in her study of the merchants of colonial Massachusetts, writes that they "gradually accumulated political power to match their wealth."[64]

This was the world of Gertrude's and David's ancestor, Francis Willoughby (c. 1613–1671), who is usually referred to as "Deputy Governor Francis Willoughby." Born in England, he first arrived in Charlestown, Massachusetts, in 1638. He had a long career in public service, beginning in 1640 by being chosen as a selectman. From 1665 until his death in 1671, he was Deputy Governor of the Massachusetts Bay Colony, serving under Governor Richard Bellingham. As early as 1641, he owned a shipyard, was building a ship, and was investing in the building of warehouses and wharves to facilitate the landing of goods, "not only from about home but from further parts."[65] Deputy Governor Francis Willoughby went back to England in 1651, where he served as a Commissioner of the Navy and also as a Member of Parliament, before returning to Massachusetts in 1662.[66] He was widowed twice before marrying Margaret Locke, herself a young widow, about 1659. (Appendix B) A successful merchant, Willoughby was a wealthy man when he died in 1671. A description of his estate lists a "mansion," a warehouse, a wharf, "large collections of ship stores," and more than 2,000 acres of land. His household goods were said to include furniture, carpets, several sets of hangings, curtains, valances, chair cushions, pictures, books, and many other items. Frustratingly, this description did not mention quilts—nor any type of bed covering.[67] But, it is clear that Deputy Governor Francis Willoughby had the means to purchase the quilt, and he could have done so when he was in London, or as part of his mercantile activities.

However, Margaret Locke's deceased first husband, Daniel Taylor, was a wealthy London merchant.[68] Deputy Governor Francis  noted in his will

Appendix B: Selective Willoughby/Lynde Family Tree

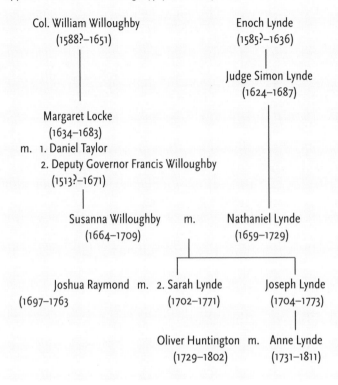

that "my dear wife hath brought a considerable estate with her. . ." and stipulated that, "I doe *[sic]* freely confirm her right in, and accordingly bequeath unto her all that household goods, plate, and Jewells *[sic]* which she brought with her. . ."[69] It is possible that the quilt was originally acquired by Daniel Taylor, and his widow brought it with her when she married the Deputy Governor.

Deputy Governor Francis and Margaret Locke Willoughby had several children, including a daughter, Susanna. In 1683, Susanna married Nathaniel Lynde, whose father was known as Judge Simon Lynde of Boston. (Appendix B) Judge Simon Lynde's father, Enoch Lynde, was born about 1585. Enoch's parents were apparently originally Dutch, but had emigrated to England. "While a resident of London, Enoch Lynde was a merchant engaged in foreign trade, and was for some years connected with the postal service between England and Holland."[70] Enoch died in

1636 when Simon was only twelve years old, but Simon initially followed in his father's footsteps and "was for a time apprenticed to a Mr. Delaney, a merchant of London . . . He subsequently went to Holland, where he still followed mercantile pursuits."[71] Judge Simon Lynde came to New England in 1650. After a distinguished legal career, he died in 1687, "possessed of a large estate."[72] Either Enoch Lynde or Judge Simon Lynde could have acquired the quilt in either the Netherlands or England.

It is plausible, therefore, that either Susanna Willoughby Lynde or her husband, Nathaniel Lynde, received the quilt as a gift, or through inheritance. The quilt may then have passed down to one of their grand-daughters, Anne Lynde. Anne could have brought the quilt with her when she married Oliver Huntington, a "farmer and shoemaker," in Lebanon, Connecticut, in 1761. Oliver and Anne Lynde Huntington were the great-great-grandparents of David Lynde Huntington and Gertrude Huntington, the donor of the quilt (Appendix A).[73]

However rare and appreciated the quilt may have been originally, it was undoubtedly folded and put away at some point. It is unlikely that it would have survived two or three hundred years of continuous use, and there are, unfortunately, clear marks on it that suggest that it was kept folded for a long period of time. Averil Colby, in her study of quilting in England and Wales, offers an explanation that may be applicable to this quilt: Colby refers to the popularity of colorful chintz fabric from India during the seventeenth century.[74] This popularity increased as time went on, resulting in an "enormous increase" in chintz exports to Europe between 1680 and 1685, as John Irwin and Katherine B. Brett noted in their classic text, *Origins of Chintz*.[75] After a temporary lull related to the French ban on chintz imports in 1686, English East India Company orders for chintz again surged by 1694.[76] Colby speculated that, "The furore [sic] created by the 'novelty' of the coloured quilts may have been the reason for the preservation of some others of the time, which may have been considered to be sad in appearance. Their monochrome colours, such as indigo, dull yellow, or drab, or a light coffee colour, would not have pleased the mood of the Restoration period [generally 1660–1688] and perhaps they were banished to the bottom of the linen chest, while the more favoured, with branches and flowers on a light ground, graced the beds."[77] Colby then offers as an example a seventeenth-century mono-chromatic Portuguese quilt which survived in apparently very good condition. Perhaps, the subject of this paper was also carefully put away when colorful chintz fabric was the height of fashion, thus helping to preserve it.

Gertrude Huntington was probably the author of the note that links the quilt to the Willoughby family of Norwich, Connecticut in 1693, and the court of Elizabeth I. The penmanship in the note is similar to that of a letter written by her in 1942.[78] Although the information in the note is not completely accurate, it is not a complete fiction, either. Rather, it appears that family stories and historical events were blended together over time to form a narrative that contained pieces of the truth.

The author—presumably Gertrude—sounds understandably cautious when writing, *Said to have been embroidered by some of Queen Elizabeth's Maids of Honor,* but the attribution is actually somewhat plausible: Many embroidered items survive from the Elizabethan era, and both Queen Elizabeth I and her father, Henry VIII, owned quilts.[79] However, Gertrude did not need to know this because there was another reason for her to connect the quilt with the Queen.

Gertrude, who was born in 1873, may have heard family stories about objects that were handed down through the descendants of Deputy Governor Francis Willoughby. The objects were described in an article published in *The New England Historical and Genealogical Register* in 1886. The author of the article, Evelyn McCurdy Salisbury, herself claimed descent from Susanna Willoughby and Nathaniel Lynde.[80] In the article, she quotes another descendant as saying, "I have heard my aunt, who lived to be ninety-two, speak of her remembrance of articles of value said to have come down from noble Willoughby relatives in England."[81] A third descendant provided a description of "a tablecloth composed of fine linen, with two rows of exquisite needlework across it, said to have been wrought by Queen Elizabeth when she was confined in the Tower in her sister Mary's reign, and given by her to Francis Lord Willoughby, who was a relative and thus handed down." (This is a reference to Sir Francis Willoughby, who lived in the sixteenth century, not Deputy Governor Francis Willoughby.) Supposedly, the initials "F. M. W." were embroidered on one end of this tablecloth. A fourth descendant had told the author the "tradition that the tablecloth wrought by Queen Elizabeth in the Tower was given to a Maid of Honor of hers, who was one of the Willoughbys, by whom it came down in the family." Also described was "a very large, massive, richly carved chest . . . in which the tablecloth and other articles are said to have been brought from England." Evelyn McCurdy Salisbury went on to identify the sister of Sir Francis Willoughby, Margaret

Willoughby of Wollaton, as the "Maid of Honor," and concluded with a discussion of how Colonel William Willoughby (the father of Deputy Governor Francis Willoughby) may have been related to either of two noble families who were connected to the court of Elizabeth I: The Willoughbys of Wollaton (the family of Sir Francis Willoughby and Margaret Willoughby of Wollaton) or the Willoughby de Eresby family.[82] Mrs. Salisbury and her husband, Edward Elbridge Salisbury, repeated these stories in an 1892 publication.[83]

In 1928, a photograph of the carved chest appeared in an Ohio newspaper, accompanied by an article. The article offered an extensive history of the chest, stating that it was originally acquired by Col. William Willoughby, and that it was passed down to one of his great-granddaughters, Sarah Lynde Raymond (1702–1771).[84] (Appendix B) This chest is now in the permanent collection of the Wadsworth Atheneum Museum of Art in Hartford, Connecticut.[85] The article also repeated the history of the table cloth, which was referred to as the "Queen Elizabeth Table Cloth," and described as it as made of "the finest damask." At the time, it was owned by a "prominent" resident of Toledo, Walter J. Sherman, who was a direct Willoughby descendant.[86]

Whether or not these items actually had anything to do with Queen Elizabeth I, there were clearly family stories suggesting a connection. Over time, the true provenance of the quilt was probably forgotten, and it was falsely assumed to be one of the "articles of value" handed down from noble Willoughbys, and associated with the Queen. The story of the "Maid of Honor" became some of Queen Elizabeth's Maids of Honor.

Nevertheless, the family stories do contain historical truth: Sir Francis Willoughby (1547–1596) and his sister, Margaret Willoughby of Wollaton (b. 1544), were distantly related to Queen Elizabeth I (1533–1603).[87] As a princess, Elizabeth was imprisoned for three months in the Tower of London during the reign of her half-sister, Mary Tudor. The following year, 1555, Margaret Willoughby of Wollaton became an attendant of Elizabeth.[88] Elizabeth came to the throne after the death of Mary Tudor in 1558. Margaret now became "a fixture at court . . . In 1559 she married Sir Matthew Arundell, a young courtier with whom she could make a career of attendance in the royal household."[89] Meanwhile, Francis became heir to the Wollaton estate following the death of their older brother. As Sir Francis Willoughby ("Francis Lord Willoughby" in the article), he became very wealthy through wise investments and the mining of coal on his properties. Frequent entries in his household accounts record "the purchase of books, fabrics, or other luxury goods in London."[90] Therefore, it is quite credible that either Margaret Willoughby of Wollaton (later Lady Arundell) or her brother, Sir Francis Willoughby, could have owned items associated with Queen Elizabeth I or other "articles of value."[91]

However, there is no solid proof that Deputy Governor Francis Willoughby was actually related to either of the noble Willoughby families. His ancestry remains unproven because the parentage of his father, Col. William Willoughby (c. 1588–1651), is not confirmed, despite attempts to do so.[92] Regardless of what the 1886 article implied, it appears that Deputy Governor Francis and Colonel William were not related to the Willoughbys of Wollaton.[93] They were apparently not related to the Willoughby de Eresby family, either, although the 1886 article noted similarities between the seal used by the Deputy Governor and the coat of arms of the Willoughby de Eresby family.[94]

Still, the possibility that Col. William Willoughby was a member of the nobility should not be completely dismissed. Noble English families tended to intermarry during the sixteenth century, leading to complicated family trees, and published sources often include only the siblings and children of the individuals who inherited titles, not their nieces and nephews or cousins. Another possibility is that Col. William was disowned by his family during the English Civil War, when Parliamentarians, led by Protestant Puritans, fought against Royalists, who supported King Charles I.[95] Colonel William fought on the side of the Parliamentarians, who prevailed. Two weeks after the King was executed in 1649, the House of Commons approved the appointment of Colonel William Willoughby as a Commissioner of the Navy, and he subsequently took charge of the dockyard at Portsmouth.[96] The appointment would almost certainly have caused a rift with Royalist relatives.[97]

How much truth is in the claim that the Willoughby family of Norwich, Connecticut, brought the quilt to America in 1693? As discussed above, associating the quilt with the Willoughbys makes sense, given the family history. However, the Willoughbys were not actually "of Norwich." The assumption of a Norwich connection probably arose because William B. Goodwin, from whom the Wadsworth Atheneum later acquired the chest, purchased it from the son of Theodore Raymond around 1924.[98] Theodore Raymond (1822–1885), a direct descendant of Nathaniel and Susanna Willoughby Lynde, inherited the chest during the mid-nineteenth century and brought it with him when he moved to Norwich around 1860.[99] Possibly, Gertrude Huntington knew something about this and

Appendix C: Selective Huntington Family Tree

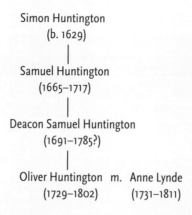

Simon Huntington
(b. 1629)

Samuel Huntington
(1665–1717)

Deacon Samuel Huntington
(1691–1785?)

Oliver Huntington   m.   Anne Lynde
(1729–1802)            (1731–1811)

associated the Willoughbys with Norwich. Another possibility is that Gertrude linked the Willoughbys with Norwich because she confused them with family stories about the Huntingtons: Her direct ancestor, Simon Huntington, was actually one of the founders of Norwich in 1659.[100] (Appendix C.)

Research has so far not revealed the significance of the year 1693. The quilt was almost certainly brought to America before then. But, for whatever reason, 1693 was combined with *The Willoughby family; Norwich, Connecticut;* and some of Queen Elizabeth's Maids of Honor to form a new narrative about the quilt.

## Conclusion

Indian cotton was long famous for its quality. The cloth and thread used in this quilt are in very good shape with few stray threads, making it challenging to obtain samples for fiber identification. The few holes found in the quilt are very tiny and the seams are tight. The author is inclined to agree with Eric Broudy, who, in describing the production of early Indian handwoven cloth, asks, "How did they achieve such fine weaving? It is worth recounting for it is an art that the world may never see again."[101] Nevertheless, time has taken its toll on the quilt's appearance. It is discolored in places. There are stains. The elaborate stitching is hard to see from a distance, especially in bright light. However, in a dark room, with one spotlight angled to the side, the silk embroidery reflects the light in perhaps the same way it reflected candlelight centuries ago. In that indirect light this quilt absolutely sparkles.

Although it is doubtful that the provenance of this quilt will ever be completely certain, it is possible to summarize a plausible history for it: The quilt's materials, construction, overall layout, and motifs all strongly support a seventeenth-century Bengali provenance. It thus represents the long tradition of Indian textiles, which for centuries dominated the world's markets. It also reflects the widespread and enduring influence of Persian design. It was exported to England (or the Netherlands), as part of an international trade in Indian textiles that increased rapidly during the seventeenth century. Someone—most likely a member of either the Willoughby or Lynde families—then brought it to colonial Massachusetts, where it would have been costly and uncommon. It was valued enough to be cared for and passed down through generations until, finally, a descendant brought it to Spokane. The true facts of its making were forgotten over the course of several centuries, leading to a false narrative that blended pieces of the truth. Carefully preserved, this quilt is now most likely one of the oldest surviving quilts in the United States.

## Acknowledgments

The author sincerely thanks the staff of the Northwest Museum of Arts and Culture/Eastern Washington State Historical Society in Spokane, Washington for their assistance with research, especially Marsha Rooney, Valerie Wahl, and Brooke Wagner. Appreciation is also extended to Linda Baumgarten, Rosemary Crill, Dr. Hang Liu, Gail Bakkom; Lisa Evans; Laurel Horton; and Susan Underwood for generously sharing their time and expertise.

## Notes and References

1. Written comments are in "888.1" file in Archives at the Northwest Museum of Arts and Culture, Spokane, Washington.
2. Lisa Evans, email message to author, January 5, 2014.
3. Satarupa Durra Majumder, "Satgaon Quilts: A Study," in *Textiles from India: The Global Trade,* Rosemary Crill, ed., (Calcutta, India: Seagull Books, 2006), 317.
4. Ibid., 320.
5. Ibid., 322. Majumder states that "more rarely backgrounds of silk backed with cotton are encountered." See also: Patrick J. Finn, "Indo-Portuguese Quilting Tradition: The Cross-Cultural Context. *Proceedings of the 4th Biennial Symposium of the International*

*Quilt Study Center & Museum* (2009), 5. Available at: http://digitalcommons.unl.edu/iqsc4symp/2/

6. Majumder, "Satgaon Quilts: A Study," 322.

7. Ibid., 322. Majumder states that they are "mostly layered, quilted bedspreads of very large dimensions, often 2.6m x 3.4m" (roughly 8'6" x 11") See also: George Michell, "1400–1600: India" in *History of Design: Decorative Arts and Material Culture, 1400 2000,* ed. Pat Kirkham and Susan Weber (New Haven: Bard Graduate Center, 2013), 41. Michell states that they often measured "in excess of 9 feet long."

8. Michell, "1400–1600: India," 41. See also: Majumder, "Satgaon Quilts: A Study," 322.

9. Majumder, "Satgaon Quilts: A Study," 325; see also: Rosemary Crill, "The Earliest Survivors? The Indian Embroideries at Hardwick Hall," in Crill, *Textiles from India: The Global Trade,* 251; see also Rosemary Crill, "Textiles for the Trade with Europe," in Ruth Barnes, Steven Cohen, Rosemary Crill, *Trade, Temple & Court: Indian Textiles from the Tapi Collection* (Mumbai, IND: India Book House Pvt Ltd., 2002), 90, 94; see also: Barbara Karl, "The Narrative Scheme of a Bengal *Colcha* Dating from the Early 17th Century Commissioned by the Portuguese" (Textile Society of America Symposium Proceedings, Paper 352, 2006), 438–448, http://digitalcommons.unl.edu/tsaconf/352.

10. Different dates are given in the literature for the establishment of Satgaon. See: Crill, "The Earliest Survivors?," in Crill, ed., *Textiles from India: The Global Trade,* 257. Crill gives a date of 1536. See also: George Michell, "1400–1600: India" in Kirkham and Weber, *History of Design,* 34. Michell gives a date of 1535.

11. Majumder, "Satgaon Quilts: A Study," 317, 326. On page 326, Majumder states that these quilts were "traded in until perhaps the late seventeenth century or mid eighteenth century." See also: Crill, "The Earliest Survivors?," 258. Crill states that they were "certainly made up to the middle of the seventeenth century." See also: Patrick J. Finn, *Quilts of India: Timeless Treasures* (New Delhi: Niyogi Books, 2014), 43. Finn states that they were predominately made between 1550 and 1650.

12. Bengal as an early center of commerce is in Nick Robins, *The Corporation that Changed the World,* 2nd ed. (London: Pluto Press, 2012), 11.

13. Stephen Yafa, *Cotton: The Biography of a Revolutionary Fiber* (New York: Penguin Books, 2005), 18–19.

14. John Guy, Woven Cargoes: *Indian Textiles in the East* (New York: Thames & Hudson, Ltd, 1998), 28, 41. Margaret Hall, "India and Pakistan: Historical Development and Trade," in *Textiles, 5,000 Years: An International History and Illustrated Survey,* ed. Jennifer Harris (New York: Harry N. Abrams, Inc., 1993), 103–104; see also: John Gillow and Nicholas Barnard, *Indian Textiles,* (London: Thames & Hudson, 2008), 20.

15. Guy, *Woven Cargoes,* 39, 41–42; see also: John Guy, "One Thing Leads to Another: Indian Textiles and the Early Globalization of Style," in *Interwoven Globe: The World Textile Trade 1500–1800,* ed. Amelia Peck (New York: The Metropolitan Museum of Art, 2013), 13.

16. Gillow and Barnard, *Indian Textiles,* 21–22; Guy in Peck, *Interwoven Globe,* 13–15; Guy, *Woven Cargoes,* 14–15, 38–39.

17. India's domination of global cotton textile markets is discussed in Sven Beckert, *Empire of Cotton: A Global History* (New York: Alfred A. Knopf, 2014), 75.

18. Marco Polo is quoted in Beckert, *Empire of Cotton,* 8.

19. Nigel Cliff, *The Last Crusade: The Epic Voyages of Vasco Da Gama* (New York: Harper Perennial, 2011), 390.

20. Ruby Ghuznavi, "Muslins of Bengal," in Crill, *Textiles from India: The Global Trade,* 307. Ghuznavi gives the source as R. Eden, tr., *Voyages of Lewis Vertomannus, A Gentleman of Rome AD 1503* (London, 1576), quoted in James Taylor, *A Descriptive and Historical Account of the Cotton Manufacture of Dacca in Bengal* (London, 1851), 117–118.

21. Robins, *The Corporation that Changed the World,* 11.

22. Ibid.

23. Beckert, *Empire of Cotton,* 36, 46.

24. Linda Baumgarten, Curator of Textiles and Costumes at the Colonial Williamsburg Foundation, identified samples of the face fabric weft, backing warp and weft, binding tape, and coarse inner layer as cotton. Linda Baumgarten, email message to author, December 12, 2014. (Because a quilt's binding tape can be replaced at a later date, the author does not consider the cotton binding on this quilt as necessarily supportive of a Bengali provenance.) The face fabric warp was identified as cotton by Dr. Hang Liu, Assistant Professor of Apparel, Merchandising, Design and Textiles at Washington State University, in the presence of the author on the campus of WSU in Pullman, Washington, on March 22, 2016. A sample of the piecing thread was not removed at that time for fear of damaging the quilt. However, Dr. Liu examined a seam under a microscope and stated that the piecing thread appears to be the same fiber as the face fabric (cotton).

25. Linda Baumgarten, Curator of Textiles and Costumes at the Colonial Williamsburg Foundation, identified a sample of the embroidery thread as silk. Linda Baumgarten, email message to author, December 12, 2014.

26. For a discussion of quilts from different regions of India, see: "Chapter I: Indian" in Linda Baumgarten and Kimberly Smith Ivey, *Four Centuries of Quilts: The Colonial Williamsburg Collection* (New Haven: Yale University Press in association with The Colonial Williamsburg Foundation, 2014), 12–20.

27. The quilt in Hardwick Hall as one of the only two "early examples" is in Rosemary Crill, ed., *The Fabric of India* (London: V&A Publishing, 2015), 162. Images of the quilt in Hardwick Hall and its identification as "Late sixteenth century," are in Rosemary Crill, "The Earliest Survivors?," 255–256.

28. Rosemary Crill, email message to author, July 15, 2014.

29. For example, one of the motifs can be seen in a photograph of the vaults of the exterior galleries of the fourteenth-century Tomb of Uljaytu (built 1307–13) in Sultaniyya (Soltaniyeh), Iran, in Sheila S. Blair and Jonathan M. Bloom, *The Art and Architecture of Islam 1250–1800* (New Haven: Yale University Press, 1994), 9.

30. *Persian* and *Iranian* are often used interchangeably. This paper refers to the geographic area and people as *Iran/Iranian* and to the language and art as *Persian.*

31. Blair and Bloom, *The Art and Architecture of Islam,* 1.

32. Suzan Yalman. Based on original work by Linda Komaroff. "The Art of the Ilkhanid Period (1256–1353)." In *Heilbrunn Timeline of Art History* (New York: The Metropolitan Museum of Art, 2000) http://www.metmuseum.org/toah/hd/ilkh/hd_ilkh.htm

33. Decorative arts of the Timurid Period are in Blair and Bloom, *The Art and Architecture of Islam,* 69. Influence on Safavid, Ottoman, and Mughal art is in Aimée E. Froom, "1400–1600: The Islamic World" in Kirkham and Weber, *History of Design,* 55.

34. Mughal wealth is in Blair and Bloom, *The Art and Architecture of Islam,* 267. Mughal conquest of Bengal is in Muzaffar Alam and Sanjay Subrahmanyam, "Mughal Expansion in the Deccan, 1570-1605: Contemporary Perspectives," in Vasallo e Silva, Nuno and

Flores, Jorge, eds., *Goa and the Great Mughal* (London: Scala Publishers Ltd. In conjunction with the Calouste Gulbenkian Foundation, 2011), 16–18.

35. Wolpert, *India,* 4th ed., 41.

36. John Irwin, "Indian Embroidery" in *Victoria and Albert Museum Indian Embroidery* (London: His Majesty's Stationery Office, 1951), 4.

37. Ibid.

38. Susan Stronge, "The Land of 'Mogor," in Nuno Vassallo e Silva and Jorge Flores, eds., *Goa and the Great Mughal,* (London: Calouste Gulbenkian Foundation in association with Scala Publishers), 143.

39. Steven Cohen, "Materials and Making" in Rosemary Crill, ed., *The Fabric of India* (London: V&A Publishing, 2015), 20–23.

40. Crill, "Textiles for the Trade with Europe," in Barnes, Cohen, Crill, *Trade, Temple & Court,* 90, 94.

41. Patrick J. Finn, *Quilts of India,* 44.

42. Stronge, "The Land of 'Mogor," 141.

43. Blair and Bloom, *The Art and Architecture of Islam,* 293.

44. Loan Agreement, Letter to Gertrude Huntington, and her reply presenting the quilt can be found in "888.1" file in Archives at the Northwest Museum of Arts and Culture, Spokane, Washington.

45. "President D. L. Huntington Called by Death," *The Illuminator* (October 1929). Found in "Huntington Family Papers 1921–ca. 1950." Manuscripts, Archives, and Special Collections at Washington State University libraries, Pullman, Washington. See also: "D. L. Huntington Dies," *The Spokesman-Review* (September 28, 1929).

46. Lynne Zacek Bassett, "Early Quilts and Quilted Clothing," in Lynne Zacek Bassett, ed., *Massachusetts Quilts: Our Common Wealth* (Lebanon, NH: University Press of New England, 2009), 3.

47. Sven Beckert, *Empire of Cotton,* 33.

48. Extensive information about the EIC and the VOC can be found in: Xenia E. Cord, "A Brief History of Chintz," in Kay Triplett, Lori Lee Triplett and Xenia Cord, *Chintz Quilts from the Poos Collection* (St. Étienne de Montluc, France: *Quiltmania,* 2013); An Moonen, "The Seventeenth Century," in *A History of Dutch Quilts* (Westervoort, The Netherlands: Van Gruting Publishers, 2010); and Robins, *The Corporation That Changed the World.*

49. Gloria Seaman Allen, *First Flowerings: Early Virginia Quilts* (Washington DC: DAR Museum, 1987), 6.

50. Sally Garoutte, ""Early Colonial Quilts in a Bedding Context," in Sally Garoutte, ed. *Uncoverings 1980* (San Francisco: American Quilt Study Group, 1981), 23, 26.

51. Inventory of Peter Walker, Northampton County VA, Deeds, Wills, and Inventories, no, 5 (1654–1655), Virginia State Library, Richmond, in Baumgarten and Ivey, *Four Centuries of Quilts,* 14, 20.

52. Garoutte, "Early Colonial Quilts," 22–23. Garoutte found a total of 551 blankets, 158 ruggs, 159 coverlets, and 10 quilts.

53. George Francis Dow, "The Patchwork Quilt and Some Other Quilts," *Old Time New England,* Vol. 17, no. 4, April 1927 quoted in Garoutte, "Early Colonial Quilts," 25. According to Garoutte, Dow wrote: "coverlets are mentioned 142 times and ruggs 157 times while quilts are listed only four times."

54. Garoutte, "Early Colonial Quilts," 26.

55. Richard Zacks, *The Pirate Hunter: The True Story of Captain Kidd* (New York: Theia, 2002), 11.

56. The original source of the inventory of Captain William Kidd's household effects appears to be Alice Morse Earle, *Colonial Days in Old New York* (1896; reprint edition, Port Washington, NY: Ira J. Friedman, 1962), 102–103. Marie Webster referred to it in 1915: Marie Webster, *Quilts: Their Story and How to Make Them,* new edition with notes and biography of the author by Rosalind Perry (Santa Barbara, CA: Practical Patchwork, 1990), 70–71. The information was repeated by Patsy and Myron Orlofsky in *Quilts in America* (New York: McGraw-Hill, 1974), 10, and Jinny Beyer in *Medallion Quilts* (McLean, VA: EPM Publications, Inc., 1982), 19.

57. Linda R. Baumgarten, "The Textile Trade in Boston, 1650–1700," in *Arts of the Anglo-American Community in the Seventeenth Century,* Winterthur Conference Report 1974, ed. Ian M. G. Quimby (Charlottesville: University Press of Virginia for the Henry Francis du Pont Winterthur Museum, 1975), 219.

58. Garoutte, "Early Colonial Quilts," 22.

59. Garoutte, "Early Colonial Quilts," 26.

60. Nathaniel Philbrick, *Mayflower* (New York: Penguin Books, 2006), 199.

61. Lorinda B. R. Goodwin, *An Archaeology of Manners: The Polite World of the Merchant Elite of Colonial Massachusetts* (New York: Kluwer Academic/Plenum Publishers, 1999), 62. Goodwin gives as her source for the hierarchy: J. T. Main, *The Social Structure of Revolutionary America* (Princeton, NJ: Princeton University Press, 1965), 83.

62. Goodwin, *An Archaeology of Manners,* 62.

63. Ibid., 62, 65.

64. Ibid., 62.

65. Richard Frothingham, *The History of Charlestown, Massachusetts* (1845; reprint edition, Boston: Harvard Book Store, 2016), 104.

66. Evelyn McCurdy Salisbury (Mrs. Edward Elbridge Salisbury), "Suggestions and Inquiries Respecting the Ancestry of Col. William Willoughby, Father of Deputy Governor Francis Willoughby of Massachusetts," *The New England Historical and Genealogical Register,* XL (1886) (Facsimile Reprint Published 1996 by Heritage Books, Inc., Bowie, MD), 51–52.

67. Edward Elbridge Salisbury and Evelyn McCurdy Salisbury, *Family Histories and Genealogies, Volume First, Part Second Containing a Series of Genealogical and Biographical Monographs on the Families of Lynde, Digby, Newdigate, Hoo and Willoughby and Notes on the Stories of Locke and Cole* (Privately Printed: 1892), 547. Available at: https://books.google.com/books?id=fJVQAAAAYAAJ&pg=PA565&lpg=PA565&dq=Sarah+Lynde+Raymond&source=bl&ots=kBZBYPV2kn&sig=uozmGjhjcUHXc_g1KxtDLr6Tlsw&hl=en&sa=X&ved=0ahUKEwjMjMHN5JjSAhVE-mMKHQVICAMQ6AEIMTAH#v=onepage&q=Sarah%20Lynde%20Raymond&f=false

68. Information from "Francis Willoughby, Deputy-Governor of Massachusetts," Family Search, https://histfam.familysearch.org//getperson.php?personID=19837&tree=Nixon and Salisbury, "Suggestions and Inquiries Respecting the Ancestry of Col. William Willoughby," 52. Daniel Taylor is also in Salisbury, 52.

69. Edward Elbridge Salisbury and Evelyn McCurdy Salisbury, *Family Histories and Genealogies,* 544.

70. Information about Enoch and Simon Lynde is from: Benjamin Lynde, *The Diaries of Benjamin Lynde and of Benjamin Lynde, Jr. with an Appendix* (Cambridge, MA: Riverside Press, 1880), iii, v, vi, vii.
https://books.google.com/books?id=H3ZWfjPnDtEC&pg=PA221&dq=The+diary+of+Benjamin+Lynde&hl=en&sa=X&ved=0CCcQ6AEwAGoVChMI5c_yy5aQxgIVSZeICh0NkwA4#v=onepage&q=The%20diary%20of%20Benjamin%20Lynde&f=false

71. Ibid.

72. Information was compiled from: Ancestry. com., and Benjamin Lynde, *The Diaries of Benjamin Lynde and of Benjamin Lynde, Jr. with an Appendix* (Cambridge, MA: Riverside Press, 1880), iii, v, vi, vii.
viihttps://books.google.com/books?id=H3ZWfjPnDtEC&pg=PA221&dq=The+diary+of+Benjamin+Lynde&hl=en&sa=X&ved=0CCcQ6AEwAGoVChMI5c_yy5aQxgIVSZeICh0NkwA4#v=onepage&q=The%20diary%20of%20Benjamin%20Lynde&f=false

73. Genealogical information for the Huntington and Lynde families was compiled from the following sources: Ancestry.com; U.S. Census records for 1880 and 1940, and Elijah Baldwin Huntington, *A Genealogical Memoir of the Huntington Family in this Country: Embracing all the known descendants of Simon and Margaret Huntington, who have retained the family name* (Stamford, CT, 1863), https://books.google.com/books?id=3mdVAAAA-MAAJ&dq=inauthor:%22Elijah+Baldwin+Huntington%22&source=gbs_navlinks_s

74. Averil Colby, *Quilting* (London: B. T. Batsford, 1972), 100-101.

75. John Irwin and Katharine B. Brett, *Origins of Chintz, with a catalogue of Indo-European cotton-paintings in the Victoria and Albert Museum, London, and the Royal Ontario Museum, Toronto* (London: Her Majesty's Stationery Office, 1970), 5.

76. Ibid.

77. Colby, *Quilting*, 100-101.

78. Correspondence found in "888.1" file in Archives at the Northwest Museum of Arts and Culture, Spokane, Washington.

79. The wealth of surviving Elizabethan textiles is discussed in Thomasina Beck, *The Embroiderer's Story: Needlework from the Renaissance to the Present Day* (Newton Abbot, UK: David & Charles, 1999), 8. For discussion of Elizabeth I's quilts, see: Anna Whitelock, *The Queen's Bed* (New York: Sarah Crichton Books/Farrar, Straus & Giroux, 2013), 84. The inventory of Henry VIII's possessions is described in Lisa Evans, "The Same Counter-poincte Beinge Old and Worene': The Mystery of Henry VIII's Green Quilt, in *Medieval Clothing and Textiles: Volume 4,* ed. Robin Netherton and Gale R. Owen-Crocker (Wood-bridge, UK: The Boydell Press, 2008), 193.

80. Edward Elbridge Salisbury and Evelyn McCurdy Salisbury, *Family Histories and Genealogies,* 515-516.

81. Evelyn McCurdy Salisbury, "Suggestions and Inquiries Respecting the Ancestry of Col. William Willoughby," 52.

82. Ibid., 53-56.

83. Edward Elbridge Salisbury and Evelyn McCurdy Salisbury, *Family Histories and Genealogies,* 507-604.

84. "Dutch Chest, Prized Salvage of Armada, Is Linked Here: Walter J. Sherman Lineal Descendant of Owner Who Presented Treasure to Eastern Museum; Mate in London," The byline is: "By the Rambler," The article was apparently published on January 23, 1928. A copy of the article is in the "1950.712" file in the Archives of the Wadsworth Atheneum

Museum of Art, Hartford, Connecticut. The name of the newspaper does not appear in the article, but the contents suggest that it was published in Toledo, Ohio.

85. Accession number 1950.712.

86. "Dutch Chest," January 23, 1928, newspaper unknown. Walter J. Sherman's daughters were contacted in 1973, but they "could not or would not" add any information, according to a letter from Clarissa Nevins Hayes to Luci S. Kincanon, April 26, 1973. Letter in "1950.712" file, Wadsworth Atheneum Museum of Art, Hartford, Connecticut.

87. Elizabeth Woodville was the Wollaton Willoughbys' great-great-grandmother through her first marriage to Sir John Grey. Through her second marriage to Edward IV, Elizabeth Woodville was the great-grandmother of Elizabeth I.

88. Alice T. Friedman, *House and Household in Elizabethan England: Wollaton Hall and the Willoughby Family* (Chicago: University of Chicago Press, 1989), 16–18.

89. Ibid., 21.

90. Ibid., 27–28. In 1890 an exhibition was held in London in which items from the reigns of Henry VII through Elizabeth I were displayed. The catalogue for that exhibition includes a description of "Item 1057" ("Lent by the Lady Middleton"): "Coverlid of Lace and Needlework, worked by Queen Elizabeth, when Princess, and her kinswoman, Margaret Willoughby, of Wollaton, afterwards Lady Arundell of Wardour."

91. Catalogue for "Exhibition of the Royal House of Tudor" held at The New Gallery on Regent Street (London: The New Gallery, 1890), 207. books.google.com. https://books.google.com/books?id=cGgPAAAAYAAJ&pg=PA149&source=gbs_toc_r&cad=3#v=onepage&q&f=false

92. In 1892, Edward Elbridge Salisbury and Evelyn McCurdy Salisbury devoted many pages to the circumstantial evidence linking Col. William and Deputy Governor Francis to the noble Willoughbys. See: Edward Elbridge Salisbury and Evelyn McCurdy Salisbury, *Family Histories and Genealogies*, 507–604. However, this was disputed by Kimball Grant Everingham in 1980. A discussion of this can be found in "Col. William Willoughby and Family in Stepney," WikiTree, http://www.wikitree.com/wiki/Willoughby-311

93. Colonel William was not a son of Sir Francis Willoughby; none of Sir Francis' male children survived him. Sir Francis' daughter, Bridget married a distant relative, Sir Percival Willoughby of Bore Place in Kent (c.1560–1643), and Sir Francis made Percival his heir. Bridget and Percival had five sons, none of whom were named William, and the eldest (another) Sir Francis Willoughby (1588-1665) succeeded Percival. It does not appear that Col. William was descended from any of Percival's brothers. Genealogical information found in the University of Nottingham Manuscripts and Special Collections, online: https://www.nottingham.ac.uk/manuscriptsandspecialcollections/collectionsindepth/family/middleton/biographies/biographyofsirfranciswilloughby(1546-1596).aspx https://www.nottingham.ac.uk/manuscriptsandspecialcollections/collectionsindepth/family/middleton/biographies/biographyofsirpercivalwilloughby(d1643).aspx https://www.nottingham.ac.uk/manuscriptsandspecialcollections/collectionsindepth/family/middleton/biographies/biographyoffranciswilloughby(1588-1665).aspx

94. Salisbury, "Suggestions and Inquiries," 51–55.

95. Salisbury, "Suggestions and Inquiries," 54.

96. Great Britain House of Commons, *Journals of the House of Commons from September the 2nd 1648, In the Twenty-fourth Year of the Reign of King Charles the First, to August the 14th 1651.* (Reprinted by Order of the House of Commons: 1803), 144. Although Col.

Willoughby was appointed in 1649, this appears in the record of 1648, because England used the Julian calendar at that time. https://books.google.com/books?id=exNDAAAA-cAAJ&pg=PP9&lpg=PP9&dq=Journal+of+the+House+of+Commons+from+September+the+2d+1648&source=bl&ots=GF13nFvEa9&sig=5bO3GD7-8X61HFpFE-MUkKNw0thg&hl=en&sa=X&ved=0CB4Q6AEwAGoVChMIvp3xgLKPxgIVSziICh0NQg Aw#v=onepage&q=Journal%20of%20the%20House%20of%20Commons%20from%20Se ptember%20the%202d%201648&f=false. See also: Portsmouth Royal Dockyard Historical Trust "Dockyard Timeline: 1649-Commonwealth," http://portsmouthdockyard.org.uk/timeline/details/1649-commonwealth

97.  Robert Bertie, 1st Earl of Lindsey, who was the only known son of Lord Willoughby, was killed in battle in 1642 while fighting for the King. The Parham heir, Francis Lord Willoughby, initially sided with the Parliamentarians, but later took up the Royalist cause. Probably the other members of the noble Willoughby families were Royalists, as well.
98.  Information taken from: "Dutch Chest," January 23, 1928, newspaper unknown; and Letter from Luci S. Kincanon to Clarissa Nevins Hayes, May 2, 1973 in the "1950.712" file, Wadsworth Atheneum Museum of Art, Hartford, Connecticut.
99.  Information from: ancestry.com, and "Dutch Chest," January 23, 1928, newspaper unknown.
100.  Frances Manwaring Caulkins, *History of Norwich, Connecticut: From its Possession by the Indians to the Year 1866. . .* (Hartford, CT: Case, Lockwood, and Brainard, 1874), 60–62, 67. https://books.google.com/books?id=DlWDnPZ04K0C&printsec=frontcover&dq=A+History+of+Norwich+CT&hl=en&sa=X&ei=wsIMVaaWJ833oASl4DYCA&ved=0CCAQ6AEwAA#v=onepage&q=A%20History%20of%20Norwich%20CT&f=false101. Eric Broudy, *The Book of Looms: A history of the hand loom from ancient times to the present* (Hanover, NH: University Press of New England, 1979), 107.

Figure 5. Quilt top #2, constructed in part by Franklin R. Cushman. Cotton. 98 x 60 inches. Historic Textile and Costume Collection, University of Rhode Island, gift of Franklin R. Cushman, 1952.63.125.

# The Cushman Quilt Tops: A Tale of North and South

Rachel May and Linda Welters

*The Cushman Collection in the University of Rhode Island's Historic Textile and Costume Collection includes three unfinished quilt tops and two fabric swatch books, along with over 500 other artifacts. The quilt tops, which were begun in 1833, reveal a family story of North and South that spans two hundred years. The tops were similarly constructed of hexagons with a central star motif, made with the template-pieced mosaic patchwork method. Many of the paper templates remain in the backs of the quilt tops. Dates in the paper fragments range from 1775 to 1940, revealing generations of history from the colonial and antebellum periods to the Colonial Revival movement. The fabrics in the quilt tops and swatch books mark the transition from hand-spun and hand-woven cloth to machine-made textiles. Further, the quilt tops, swatch books, and related archival materials shed light on deeply intertwined family relationships between those who lived in Providence, Rhode Island, and Charleston, South Carolina, and their connection to larger themes in the Atlantic world, notably capitalism, trade, and slavery.*

## Introduction

In 1952, siblings Franklin R., Charles, and Julia Cushman donated three quilt tops along with over 500 other objects and items of clothing to the University of Rhode Island's Historic Textile and Costume Collection. The quilt tops were begun in 1833 in Charleston, South Carolina, by the Cushmans' great-aunt, Susan McPherson Sibley (Williams) Crouch, a young bride. Her husband, Hasell Wilkinson Crouch, a doctor in Charleston, assisted with the design and piecing. After his premature death on December 6, 1836, his widow returned to her family home in Providence with her daughter Emily, along with the unfinished quilts, cut pieces, and extra fabrics, which were kept in a trunk. They were discovered in 1917 by Susan Crouch's grandnephew Franklin R. Cushman, a teacher of industrial design and history. He started making two fabric swatch books in 1917 for use in his classes, connecting some of the fabrics in the swatch books with the fabrics in the quilts, adding dates of the fabrics' production, and explaining from whom each fabric came. He began work on the quilt tops, sewing the pieces together in the summers from 1930 to 1940. Franklin noted that his relatives helped to stitch the quilt tops together.[1]

The three quilt tops and two fabric swatch books reveal the story of two interconnected families, one with roots in Providence, Rhode Island, and the other in Charleston, South Carolina. Through the quilt tops, swatch books, and related archival documents, the lives of family members are connected to larger themes in the Atlantic world during the eighteenth and nineteenth centuries, notably capitalism, trade, and slavery.

### The Williams/Crouch/Cushman Family

Quiltmaker Susan McPherson Sibley Williams (1813–1902) was born April 13, 1813 in Providence, Rhode Island, to an old New England family. Her parents were Jason (1774–1863) and Sarah (Rose) Williams (1778–1863). Her grandparents, both from Pomfret, Connecticut, were Elijah (1744–1825) and Abigail (Chandler) Williams (1747–1834). Susan was the fifth of eight children born to Jason and Sarah, seven of whom survived to adulthood. Susan's older sister Emily married William Jenkins Harris, a descendent of Roger Williams, founder of the colony of Rhode Island.[2] It was Emily and William's grandchildren who donated the artifacts to the URI Historic Textile and Costume Collection. Susan McPherson Sibley (Williams) Crouch was their great aunt. (See family tree in the Appendix.)[3]

The Crouch family, whom Susan married into on October 11, 1832, had equally deep American roots, but in the South. Susan's husband, Hasell Wilkinson Crouch (1809–1836), was raised in Charleston, the South's largest port. He graduated from Providence's Brown University in 1830, and returned home where he earned his medical degree at the University of South Carolina and became a doctor.[4] Hasell's father, Abraham Crouch (1765–1825), was a lawyer and a notary public in the Customs House in Charleston. Hasell's mother, Sophia Withers (1788–1809), was born in Wilmington, North Carolina in 1788 and died September 10, 1809, a month after Hasell was born.[5]

Figure 1. Jean François Vallée, Abraham Crouch, c. 1805. Watercolor on ivory. Gibbes Art Museum/Carolina Art Association, 1967.025.0001.

Susan and Hasell Wilkinson Crouch had two children of their own, Hasell Charles (1833–1836) and Emily Hasell Crouch (1836–1926). The eldest, Hasell Charles, had been ill for months after falling from his crib, and died when he was just three years old. Susan had written to her family that little Hasell had not been "right since he fell out of the crib the first night he slept in it," and, three months later, he fell a second time.[6] In what must have been a devastating moment, the death certificate of little Hasell Charles was signed by his own father, Dr. Crouch, with the cause of death listed as "Inflamm Brain."[7] Emily was born on February 7 of 1836, just months before her brother died. Hasell Wilkinson, Susan's husband, died shortly afterwards, of yellow fever. Susan Crouch returned to Providence with her daughter Emily to live with her parents, remaining there until her death in 1902; Emily continued to reside there until 1917.

How did Hasell, a native of Charleston, and Susan, from Providence, meet? Several possibilities exist because the South Carolina Crouches had connections to Rhode Island, and the Williamses in Providence had business interests in Charleston. Hasell's grandfather, Charleston native Charles Crouch, had moved to Providence as a journeyman printer in 1762, where he met Mary Wilkinson of Smithfield, Rhode Island. They married in 1763 and moved to Charleston the following year, where he began the *South Carolina Gazette and Country Journal*.[8] Mary is known to have summered in Newport, Rhode Island, with her children William and Abraham in 1770, 1773, and probably 1775.[9] It was customary for prosper-

Figure 2. Artist unknown, Mrs. Abraham Crouch (Sophia Jane Withers), c. 1805. Watercolor on ivory. Gibbes Art Museum/ Carolina Art Association, 1967.025.0002.

ous South Carolinians to escape the swampy conditions of the rice-growing Lowcountry by sailing north to Newport in June and returning to Charleston at the end of mosquito season, as late as November.

On August 24, 1775 Charles drowned at sea when the vessel he was traveling on sank.[10] He had been en route to Philadelphia to purchase printing supplies. Mary was in Rhode Island at the time, but returned to Charleston where she began publishing her own newspaper, the *Charleston Gazette.* Just before the British laid siege to Charleston in 1780, Mary packed up and moved to Salem, Massachusetts, to start a newspaper. By 1781 Mary was living with her two sons in Providence. They remained in the city while Abraham, Hasell's father, studied at Brown University. He graduated in 1787.[11] Abraham continued his studies, earning a master's degree at Brown in 1790. It is probable that Abraham stayed in Providence after graduation to practice law, because he is listed as a "lawyer from Providence" in the accession records of the Gibbes Museum of Art where his miniature portrait resides (fig. 1). That miniature was painted in 1806, the year the forty-one year-old lawyer and customs house clerk married eighteen-year-old Sophia Withers of Wilmington, Delaware (fig. 2). That same year he purchased the Tucker-Ladson house at 8 Meeting Street, one of Charleston's most prestigious addresses.[12] There the couple had two sons, Charles (1807–1880) and the afore-mentioned Hasell (1809–1836). After Sophia's death in 1809, Abraham never remarried. He sold the Meeting Street house in 1821. He must have continued traveling to Providence, however, because that is where he died on November 2, 1825. Both of his

Figure 3. Jason Williams/Crouch House, 51 George Street, Providence, RI. Brown University's Littlefield Hall was built on the site in 1925.

sons graduated from his alma mater, Brown University—Charles in 1829 and Hasell in 1830.[13]

Susan's grandparents, Elijah and Abigail Williams, lived in Pomfret, Connecticut, after their marriage in 1770.[14] In 1795, the Williamses moved to Providence with two of their sons, Jason and William Hilton. The third, a doctor, remained in Connecticut to oversee the family farm until it was sold.[15] Elijah Williams built a house in 1795 at 51 George Street near Brown University that eventually passed into Jason's hands (fig. 3). One of Elijah's sons, William Hilton, attended Brown University, graduating in 1799.[16] Elijah had run a general store in Pomfret; he and his son Jason operated a grocery store after settling in Providence. That business was dissolved in 1799, about the time Elijah and his sons began partnering with other Providence merchants in various coastal trading ventures.[17] Between 1798 and 1809, father and sons were listed as co-owners on seven sloops, schooners, or brigantines that sailed from Providence to ports south, including Charleston, and beyond to the West Indies.[18] One of Elijah's sons, William Hilton, the Brown University graduate, served as a supercargo (an officer on board a merchant ship in charge of cargo) on a coastal vessel. He died of "fever" in Surinam in 1800 at the age of twenty.[19] In 1808, one brig owned by the Williamses, the Mount Vernon, was seized by customs in Sag Harbor, New York, for violating the 1807 Embargo Act, ending the family's shipping ventures and landing them in bankruptcy court.[20] Elijah, the father, had already moved to Athens, New York, in 1807, where he farmed and operated a tavern.

In 1802, Jason Williams, the merchant, married Sarah Rose, with whom he had eight children, including our quiltmaker Susan. At least one of his sons, Elijah Hilton Williams (1809–1884), known as Hilton, was a good friend of Hasell Wilkinson Crouch. It would seem that the Williamses and the Crouches knew each other for years, because the children socialized together during their young adulthood, leading to the marriage of Hasell and Susan. After the 1809 bankruptcy, Jason returned to his former career as a store owner and began renting rooms in his George Street house, probably to Brown University students.[21] The two Crouch boys might have boarded there. However, it is also possible that Jason and Abraham knew each other from the years between 1795 and 1806, when both Williamses and Crouches lived in Providence, a city of around 7,000 residents. Citizens of similar social standing, like the Williamses and Crouches, would have socialized together, especially considering their Brown University connections. When Abraham Crouch died in Providence in 1825, it was Jason Williams who paid his funeral expenses.[22]

The two families were about to become further intertwined. Letters from the late 1820s document the friendship between Charles and Hasell Crouch and the Williams siblings. Hasell and Susan married in 1832 in Providence and moved to Charleston soon thereafter. Both of Susan's brothers settled in Charleston; Hilton bought a lumberyard in 1831, and Winthrop worked for a general store before becoming a cotton broker. These details of the Williams-Crouch story illuminate the close connections between families from the North and the South during the colonial era and in the years leading up to the Civil War. Providence and Charleston were both leading port cities, about a ten-day sea voyage from each other. During the colonial period, nearby Newport, Rhode Island, served as Charleston's summer resort; in the post-Revolutionary years Providence's economy boomed from shipping and manufacturing enterprises (including rum and cotton); at the same time Charleston became the Lower South's leading port for the exchange of rice, indigo, cotton, and slaves. This historical backdrop provides the context for the quilt tops and swatch books as well as a window into the dynamics of a family with roots in both the North and the South.

### The Quilt Tops

Susan started the quilt tops in Charleston. The accession notes of 1952 read, "these quilts were begun by Mr. Cushman's grandmother's sister, a Charleston, N.C. [*sic*] bride in 1833. Her husband, a young physician, Dr. Hasell N. [*sic*] Crouch, planned the design and color scheme."[23]

Quilt #1 (fig. 4, color plate 1) is thought to be the oldest of the three tops.[24] The accession tag attached to the quilt reads, "Planned and sewn by

Figure 4. Quilt top #1, Hexagon Mosaic, "Planned and sewn by Dr. and Mrs. Hasell Crouch." Cotton. 84 x 83 inches Historic Textile and Costume Collection, University of Rhode Island, gift of Franklin R. Cushman 1952.63.124.

Dr. and Mrs. Hasell Crouch. It is said that when he had a difficult case to prescribe for, he would work on his patchwork while trying to decide what to do for his patient…." After Dr. Crouch's premature death in 1836, the unfinished quilt tops were put away with some hexagon pieces cut and ready to be stitched in place, an unknown number of mosaic "flowers," and additional fabrics for more hexagons. Both Mrs. Crouch and her daughter Emily passed away, leaving the quilts unfinished. Franklin R. Cushman and his relatives completed some of the border patches in the quilts, made new templates for old fabrics, and sewed together hexagons to form new "flowers." Their stitching is not of the same high quality as Susan's. Quilt #1 was intended for a bigger bed than quilt tops #2 (fig. 5, color plate 2) and #3 (fig. 6). The original hexagons were to be assembled into a large quilt for Hasell and Susan's bed; the largest of the three tops was the beginning of that quilt. A letter in the Cushman file reveals that Franklin decided to sew the remaining pieces together with those that he made for two quilts in twin bed size; these were sewn together by Franklin and his relatives in 1936.[25] These are tops #2 and #3. Emily never married, and she lived with her mother in Providence; according to census records from 1880, she worked as an art teacher.[26] In fact, the Cushman collection at the University of Rhode Island includes a large box of watercolors, some signed by Emily.

All three quilt tops are constructed of mosaic patchwork, in which fabric pieces were folded over hexagonal paper templates, and then basted to hold the shape in place until multiple pieces were whip stitched together. Mosaic patchwork originated in England; the earliest surviving example is a silk patchwork coverlet dated 1718.[27] British emigrants brought the technique to the American colonies in the eighteenth century, and several late eighteenth-century examples exist.[28] Thus, this was neither a new piecing method nor a new pattern in 1833. Hexagon quilts were very popular in the South Carolina Lowcountry well into the nineteenth century. The Charleston Museum has thirty pieced mosaic patchwork artifacts, which were exhibited in 2002; Sharon Pinka included a hexagonal quilt top dated circa 1840 in her report on Lowcountry chintz.[29]

The Hexagon pattern, also called Mosaic or Honeycomb, increased in popularity in the United States in the early 1830s with its publication in 1831 by Eliza Leslie in *The American Girls' Book,* and again in 1835 by *Godey's Lady's Book.*[30] When the Cushman quilts were started in 1833, industrial textile production had taken hold in Rhode Island, Massachusetts, Pennsylvania, and other eastern seaboard states; printed cotton goods

Figure 6. Quilt top #3, constructed in part by Franklin R. Cushman. Cotton. 98 x 60 inches. Historic Textile and Costume Collection, University of Rhode Island, gift of Franklin R. Cushman, 1952.63.126.

constituted a lively trade up and down the coast, and across the Atlantic through America's major ports: Boston, New York, Baltimore, and Charleston.[31] Susan Crouch and her relatives would have had easy access to these early machine-produced textiles to assemble their quilts.

In the mosaic patchwork method, once the quilt top was finished, the quilter generally removed the paper templates from the back and added batting and backing to the quilt top. However, the earliest extant American examples did not have the papers removed.[32] Mosaic patchwork often was joined to the backing without batting, which required no quilting.

The three quilt tops are similarly composed, with a central star motif and "flowers" of hexagons arranged on the rest of the quilt separated by rows of white hexagons. The individual hexagons measure approximately 1 5/8 inches to 1 7/8 inches point to point. Quilt top #1 has hexagons pieced into triangular units that form stars around the central "flower," and quilt top #3 includes smaller star motifs. Two of the quilt tops, #2 & #3, include newer fabrics than the first quilt top (the one with fewer papers). Furthermore, quilt top #1 has a simpler central star surrounding the "flower," with just an outline of colorful hexagon pieces constituting the star, and a white center. Quilt tops #2 and #3 have more complex central star patterns, with no white space and several rows of colorful hexagon pieces spreading outward to create the star shape. The central stars in these two quilts also include older fabrics, some from about 1800; one of the fabrics in the quilt, with a leaf motif characteristic of the early 1830s, is represented in three colorways. Many pieces of a glazed chintz dated 1829 commemorate the inauguration of President Jackson; fabrics from a black-and-white plate print of two parrots perched on the branches of a fruit-bearing tree (one parrot is eating the fruit) were in production from 1774 to 1811.[33] The tops are a veritable encyclopedia of the checks, stripes, indigos, chintzes, calicos, drabs, and rainbow prints that characterize early nineteenth-century quilts; all three of the main printing technologies of the period—block, plate, and cylinder—are evident.

In their selection of mosaic patchwork for their bed quilt, Susan and Hasell echoed the choices of other Charlestonians. As Laurel Horton has noted, evidence suggests that quiltmakers in Charleston started to practice the technique of mosaic patchwork in the early nineteenth century. It was practiced by upper-class women who came from or married into "families of wealth, education and influence."[34] The framed center orientation of Susan and Hasell's quilt is characteristic of other mosaic patchwork quilts made in South Carolina, as are the fabric choices: chintz and small-figured

Figure 7: Paper hexagon templates. One has the name "Hasell" and the words "her book," another the word "month," and a third shows penmanship practice of the phrase "keep." Historic Textile and Costume Collection, University of Rhode Island (1952.63.124).

calicoes.[35] Unlike most of the published South Carolina mosaic patchwork quilts, however, a great deal is known about Susan and Hasell Crouch and the history of the quilt tops. Interestingly, correspondence with family members in Rhode Island revealed that Susan's two sisters-in-law living in Charleston were also planning mosaic patchwork quilts.[36]

### The Paper Templates

Because the quilt tops were made in the paper-piecing method and were not yet finished, the papers remaining in the back of the quilts reveal snippets of letters, contracts, magazine clippings, musical scores, envelopes with postmarks, and even a child's penmanship practice, with phrases and words repeated in the same fragment (fig. 7). The papers give tantalizing clues to the family's lives across time and their ties to trade.

These papers reveal dates from 1775 to 1940, as well as names of family members, evidence of shipping records from Charleston or Providence to Havana and Barbados (with mention of "shugar," casks, and lists of calculations), family letters, clippings from Franklin's high school, musical scores, and even old dictionary entries. The papers indicate dates ranging from the eighteenth century to the twentieth century, with the latter dates pointing to the sections that Franklin had a hand in finishing.

Quilt top #1 has the fewest papers, which remain only around the border. In quilt tops #2 and #3, the papers are clustered in a pattern. The older pieces of paper are identifiable by the color of the paper and the references and dates written on the paper.[37] The earliest date written on one of these older pieces is 1775.[38] Other dates in all three tops are 1798, 1802, 1813 (repeated on three pieces of paper in the quilt tops), 1817, and 1824. Then, the dates jump to 1931, 1934, and 1935, which are repeated five times in the quilt tops. One template has the date 1940; another is cut from an envelope bearing Franklin's name and address at 19 Bellevue Avenue in Providence. The older dates correspond to the older fabrics—those recorded in the fabric swatch books. But newer paper templates also back the older fabrics. The older dates and pieces of paper are clustered together on hexagons of about five rows. It is likely, then, that Susan Crouch and her husband Dr. Hasell Crouch pieced most of the hexagons in the quilt top #1.[39] The more recent fabrics surround hexagons made from the older fabrics and paper templates, implying that Franklin Cushman did some work on quilt top #1 around the edges, but most of the work assembling quilt tops #2 and #3.

### The Fabric Swatch Books

The fabric swatches are contained in two loose-leaf binders, with individual fabric swatches attached to each page and handwritten notes written beneath each one (fig. 8). The inside front cover of one of the fabric swatch books reads, "Patches from the pocket of Abagail [sic] Chandler, wife of Elijah Williams, handspun and handwoven about 1775." (A pocket is a separate article of clothing worn under a petticoat or gown to hold valuables; it tied on at the waist, often in pairs.) The "pocket" is referenced in a letter from Franklin to Miss Mary C. Whitlock, who managed the University of Rhode Island's Historic Textile and Costume Collection in 1952. This letter reveals that the pocket "belonged to my great, great grandmother, Abigail Chandler, wife of Elijah Williams. She died in the early [eighteen] thirties."[40] The swatch books include seven different handwoven fabrics from Abigail's pocket, samples from her daughter Sarah Rose Williams' pocket, and snippets of dress fabrics from family members. Years later, Franklin even included a few twentieth-century fabrics in his swatch books, such as a page of shirtings dated 1937. The handspun and

Figure 8. Fabric swatch with notation "Used in bed quilt Also, double gown of Eliza D. Williams" and "Crouch, before 1830. Charleston, S.C." Eliza Williams (1804–1885) was the sister of Susan McPherson Sibley (Williams) Crouch. Historic Textile and Costume Collection, University of Rhode Island.

handwoven cloth does not appear in any of the quilts; most of the fabric in the swatch books is dated (in the same hand) to the 1830s and 1840s. A few are labeled "before 1830" or "ante 1830." Underneath many of the fabrics is the handwritten name "HW Crouch," and in the bottom right corner of many pages is the date 1917, which notes the year the swatch books were begun, written in the hand of Franklin R. Cushman.

Susan's daughter, Emily, owned three trunks, from which most of the fabrics came. She had been accumulating artifacts in trunks since 1839 according to accession notes.[41] After her mother's death in 1902, Emily remained in the house, taking in female boarders as evidenced in *The Providence House Directory and Family Address Book* for the period 1905–1917.[42] Later in life, probably in 1917, she moved to the home of Franklin Cushman and his two sisters at 19 Bellevue Avenue.[43] Franklin opened the trunks in 1917, about the time she moved in with him to live out her years. The trunks and their contents were written about in a 1930 newspaper article after Emily's death; the short article featured a woman posing in one of the dresses from the trunk (Franklin refers to this article in his letter). The caption underneath the photograph reads, "An old loose gown…once worn by Mrs. Abigail Chandler Williams and packed in a sea chest which remained in the old Williams house on George St until 1917."[44] The Jason Williams Crouch house no longer stands. It was listed as vacant in 1920, and the land on which it stood now is the location of Brown University's Littlefield Hall, a student residence built in 1925.

The notebooks each hold about thirty pages of numbered fabric swatches. Some of the fabrics are identified with the source from which Franklin acquired them and the approximate date of manufacture, for example: "NY Merchant Sales—1840-50 Caroline Cromwell," and, "Mrs. Sarah Rose Williams—before 1840—front of her pocket, Providence, RI, 102 George St formerly 51 George St." Some of the fabrics are noted as being, "used in bed quilt," or, "scrap of Betsy Williams' dress—she lived in little red house in Roger Williams Park, Providence. Betsy Williams was [the great great] granddaughter of Roger Williams."[45] One plain white cotton swatch is accompanied by the caption: "sample used for setting in bed quilt—pieced in hexagonal block. H. W. Crouch, Charleston, South Carolina." Another reads, "from Mary Lee Technical High School, Purchased 1862—75c a yard." Many of the swatches are noted with mention of "HW Crouch, Charleston, SC," and either "1830-1840," or, "probably ante 1830." One drab print has a bolt stamp with the date "1830" (fig. 9). Most of the swatches in the books came from leftover fabrics stored in the trunks.

Figure 9. Fabric swatch labeled "drab" with bolt stamp dated 1830. Historic Textile and Costume Collection, University of Rhode Island.

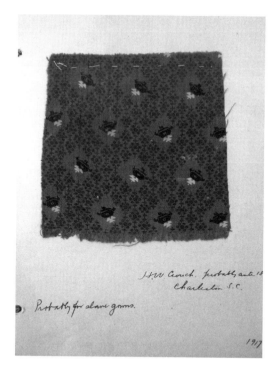

Figure 10. This page from one of the swatch books shows a simple four-cylinder cotton calico. Labeled "probably for slave gowns," it is also found in the quilts. A swatch of the same design in a different colorway (red ground) is in the swatch books. Historic Textile and Costume Collection, University of Rhode Island.

However, it appears that Franklin cut up some clothing for swatches, specifically the pockets that belonged to Abigail and Sarah, as well as the dress of Betsy Williams; the Cushman collection does not include such artifacts. Further, an 1830s dress probably belonging to Susan arrived at URI with the sleeves cut off (accession number 52.64.40); the fabric can be found in both the quilt tops and the swatch books, suggesting that Franklin may have used the sleeves for swatches.

It is significant that one of the fabrics is marked with the note, "Probably for slave gowns," and "HW Crouch probably ante 1830 Charleston, SC." (fig. 10.) Franklin probably got this information from Emily, who had learned it from her mother Susan, a first-hand witness to the clothing worn by the slaves in her husband's Charleston family. The "slave gown" print has a brown ground and features a small geometric pattern; it is found in two of the quilt tops. The calico is a simple print in the cover and pad style that would have required four cylinders. The same print on a dull red ground appears in one of the notebooks. Such designs were economical to print. According to scholars who have studied American slave clothing, field hand clothing was made of "coarse" cloth, especially os-

Figure 11. Hexagon "flower" of same fabric illustrated in Figure 8. Historic Textile and Costume Collection, University of Rhode Island.

naburg.[46] Shane White and Graham White acknowledge that most slave clothing (especially that for field slaves) was indeed "coarse" and simple, but that tremendous variation occurred in the clothes that slaves wore, as evidenced in the runaway ads posted in newspapers.[47] Patricia Hunt-Hurst researched clothing in fugitive slave advertisements in Georgia, finding that while "homespun" was the most frequently mentioned fabric in the runaway slaves' clothing, calico was the second highest: women "ran away wearing 'figured,' 'red striped,' or 'dark pongee' calico."[48] The cloth in the Cushman fabric swatch books is neither coarse nor extravagant; it is of the same quality and weight as other cottons in the swatch books and the quilt tops, though its dull color made it more practical for everyday use and labor. Probably it was intended for Susan and Hasell's seven house slaves.[49]

Most of the twenty-eight fabrics in the swatch books labeled with the Crouch name are used in the quilt tops. (fig. 11.) Franklin obtained a moiré print from another source that appears in the quilt tops. All three of the quilts share at least four of the fabrics that are also found in the swatch books. Additionally, two of the quilts share several more fabrics, but these samples are not found in the swatch books.

Franklin intended to use the swatch books in his industrial design classes at Providence Technical High School, in a state known for textile manufacturing. But the curriculum changed, and the swatch books were no longer needed as instructional materials. He gave one book to Miss Grace Whaley, a fellow teacher who went on to supervise home economics teacher training at Rhode Island State College (now the University of Rhode Island).[50] After Franklin's death, she gave the book to the Historic Textile and Costume Collection.

### Evidence of Mercantile Activity

The quilt tops and related documents reveal mercantile activity that supported the growing capitalistic economy in the Atlantic world—including the enslavement of Africans. The Portuguese pioneered the purchase of slaves on Africa's west coast for sale to plantations on coastal South America and in the Caribbean. British, Dutch, French, and Americans eventually joined in.

The British were particularly successful on Barbados with sugar plantations in the seventeenth century.[51] They planted only modest amounts of cotton. By the early eighteenth century, the Caribbean islands were getting crowded. Expansion meant moving the Barbados socio-economic model to North America's southern colonies, which established Charleston as a major port city. Indigo and rice constituted the major crops in the eighteenth century, but with the invention of textile machinery that sped up the production of cotton textiles, entrepreneurs in the young United States economy shifted their attention to cotton in the early nineteenth century. The Crouches and the Williamses participated in this economy.

Papers in the quilt tops include the words "West Indies," "casks," "shugar," "Havana," "Barbados," "Carolyna," and "Charleston." These papers are brown and crumbling with age, and the words are handwritten. The papers also include passages typeset in English, French, and Spanish, which appear to be fragments of legal documents. Examples of French wording found on paper templates include: "et prudents / Comtes / Conseillers, comme / Justiciers, et Regent / …mit ecclefiaitiques ou fecu / … res patentees. Nous…." The translations are: "and careful [or cautious] / Counts /Advisors  like / Justices, and Regents [Law-makers] / …Ecclesiastics or [   ] / […res] Patented.  We…" A fragment written in a mix of

Spanish and English reads in part, "y territorio / Par esca conv / EN testi-monio / 1798 / My Office / July 26." All but the words "My Office Jan. 26 1798" are typeset. This is clearly another sort of legal document, referencing a territory, signed in testimony.

Another language included in the fragments is Dutch; there are sev-eral mostly indecipherable handwritten Dutch (perhaps Old Dutch) frag-ments clustered together, two of which read in part, "aller geode / eldlyke die deeze / eezen: Doen wy Burge / Carolyna / son van Charleston / by foelmneelen Ee / Bygantynal," and another reads, "Carolyna Charle…" seeming to reference Charleston, [South] Carolina. These templates may have been cut from a letter, as the words translated as "go in good" sound like a greeting or sign-off of some kind.

These are some of the languages spoken in the Caribbean. This fact, along with the repeated appearance within the hexagonal paper templates of the words "West Indies," as well as references to "shugar," "weight," "lbs," "casks," "Seaman," "Sloop," "Master," "Captain," "Lists of the Vessels," "Shipping," "Helmsman," and "Property" provide evidence of mercantile transactions between the West Indies and Charleston. Hasell Wilkinson's father, Abraham Crouch, in his position as notary in Charleston's Customs House (located in the Old Exchange Building, which functioned as Charleston's slave auction site), surely witnessed the buying and selling of slaves.[52] He may have even boarded slave ships arriving from Africa, enu-merating the human cargo, prior to the 1808 law banning the transatlantic slave trade. Abraham lived in the upper strata of Charlestonian society; his home on Meeting Street was just steps away from the city's social elite, in-cluding Nathaniel Russell (1738–1820), a transplanted Rhode Island mer-chant who built a grand neoclassical home at 51 Meeting Street in 1808.[53]

The repetition of the words "shugar" and "casks" is evidence of the rum trade between the U.S. and West Indies. "Havana" and "Barbados" are mentioned—both major sources of sugar and molasses to be made into rum at the American distilleries. Merchants used Rhode Island distilleries (a major industry in the late 1700s and early 1800s) which produced a pre-ferred brand of rum. We know that Rhode Island and Charleston were in-volved in New England's nefarious "triangle trade": sugar and molasses from the West Indies were traded for manufactured goods in New Eng-land (especially Rhode Island rum) which was in turn traded for slaves in West Africa, who were sold in the West Indies.[54] No evidence exists that ties either the Crouches or the Williamses to slave ships, but Susan Crouch's family was part of the West Indies trade.[55] As previously mentioned, William Hilton Williams, Susan's uncle, died of yellow fever in Surinam. His grandmother Abigail's pocket, when discovered by Franklin, had included a silhouette of William as well as an oration on "Sympathy" that had been corrected by his tutor, Mr. Fish, at Brown University in 1798. His clothes, some of which are now in URI's collection, were returned to the family in his sea chest.

Susan's father and brothers were active in the coastal trade in the years following the American Revolution. Susan's brothers, Hilton and Winthrop, shipped goods back and forth between Providence and Charleston from the 1830s to the 1880s, when they died in Charleston. Both brothers' businesses relied on slave labor, and Winthrop continued buying and selling enslaved people into the 1850s.[56] After Susan moved back to Providence, Winthrop sold her slaves, buying one for an acquaintance. Slavery was a fact of life for the Crouches and the Williamses.

As Ronald Bailey argues, the rum trade was closely connected to the production of Caribbean sugar, spermaceti candles, cotton grown in the southern states, the ship building industry, and the slave trade—and later, the industrial production of cotton cloth. He states: "These early industries provided the foundation and part of the initial capital for the industrialization of New England."[57] Rhode Island's merchants, living in a small place with no raw materials to export, relied on trading, smuggling, and privateering in the eighteenth century. Only a handful of merchants got into the slave trade because of the expense and risk involved. "The great majority of Rhode Island vessels," like those owned by the Williamses, "were engaged in the coastal trade."[58] From the profits gained through the rum trade and the slave trade sprang the cotton textile industry that fueled New England's economy in the nineteenth century. Charleston, home to the Crouches, was the largest American receiving port for slaves during the colonial period.[59]

Recent publications have begun to address the issue of northern complicity in southern slavery over the economic juggernaut posed by cotton's growth. Madelyn Shaw and Lynne Zacek Bassett curated an exhibition and catalog titled *Homefront & Battlefield: Quilts & Context in the Civil War,* pointing out that "countless Americans maintained family and business ties across state and regional divisions," including slave traders, rum distillers, and manufacturers of negro cloth for sale to plantation owners.[60] Edward E. Baptist offered a history of the interpretation of slavery in America in *The Half Has Never Been Told,* drawing attention to the Atlantic trade, its expansion in the American South, and the cotton empire that fueled America's economy in the nineteenth century.[61] Sven Beckert globalized the history of cotton in *Empire of Cotton,* emphasizing the role of slave labor in building that empire: much of the cotton grown in America ended up in Manchester, England's cotton mills for production into inexpensive cloth sold in emerging markets.[62] Christy Clark-Pujara's *Dark Work* describes the history of slavery in Rhode Island, including the connections between northern textile mills that produced "negro cloth" and southern cotton growers.[63]

Susan and Hasell followed in the footsteps of Hasell's father, Abraham Crouch, who held twelve slaves in his household of four whites, as recorded in the 1820 census in Charleston, South Carolina. Earlier members of the South Carolina Crouch family also owned slaves; Mary Wilkinson (a Rhode Islander) and Charles Crouch owned three slaves.[64] In 1830, at Brown's Commencement Exercises, Hasell gave an oration on "Southern Slavery."[65]

The introduction of machine-printed cottons is evidenced by Susan and Hasell Crouch's acquisition of the fabrics in the quilt tops and fabric swatch books, most of which are noted to have been made between 1830 and 1840. The later shift to textile manufacture is evidenced in the fabrics that Franklin R. Cushman notes, in the fabric swatch books, were offered through "merchant sales" in New York. The fabrics from the pockets of Abigail and her daughter Susan show the transition from homemade to factory-produced cloth in New England. As Connecticut and Providence residents, the Williams family would have had access to early domestically manufactured fabrics as well as imported cloth. Several of the fabrics are represented in multiple colorways, suggesting a connection to the textile industry. Family correspondence includes numerous mentions of fabrics, some of which Susan requested from family members in Providence. Jason Williams' store carried a variety of fabrics including calicos in 1832 and 1833.[66] A letter from Hasell to Susan's family reports that she bought "a French muslin that Eliza [Susan's sister] saw at Harwoods and admired so much" and was making it into a dress.[67] Perhaps this is the fabric labeled "Eliza's double gown" in the swatch book. (Fig. 8.) Susan also requested unbleached muslin. Susan had all manner of imported and domestic fabrics available to her in Charleston's shops. But, the correspondence shows that the family shipped parcels back and forth that contained fabrics. Probably fabric prices in Rhode Island, near cotton manufacturers, were lower than Charleston's prices. Susan's shop owner father, Jason Williams, could buy both locally printed and imported fabrics at wholesale prices, which even with shipping costs were probably lower than Charleston's retail prices.

Susan's quilt tops and Franklin's swatch books represent a transitional period in America's industrial history. In the swatch books, the blue-and-white linens made by Abigail Williams speak to the pre-industrial era. The fabrics in the tops include the imported block prints and large-scale copperplate prints from the late eighteenth- and early nineteenth centuries, as well as the small-scale patterns characteristic of early cylinder printing. A few of the earliest fabrics may be printed on linen or linen-cotton blends.[68] American textile printing was in its infancy during the 1820s, and a few of the fabrics in these artifacts may have come from American print works. A few short years after these quilt tops were started, the American textile industry grew into an important economic engine for both the North, where most of the mills were located, and the South, which supplied the raw material (cotton), as well as a ready market for finished cloth.

### From the Civil War to the Colonial Revival

The files on the Cushman, Crouch, and Williams family, and the quilt tops themselves, span notable events from the Revolutionary War (with the mention of the date 1775 in one of the quilt top papers), to the Civil War, the abolition of slavery, the start of the Industrial Revolution, the Spanish American War, and World War I. Susan's two brothers who resided in Charleston lost their businesses in the Civil War; Hilton's lumber yard was ruined, and Winthrop's company—R. & J. Caldwell—was burned. Winthrop recovered, forming W. B. Williams & Son and hiring his brother as a clerk.[69] Hasell Wilkinson's grand-nephew, Hasell Wilkinson Crouch (1879–1938), fought in the Spanish American War.[70]

Years later, April 14, 1917, mention of war continues, in a letter to "Cousin Emmie," from "Trezevant":

> Well it looks like real war in Washington here! Soldiers guarding the railroad and other bridges, the water works, the Government buildings & clerks all required to show a pass to gain admittance to their offices…Germany has been killing our people & snubbing & insulting us & blowing up our factories by plots. I hope we will, with the help of England & France just entirely annihilate the Kaisir & all that he stands for.

His frustration, towards the end of the war, is clear. Later in the letter, he writes of more personal news: "I was certainly very glad to have that photo of the 'Old House.' It is a very good picture and is a quaint looking old place. I wonder *when* it was built. Do you know?"[71]

The inquiry about the house is in the spirit of the Colonial Revivalists, who celebrated the colonial houses that were previously seen as homely.[72] In fact, the Jason Williams Crouch house was included in a 1918 publication on Providence and its colonial houses.[73] Considered old-fashioned for much of the nineteenth century, people gradually became more accepting of colonial architecture, and began to celebrate it as "Picturesque," linking it to a humble, morally strong past.[74] The waves of immigration from eastern and southern Europe compelled old New England families to celebrate their long histories in North America with an emphasis on colonial heritage; they held Martha Washington teas wearing old family heirlooms and revived craft skills of olden times such as quilt-making. It was at this time that hexagon patchwork made a comeback; known as Grandmother's Flower Garden, it became one of the favorite quilt patterns of the Colonial Revival period.

In the spirit of Colonial Revivalism, Franklin R. Cushman started putting together the fabric swatch books in 1917; he began with the home-spun fabrics from the pocket of Abigail Chandler Williams. The Colonial Revival movement was at its peak in the 1920s and 1930s, when the article about the family's objects was published in 1930 under the title "Attic Treasures" in the Providence newspaper, with an image of a woman reenacting that past as she wore an antique dress and looked into a mirror.[75] She's photographed from the back, so we see her face in the mirror—an apt analogy for the Colonial Revival, re-envisioning ourselves through the past.[76] Indeed, Franklin R. Cushman, the history teacher, seemed to be fully engaged in remembering his family's past. Luckily for us, he provided the University of Rhode Island and the Rhode Island Historical Society with detailed notes on the artifacts and documents he donated.

In a coincidence of colonial revival activity, in 1921, Ethel Stanwood Bolton and Eva Johnston Coe, with the Massachusetts Society of the Colonial Dames of America, published *American Samplers*. Included in the book is documentation of samplers by Susan McPherson Sibley Williams and Emily H. Crouch, which are not pictured, but described in detail. Susan's was made when she was just seven years old, in Providence, Rhode Island, in 1820. The documentation of Susan's sampler reads:

Williams, Susan McPherson Sibley. 1820. Providence, R.I. 7 yrs. 9"
x 8 ½". 3 alphabets. Chain and cross-stitch. "Behold the child of
innocence how beautiful is the mildness of its countenance and
the diffidence of its looks." "Be good and be happy."[77]

The University of Rhode Island's Historic Textile and Costume collection
does not own the Williams samplers, but it does house dresses, shawls, and
other artifacts once used by Abigail, Susan and Emily. One dress is made
of fabric that appears in both a quilt top and the swatch books (accession
number 52.64.40). The style of another loose-fronted dress, a beautifully
stitched wrapper, is in a mid-1830s style that corresponds with the date
when Susan was pregnant with Emily (accession number 52.64.41). She
wrote home about sewing a dress for her expanding waistline.[78] Dresses
attributed to Susan after her return to Providence show that she wore
fashionable clothing in then-current fabrics. It is fascinating that the story
of this family comes full circle, starting with the history of the quilt tops,
paper templates, and swatch books, and their reference to slave dresses
and the rum trade in the West Indies, through several wars, to the early
twentieth century's interest in reviving this history in the Colonial Revival.
Franklin continued to work on the quilt tops in the 1930s as represented
by the papers in the back of the quilt tops. Fragments of documents from
the schools where Franklin taught, letters and envelopes printed with his
address (19 Bellevue Ave.), and magazine clippings mention, among many
other things, the art of Norman Rockwell.

It is remarkable that these quilt tops and fabric swatch books, and the
accompanying letters and documentation, cover such a broad span of
United States history, from the late 1700s to the early 1950s. And equally
fascinating are the stories of the people who lived through these times—
the births and deaths of their children, their travel and correspondence
from North to South, the way they sustained contact with one another
through letters and photographs, their choices to marry or to stay single,
the worry they expressed when waiting to hear from a nephew, their long-
ing to see their sisters, their sense of regret in writing of bad news. The
story of Susan McPherson Sibley (Williams) Crouch (fig. 12) holds particular intrigue. What must her life have been like for those four short years
of marriage? How did she survive the death of both her son and husband
in one year (an event not uncommon in those days, but certainly no less
difficult for the survivors), as well as the birth of her daughter in that
same year? In letters to her brothers in Charleston in her later years, she

Figure 12. Photograph of Susan McPherson Sibley (Williams) Crouch in later life. Historic Textile and Costume Collection, University of Rhode Island.

frequently mentions a male friend, so perhaps she had found love again, or at least companionship.

Did Susan feel any regret that various family members owned slaves and earned their living by servicing the plantation system? She never mentions whether she is pro or con, but she adjusted quickly to owning enslaved people. Her brother Winthrop was decidedly pro-slavery; Franklin characterized him as a "fire-breathing southerner" in his notebooks at the Rhode Island Historical Society.[79]

Conclusion

In looking at the fabrics in the quilt tops and their connection to the fabrics in the swatch books, as well as these papers in the backs of the quilt tops, we find the story of a family whose ancestors were witness to, and participated in, a rapidly shifting American economy—and because of their locations in Charleston and Rhode Island, as well as mention of "slave gowns" alongside one of the fabrics in the diary—and slavery as well. We can trace the roots of the cotton plantations in the South, and the shift to machine-spun and woven cotton in the North. Fabrics in the swatch books dated between 1830 and 1840 that match those in the quilt tops mark the early years of the textile printing industry in the United States. The quilts, papers, and letters from the family members (archived at URI and the Rhode Island Historical Society) tell the story of a family rooted in both Providence and Charleston, serving and surviving in multiple wars, sustaining their connections with letters, photographs, visits, and occasional shipments of gifts up and down the coast. And, the preservation by the Cushmans of this collection of clothes and artifacts, and their investment in recovering these stories and continuing to make the quilts, reveals their involvement in the Colonial Revival movement.

*The authors thank Professor Margaret Ordoñez, Director of URI's Historic Textile and Costume Collection, for identifying fabrics in the quilt tops, and to Susan Jerome, Collections Manager of the Historic Textile and Costume Collection for her help. Appreciation also is due to Ned Lazaro, Curator of Textiles at Historic Deerfield, for sharing information on a similar Rhode Island quilt, Linda Baumgarten for sharing information on the Cushman donations to Colonial Williamsburg, and to Matthew Haught of the University of South Carolina for sharing his research on the printer Mary Crouch. Many thanks go to Lynne Bassett for her helpful suggestions.*

## Notes and References

1. The collection came to URI in three donations, the first from Franklin R. Cushman, and the second and third from his siblings. Before his death in 1952, Franklin distributed many other pieces, including quilts and furnishing fabrics, to other museums and historical societies. Grace Whaley, who had worked with Franklin, later donated one of the two swatch books.

2. Emily and William's second daughter, Mary Elizabeth Harris, married William Allerton Cushman, a descendant of Robert Cushman, financial agent to the Plymouth Colony who arrived in America on the ship *Fortune* on November 9, 1621.

3. Genealogical information was compiled from URI accession records, Ancestry.com, Findagrave.com, MSS 34, Series F, Vol. 1-8: Franklin Cushman's Notebooks (Elijah Williams Papers, Rhode Island Historical Society).

4. *Historical Catalogue of Brown University*, 1764–1914 (Providence, RI: Brown University, 1914), 156.

5. According to an image from her grave, she had two infants at the time. "This truly amiable Lady thus early snatched away from her two infants and grieving Friends was the highly affectionate consort of Abraham Crouch Esq. of this city …." Findagrave.com.

6. Susan Crouch to Emily Williams, letter dated 7 May 1836, MSS 34, Series E, Correspondence, Elijah Williams Papers, Rhode Island Historical Society.

7. *South Carolina Death Records,* 1821–1955, www.ancestry.com.

8. Susan Henry, "Exception to the Female Model: Colonial Printer Mary Crouch," *Journalism Quarterly* 62, 4 (1985): 725–726.

9. Carl Bridenbaugh, "Charlestonians at Newport, 1767–1775," *The South Carolina Historical and Genealogical Magazine* 41, 2 (1940): 45, 47.

10. Henry, "Colonial Printer," 728–733.

11. *Historical Catalogue of Brown University,* 73.

12. Meeting Street (1–42), Charleston County Public Library, www.ccpl.org/content.asp?id=15675&action=detail&catid=6025&parentid=5747

13. *Historical Catalogue of Brown University,* 154, 156. Hasell's name is spelled "Hazell" in Brown University records.

14. George Chandler, *The Chandler Family: The Descendants of William and Annis Chandler Who Settled in Roxbury, Mass.* (Worcester, MA: Press of Charles Hamilton, 1883), 291.

15. "For Sale" advertisement listing the property of John Williams. *Providence Gazette,* 22 March 1799.

16. *Historical Catalogue of Brown University,* 70.

17. *Providence Gazette,* 21 June 1799.

18. Survey of Federal Archives, Ship Registers and Enrollments of Providence, Rhode Island, 1773–1939 (The National Archives Project, 1941).

19. *Historical Catalogue of Brown University,* 70.

20. Letters from Jason Williams to Elijah Williams, 30 August 1808 and 9 October 1808, MSS 34, Series F, Vol 1, 28–29, Elijah Williams Papers, Rhode Island Historical Society.

21. Guide to the Elijah Williams Papers, Rhode Island Historical Society.

22. Receipt, MSS 34, Series C, Jason Williams' Papers, Elijah Williams Papers, Rhode Island Historical Society.

23. Letter from Franklin R. Cushman to Miss Mary C. Whitlock, 8 March 1952, Cushman Collection, Accession Records, Historic Textile and Costume Collection, University of Rhode Island.

24. As recorded in the accession notes by Miss Mary C. Whitlock, "Practically all the pieces in the main part of the quilt are earlier than those of the 2 quilts [2 & 3]."

25. Franklin Cushman Notebooks, Elijah Williams Papers, Rhode Island Historical Society.

26. 1880 United States Federal Census Records, Providence, RI (www.ancestry.com). Additionally, in a 14 April 1917 letter from Cousin Trezevant to Cousin Emmie, he asks after her artwork and wonders if she is still painting. Series C: Jason Williams Papers (Elijah Williams Papers, Rhode Island Historical Society).

27. Bridget Long, *Elegant Geometry: American and British Mosaic Patchwork* (Lincoln, NE: International Quilt Study Center and Museum, 2011), 11.

28. Deborah E. Kraak, "Early American Silk Patchwork Quilts," in *Textiles in Early New England: Design, Production, and Consumption, The Dublin Seminar for New England Folklife Annual Proceedings,* ed. Peter Benes (Boston: Boston University, 1997), 18–20. The Newark Museum holds an unfinished top dated 1793, the Bache family of Philadelphia holds a 1790s unfinished top, and the Wadsworth Atheneum Museum of Art holds a quilt made by Sarah Ewalt Spencer (1766–1842) of Bedford, Pennsylvania, acc.no.1982.165, dated 1794. Lynne Z. Bassett, email communication, February 2013.

29. The Charleston Museum, *Mosaic Quilts: Paper Template Piecing in the South Carolina*

*Lowcountry* (Greenville, SC: Curious Works Press, 2002); Sharon Fulton Pinka, "Lowcountry Chintz: The Townsend/Pope Quilt Legacy," ed. Lynne Zacek Bassett, *Uncoverings* 2013, (Lincoln, NE: American Quilt Study Group), 76.

30. *Godey's Lady's Book* used Eliza Leslie's hexagon piecing design without crediting her. Hexagon piecing reached wide popularity and then fell from favor; in 1846, calico hexagon patchwork was dubbed "a beggar's patchwork" by author Catharine Maria Sedgwick. See: Lynne Z. Bassett and Jack Larkin, *Northern Comfort: New England's Early Quilts, 1780–1850* (Nashville, TN: Rutledge Hill Press, 1998), 62, 72.

31. Linda Welters and Margaret T. Ordoñez, eds, *Down by the Old Mill Stream: Quilts in Rhode Island* (Kent, Ohio: Kent State University Press, 2000), 29, 134–136.

32. Examples of quilt tops in which the makers left the papers in the back include the Anna Tuels quilt at the Wadsworth Atheneum Museum of Art and the Leverett-Saltonstall quilt at the Peabody Essex Museum. Lynne Z. Bassett, email communication February 2013.

33. The commemorative presidential fabric is printed in red with the date 1829. The URI Historic Textile and Costume Collection owns a length of the same fabric in blue. As for the black and white fabric with parrots, Colonial Williamsburg Foundation owns a similar piece of fabric donated by Franklin R. Cushman. The fabric in the Williamsburg collection is white and "china blue" (the pieces in the Cushman quilt are black and white), and it is dated 1774–1811. The piece at Williamsburg is said to have been a remnant from fabric used for chair and window seat covers, and window curtain tiebacks. Form No. 148, Curator's Worksheet, Accession No. 51-364, 1-2, The Colonial Williamsburg Foundation, Williamsburg, Virginia.

34. Laurel Horton, "An Elegant Geometry: Tradition, Migration, and Variation," in *Mosaic Quilts* (Charleston, SC: The Charleston Museum in cooperation with Curious Works Press, 2002), 14–15.

35. Ibid., 14–15.

36. Letter from Winthrop Williams to the Williams family, 8 November 1834, MSS 34, Series F., Vol. 7, pp. 53-54, Elijah Williams Papers, Rhode Island Historical Society.

37. The older papers have turned brown with age, and some are crumbling and falling out of the tops. Newer papers are from letters, glossy magazines, and advertisements, and remain mostly intact.

38. As Deborah Kraak points out, a dated template does not prove that a quilt was started on that date. See: Kraak, "Early American Silk Patchwork Quilts," 20.

39. A letter from Franklin R. Cushman explains further: "The work on [the two bed quilts] was begun by our grandmother's sister, a Charleston, S.C. bride in 1833. It is of block print calico with white borders. The color scheme was made by her husband, a young physician. After his death in 1936 [sic], the partly completed quilt was put away with all the pieces cut and ready to be put in place. The cut pieces were sewed in place in the summers 1930–1937, to make two quilts—twin bed size. Both Mrs. Crouch and her daughter had died leaving the quilts unfinished. Mrs. Crouch was in her ninetieth year, her daughter, an artist, had just passed her ninetieth birthday." Letter from Franklin R. Crouch to Miss Mary C. Whitlock, 8 March 1952, Cushman Collection, Accession Records, Historic Textile and Costume Collection, University of Rhode Island.

40. Letter from Franklin R. Cushman to Grace Whaley, 1 March 1952, Cushman Collection, Accession Records, Historic Textile and Costume Collection, University of Rhode Island.

41. The Cushman Collection at the University of Rhode Island includes three trunks, which may include the trunk in which the unfinished quilt tops were stored. Due to space limitations, the trunks (Trunks 4, 5, and 6) were deaccessioned when an attic storage area was deemed unusable in 2015.

42. *The Providence House Directory and Family Address Book* was viewed for 1903, 1905, 1907, 1909, 1911, 1913, 1915, 1917, and 1920, 1921–1922; available at: cdn.providenceri.com. The house number had changed to 102 George Street, but no longer existed in 1921–1922.

43. *The Providence House Directory and Family Address Book* lists E. H. Crouch as living at 102 George Street in 1917, but by the time the next directory was printed (1920), Emily H. Crouch was a member of Franklin's household at 19 Bellevue Avenue.

44. The Abigail Chandler Williams referred to in the article must be the granddaughter of the first Abigail Chandler Williams, as the dress dates to the 1840s. Her dates are 1803–1865. Newspaper clipping, Cushman Collection, Accession Records, Historic Textile and Costume Collection, University of Rhode Island.

45. The Betsy Williams Cottage is in Roger Williams Park in Providence. It is part of the National Historic District. Betsy Williams (1790–1871) bequeathed the house to the city of Providence upon her death. www.loc.gov/pictures/item/ri0275/.

46. Gerilyn G. Tandberg, "Field Hand Clothing in Louisiana and Mississippi During the Ante-Bellum Period," *Dress*, 6 (1980): 89-103; Madelyn Shaw and Lynne Zacek Bassett, *Homefront & Battlefield: Quilts & Context in the Civil War* (Lowell: American Textile History Museum, 2012), 19-25.

47. Shane White and Graham White, "Slave Clothing and African-American Culture in the Eighteenth and Nineteenth Centuries," *Past and Present,* 148 (1995): 155.

48. Patricia Hunt-Hurst, " Round Homespun Coat & Pantaloons of the Same': Slave Clothing as Reflected in Fugitive Slave Advertisements in Antebellum Georgia," *The Georgia Historical Quarterly* 83, 4 (Winter, 1999): 733.

49. The number of slaves owned by Susan and Hasell is mentioned in Franklin Cushman's Notebooks, Elijah Williams Papers, Rhode Island Historical Society.

50. Accession no. 1952.64.127.

51. Walter Edgar, *South Carolina: A History* (Columbia, SC: University of South Carolina Press, 1998).

52. "Exchange and Provost Building," www.nps.gov/nr/travel/charleston/exc.htm.

53. Nathaniel Russell House Museum, Historic Charleston Foundation, https://www.historiccharleston.org/Russell.aspx.

54. Jay Coughtry, *The Notorious Triangle: Rhode Island and the African Slave Trade, 1700–1807* (Philadelphia: Temple University Press, 1981), 6, 15.

55. Neither Williamses (or their business partners) nor Crouches are listed as owning slave ships. Ibid. 282–285.

56. MSS 34, Series E, Box 3, Folder 12, Elijah Williams Papers, Rhode Island Historical Society.

57. Ronald Bailey, "The Slave(ry) Trade and the Development of Capitalism in the United States: The Textile Industry in New England," *Social Science History,* 14, 3 (1990): 386.

58. J. Stanley Lemons, "Rhode Island and the Slave Trade," *Rhode Island History* 60, 1 (2002): 101.

59. Kenneth Morgan, "Slave Sales in Colonial Charleston," *The English Historical Review,* 113 no. 453, (1998): 906.

60. Shaw and Bassett, *Homefront & Battlefield*, 6.

61. Edward E. Baptist, *The Half Has Never Been Told: Slavery and the Making of American Capitalism* (New York: Basic Books, 2014).

62. Sven Beckert, *Empire of Cotton: A Global History* (New York, Alfred A. Knopf, 2014).

63. Christy Clark-Pujara, *Dark Work: The Business of Slavery in Rhode Island* (New York: New York University Press, 2016), 93–94.

64. Henry, "Colonial Printer," 727.

65. Reuben Aldridge Guild, *History of Brown University, With Illustrative Documents* (Providence, RI: 1867), 394.

66. MSS 34, Series 3, sub-series 2, Folder 9, 1830–32, Elijah Williams Papers, Rhode Island Historical Society.

67. Letter dated 27 June 1834, MSS 34, Series F, Vol. 2, p. 67, Elijah Williams Papers, Rhode Island Historical Society.

68. Margaret Ordoñez (URI) has been conducting research on eighteenth- and early-nineteenth-century fabrics previously assumed to be 100 percent linen, and has discovered that many of them are linen-cotton blends.

69. Elijah Williams papers, Rhode Island Historical Society.

70. The name "Hasell," which was Emily Crouch's middle name, was given to other children in the Crouch family.

71. "Cousin Trezevant" to "Cousin Emmie," 14 April 1917, Series C: Jason Williams Papers, Elijah Williams Papers, Rhode Island Historical Society.

72. W. Barksdale Maynard, "'The Best, Lowliest Style!' The Early-Nineteenth-Century Rediscovery of American Colonial Architecture," *Journal of the Society of Architectural Historians,* 59 no. 3 (2000): 338–357.

73. The Jason Williams Crouch house is pictured in Norman M. Isham, "Providence and Its Colonial Houses," *The White Pine Series of Architectural Monographs* IV, 3 (June, 1918): 7.

74. Maynard, "American Colonial Architecture," 339.

75. Newspaper clipping, Cushman Collection, Accession Records, Historic Textile and Costume Collection, University of Rhode Island.

76. Beverly Gordon wrote, "For the past two decades scholars have been exploring the meanings of the colonial revival, the movement in which Americans turned to the colonial past for images, artifacts, and symbols that seemed to give them a sense of themselves." Beverly Gordon, "Spinning Wheels, Samplers, and the *Modern Priscilla:* The Images and Paradoxes of Colonial Revival Needlework," *Winterthur Portfolio,* 33 no. 2/3 (1998): 163.

77. Ethel Stanwood Bolton and Eva Johnston Coe, *American Samplers,* (Boston, MA: National Society of the Colonial Dames, 1921), 242.

78. Letter dated 7 December 1834, MSS 34, Series E., Correspondence, Elijah Williams Papers, Rhode Island Historical Society.

79. Franklin Cushman made this comment in the correspondence he transcribed in his notebooks. See MSS 34, Series F, Vol. 2, p. 27.

Williams-Crouch Family

Elijah Williams ———————— Abigail (Chandler) Williams
(1744–1825) merchant                    (1747–1834)

1. John (1772–1842?)
doctor

3. William Hilton
(1780–1800) Surinam,
supercargo

2. Jason Williams ———————— Sarah (Rose) Williams
(1774–1863)                    (1778–1863)
merchant, shop owner

5. Susan McPherson Sibley William
(1813–1902) quiltmaker

1. Abigail (1803–1865)

2. Eliza (1804–1885)

3. Emily (1807–1875) ———————— William Jenkins Harris
(1808–1893)

4. Elijah Hilton
(1809–1884) lumber yard
owner, Charleston, SC          Mary Elizabeth Harris ——— William Allerton Cushman
(1838–1917)                    (1829–1893)
6. Winthrop Bowen
(1814–1886) cotton broker,
Charleston, SC                 Franklin R. Cushman (1870–1952)
technical high school teacher &
7. Sophia Jane (1818–1818)     colonial revivalist, finished the
quilt tops, assembled swatch
8. Sarah Rose (1822–1854)      books, donated to URI & other
archives

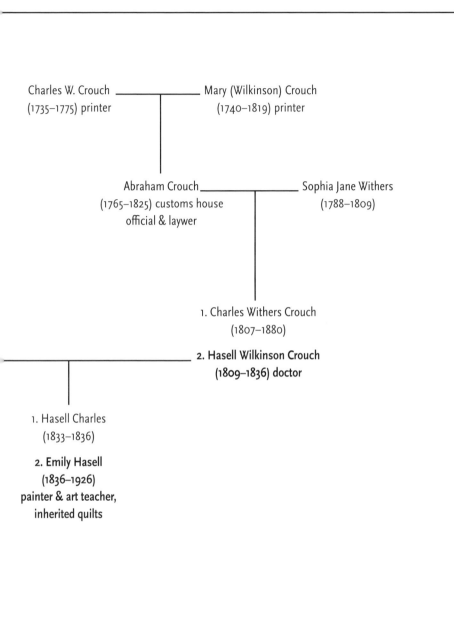

Charles W. Crouch ——————— Mary (Wilkinson) Crouch
(1735–1775) printer                (1740–1819) printer

Abraham Crouch———————— Sophia Jane Withers
(1765–1825) customs house          (1788–1809)
official & laywer

1. Charles Withers Crouch
(1807–1880)

**2. Hasell Wilkinson Crouch**
**(1809–1836) doctor**

1. Hasell Charles
(1833–1836)

**2. Emily Hasell**
**(1836–1926)**
**painter & art teacher,**
**inherited quilts**

Fig. 1. Acadian *cotonnade* quilt made by Eve Vidrine Thompson (Laf Sci Thompson in the appendices), c. 1930, 88 x 58 inches, Lafayette Science Museum 1985.3c.1950. Photograph courtesy of Lafayette Science Museum.

# Louisiana Acadian Cotonnade Quilts: Preserving the Weaving Heritage of a People

Dale Drake

*Two hundred fifty years ago Acadian refugees from Nova Scotia settled in Louisiana, bringing their weaving traditions with them. Over the next 150 years they wove* cotonnade *fabrics for clothing and bedding, and by the end of the nineteenth century they were making quilts from the scraps. Twenty-four of these quilts from private and public collections were studied in this project, which the author grouped by piecing format and textile type: Acadian format or block format, constructed of either clothing- style or household-textile-style* cotonnades. *Traditional Acadian values of self-sufficiency, frugality, cultural conservatism and family loyalty are evident in the quilts. They are important cultural artifacts, documenting the wide variety of fabrics the weavers created as they cared for their families, and preserving that weaving tradition and those cultural values in a new form.*

## Introduction

This is the story of the Acadians of Louisiana, their weaving heritage, and the quilts that preserve the fabrics the Acadians wove as they created clothing and bedding for their families. This research began with a chance mention of their signature fabric, *"cotonnade"* (cotton broadcloth), and led the author to private homes, warehouses and museums across southwest Louisiana in search of quilts constructed from fragments of fabric woven for other purposes. Very few quilts constructed of Acadian *cotonnade* fabrics now exist. As is the case with most quilts made for utilitarian purposes, many were probably used until they were used up and thrown away, and it is likely that few were made in the first place: the Acadians traditionally used blankets as bedding, not quilts. Some are now in private and public collections, and most of these have no provenance except for

Fig. 2. Acadian cotonnade quilt made by a member of the Thompson family (Miller Wholecloth), c. 1910, 85 x 62 inches, private collection. Photograph courtesy of Lafayette Science Museum and the Miller Family.

the important fact that they were collected from the area of southwest Louisiana known as Acadiana.

Two quilts, however, have survived with documentation that establishes who wove the fabrics and made the quilts. The first, probably made by Eve Vidrine Thompson around 1930 for her son Voorhies, is now in the collection of the Lafayette Science Museum in Lafayette, Louisiana. (Fig. 1, color plate 3.) The collection card that accompanies this quilt documents not only the maker of the quilt, but also the weavers of its fabrics. This collection card led the author to the second quilt with provenance, made from fabrics woven in the same extended household as the first and passed down through the generations to its current private owner. (Fig. 2.) The quilts that Acadian women made from hand-spun and handwoven *cotonnade* fabrics are a side note to the larger weaving tradition of the Acadians, but they are significant artifacts, documenting the many fabrics woven and traditions preserved by these weavers.

## Acadian History

The colony of Acadie, located in current Nova Scotia and New Brunswick, was settled by French immigrants from the coastal region of central France in the mid-1600s.[1] Over the next 100 years they thrived and developed a separate culture from the other French colonies in the New World, calling their land Acadie and themselves Acadians. High birth rates and low infant mortality rates led to dramatic population growth; a population of roughly 350 in 1654 had grown by 1755 to over 14,000.[2]

The area passed between French and British hands ten times between 1604 and 1710. During these years the Acadians swore conditional allegiance to the King of England, asking only that they not be asked to fight against the French or Native Americans. They became known as the French Neutrals and this conditional allegiance was tolerated until the onset of the Seven Years War (in the American theater, called the French and Indian War) in 1755.[3]

With tensions escalating between Britain and France, newly appointed Governor Charles Lawrence decided that the Acadians had to be removed. In the fall of 1755, Acadians in the most densely populated areas were forced onto transport ships with only hand baggage. Their houses and barns were burned and the ships dispersed among the other British colonies (not to Louisiana, a common misconception). The other colonial governors were not warned in advance and were not pleased with the

Fig. 3. The twenty-two parishes of Acadiana. Wikimedia Commons, commons. wikimedia.org/ wiki/File%3AAcadiana_parishes_map.png.

appearance of these Roman Catholic, French-speaking refugees on their doorsteps; they imprisoned some and enslaved others. Some ships were rejected outright. Some ships sank. Epidemics killed many of the refugees. Most Acadians who escaped the initial deportations fled into the woods, attempting to reach other French settlements. Over the next eight years most escapees were tracked down, died of exposure, or surrendered. This tragic event, romanticized by Longfellow in the poem "Evangeline," is *Le Grand Dérangement*—The Great Upheaval.[4]

Colonial governments that did accept Acadian refugees refused to release them during the Seven Years War, citing concern that they would join the French forces. Some colonies attempted to assimilate the Acadians, but most Acadians in exile retained their language, religion and culture.[5] At the end of the war in 1763, the Acadians in exile were encouraged to leave the British colonies. None were permitted to return to their homes, which were now in the hands of British subjects. Most who returned to the Canadian Maritimes established homes in New Brunswick. Many joined the French in Quebec, who had not been deported. Others removed to France or its colonies in the New World, including Louisiana, which had passed into Spanish hands.[6]

The Spanish were happy to accept the Acadians into their newly acquired territory, hoping to gain settlers and potential militia members to defend the west side of the Mississippi River against the British, who held the lands east of the river. At their invitation, over 2,500 refugees made their way from the eastern seaboard colonies to Louisiana between 1764 and 1788.[7] In the new Spanish territory they flourished in cultural and linguistic isolation. Their experience of betrayal and heartbreak created a deeply self-reliant people, now known as the Cajuns, who are loyal to their Acadian traditions and their community of extended family groups.[8] (Fig. 3.)

### The Weaving Tradition—From Acadie to Louisiana

While essentially no material culture of the Acadians survived *Le Grand Dérangement,* early-eighteenth-century accounts by visitors to pre-deportation Acadie indicate that the Acadians were known for their self-sufficiency and cultural conservatism in all areas, and particularly in textile production, using flax and wool. Sieur de Dièreville, a young French surgeon, reported in the published memoirs of his trip to Acadie in 1700 that "There's nothing which they cannot produce. They make the things they lack," creating clothing "in no way distinguished by new fashions . . . [but] made for comfort."[9] In 1717 a French official wrote: "They themselves make the cloth and the fabrics in which they are dressed."[10] Other visitors remarked on the traditional manner of the Acadians' dress; in the Maritimes they retained old French styles of dress into the nineteenth century.[11] This tendency of the Acadians to cling to traditional customs is noted by Dr. John Holden in his book *Furnishing Louisiana;* he refers to the Louisiana Acadian style of furniture production as *retardataire*—literally, late-comer. "Age-old French forms, recalling eras long departed and fashions long eclipsed, have a surprising way of turning up in Acadian chairs, beds, tables, and armoires. The knowledge necessary to craft these pieces illustrates the persistence of cultural memory in isolated communities such as those established by Louisiana's 'Cajuns.'"[12]

In *The Comfortable Arts: Traditional Spinning and Weaving in Canada*, Dorothy Burnham documents the dispersal of traditional weaving techniques with *Le Grand Dérangement*. "The Acadians of Louisiana were separated from the Acadians of the Atlantic Provinces by two thousand miles for two centuries, yet a bed covering woven in 'Cajun' country is a recognizable cousin of a bed covering woven in an Acadian community in Canada."[13] While one community worked in wool and flax and the other in cotton, similarities are evident. They both produced tabby weave fabric on two-harness looms and created patterns of mirror image weft banding. They retained the traditions of creating *couvertures du mariage,* all-white bridal coverlets with hand-netted fringes, and *catalognes* (rag rugs) using salvaged strips of material. And they incorporated weft manipulation techniques: *cordonné,* a regular pattern of heavier threads, creating textured ridges and windowpane effects; *boutonné,* wherein heavier threads are pulled up in loops; *chenilles* (literally "caterpillars"), the insertion of short strips of a contrasting color; and *dublé,* a barber-pole effect created by plying two threads of different colors together. (Fig. 4.) Burnham points out: "The family connection is unmistakable. We can therefore only conclude that the Canadian Acadian and Louisiana Acadian weaving traditions date back to a common origin."[14]

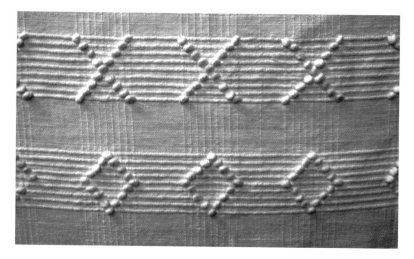

Fig. 4. Detail, couverture du mariage with cordonné and boutonné made by weaver Thèrése Meyers Dronet, c. 1930, Acadian Museum, Erath, Louisiana. Photograph by the author.

By 1769 the Acadians in Louisiana were growing cotton, which they wove into *cotonnade* (cottonade in English). "Throughout Louisiana, Acadian *cotonnade* (cotton broadcloth) quickly became synonymous with excellence."[15] In 1812 Territorial Governor Claiborne sent a "Cotton Blanket manufactured by a very amiable Lady of the county Attakapas within this Territory" to First Lady Dolley Madison.[16]

*Cotonnade* was fashioned into all manner of clothing: men wore collarless, loose-fitting shirts and pants, and women wore ankle-length striped skirts, cotton corsets, *carmagnolles* (decorated vests) and *garde-soleils* (sun bonnets). With the large expenditure of energy required to create *cotonnade,* clothing was worn, patched and worn again until it disintegrated. Louisiana Acadian scholar Carl Brasseaux notes that "[m]any if not most of the garments listed in Spanish-period estates were either *mauvaises* (tattered) or *usées* (threadbare)."[17] The earliest surviving article of clothing from the nineteenth century is a blue and white checked *cotonnade* dress dated around 1830; very few other garments have been preserved.[18] The Acadian textiles in the privately held Holden Family Collection include a shirt and a pair of pants. (Fig. 5.)

Early-nineteenth-century importation of manufactured cloth to the river parishes impacted cloth production in some Acadian households, where a decline in the number of spinning wheels and looms is found.

Fig. 5. Man's trousers and shirt of Acadian cotonnade in color-and-weave patterns, c. 1890, Holden Family Collection. Photograph by Jim and Reni Zeitz, modeled by Reni Zeitz.

This corresponds with trends in other areas of the country, with inexpensive commercial fabric replacing homespun textiles.[19] Many Acadians, however, particularly in the parishes west of the Atchafalaya Swamp, continued to produce their own clothing, sheets, blankets, mosquito netting and mattresses until at least the end of the century.[20] The anonymous *Breaux Manuscript,* an account of nineteenth-century Acadian culture written in 1901, includes a mention of quilts: "Before the Civil War, the country habitant dressed from head to foot in home-grown products.... The capot vest and trousers were made of *cotonnade.* The women wove the material for quilts, striped coverlets, bed-sheets, shirts, and so forth.... Nowadays all these home-made objects are so easily come by that people prefer to buy the commercial product. Home industry does not generally pay; however, *cotonnade* of great regional renown is still being manufactured."

As the weaving tradition died out, a few of the weavers of Acadian textiles were documented by reporters and historians. Widely considered to be the last of the traditional Acadian weavers, Gladys LeBlanc Clark (1918–2011) demonstrated spinning at the 1984 World's Fair in New Orleans, and won a Master Artist National Endowment for the Arts Award in 1997.[22] Gladys grew her own brown and green cotton and spun a single marbled brown/white thread in a special *doublage* technique learned from her mother, Colastie Hébert LeBlanc; *portières* woven from this thread are hanging at the windows of the weaving house in Vermilionville Historic Village in Lafayette.[23] Gladys trained new weavers through apprenticeships funded by the Louisiana Division of the Arts, passing along not only her knowledge of spinning and weaving, but also how to grow the cotton and dye the thread.

## Acadian *Cotonnade*

Acadian *cotonnade* is homespun cotton fabric made for clothing and household textiles such as sheets, curtains, and towels; Acadian spinners also created a heavier thread which was woven into cloth for blankets. In her 1999 *Uncoverings* article, Dr. Jenna Kuttruff said: "*Cotonnade* is noted for its durability, as indicated by the Cajun expression *il n'y a pas fin de cotonnade,* or there is no end to *cotonnade.*" A nineteenth-century Acadian folk song, "Le Bon Vieux Temps," recounts that "clothing made from homemade fabrics wore for a century."[25]

Acadian *cotonnade* was traditionally woven with three colors: white, blue (from white cotton dyed with indigo) and a rich warm tan from *coton jaune* (literally "yellow cotton"), a naturally occurring brown cotton.[26] White cotton, being of better commercial quality, was grown for both home use and as a cash crop; *coton jaune,* with its shorter staple length and inferior lint content, was grown in home gardens solely for weaving. Traditionally, mothers passed seeds of *coton jaune* on to their daughters.[27] There is concern now that, without home production for weaving, the variety could die out.[28] Revivalist artisans such as Elaine Larcade Bourque and Charlene Vizena Quinilty and colored cotton marketers are working to perpetuate and improve the variety.[29]

Archaeological findings show that brown cotton was cultivated in the Yucatan peninsula 1,000 years ago. Colonial trading could have brought this variety directly to Louisiana, or it could have been taken to West Africa by the French or Portuguese and then found its way back to Louisiana through the slave trade.[30] Botanical analysis of Louisiana's brown cotton has established that it is a New World cotton, with fifty-two chromosomes, and not a variant of "nankeen," or Chinese brown cotton, which has twenty-six chromosomes.[31] Botanist J. O. Ware studied this variety and designated it "Acadian Brown" in the 1940s. Ware observed: "This variety presumably has been maintained intact and in isolation from regular commercial stocks since its introduction from a foreign source in Colonial times. [It was used] in home manufacture by the French Acadians of the Teche country of Louisiana." He and other botanists found that Acadian Brown cotton has a recessive gene characteristic of smooth seeds that is linked to its brown color.[32] Dr. Ray Brassieur believes that the Acadians cultivated this characteristic to further establish their independence; smooth seeds are easy to hand gin, whereas the more common fuzzy seeds stick to the cotton fibers like Velcro®.

*Coton jaune* was spun in two sizes of thread, for blankets and for *cotonnade.* Contemporary Acadian weaver Elaine Bourque says that "the size of the cotton for a blanket is the size of my little finger."[33] These blankets were warm and durable, and can be found in public and private collections in the area.  Some are simple solid tan; others incorporate stripes of white or other colors.

Acadian weavers dyed their threads with other dyes in addition to indigo. Some *cotonnade* fabrics in this study include red threads, possibly created using horse liniment, which contains "cuperous," according to Gladys Clark.[34] This is probably copperas, or ferrous sulfate, which was often used as a dyeing agent.[35] Traditional weaver Joséphine Gary dyed her

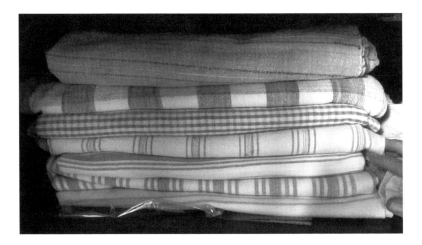

Figure 6: Armoire with cotonnade sheets, Holden Family Collection. The top sheet has cordons of red and white. Photograph by the author.

threads with coffee.[36] *Coton jaune* was sometimes dyed with indigo, creating a dark teal color.[37] And the author has observed *cotonnade* with dark brown threads; most of these, when present, are disintegrating, probably from walnut dye and/or iron mordant.

Acadian weavers wove the thick thread they had spun into blankets. They wove the lighter weight thread into *cotonnade* for both clothing and household textiles such as sheets, towels and curtains. The difference between clothing and household textile *cotonnade* is in pattern scale. Gladys Clark brought this distinction to the attention of Dr. Kuttruff, who included a quantitative analysis of the two types of fabrics in her 1999 study for *Uncoverings*. Small color-and-weave effect patterns, usually dark blue, light blue or tan, were used in clothing.[38] Solids, large stripes and plaids visible from a distance, often including white, fit into the household textile category. (Fig. 6.)

Acadian weaving tools were usually hand made, and included carding paddles, wheels, reels, and swifts. Warping boards accommodated warps long enough to weave a dozen blanket lengths. One unusual item, the *arc-de-coton,* is a small bow whose string is twanged with the fingers while being held in the hand-ginned cotton; this fluffs and cleans the fibers and prepares them for carding.[39] Two-harness looms with string heddles were often shared by members of the extended family, and weavers had multiple sets of harnesses and reeds to accommodate different sizes of thread.

The large looms were constructed with pegs, and could be moved from household to household as needed.[40]

Fabric production was a family affair. In one family, each child had to fill a demitasse cup with cotton seeds before bed.[41] Weaver Charlotte Lindsay describes the scene: "The Acadian loom would be dressed with 'miles' of warp. The families would sit around in the evenings (men playing instruments and singing) while the women and children hand ginned the cotton, carded it and created many a *rolag* [a hollow tube of carded cotton for spinning]. All would be spun by the end of the evening. Someone was always at the loom to weave off what had been spun the night before."[42]

Woven textiles were an important component of the social fabric of the community, and the tradition of *L'Amour de Maman* expressed the strong family ties important to the Acadians. At her marriage, each daughter in an Acadian household traditionally received a *cotonnade* trousseau, typically consisting of "12 blankets, 12 bedspreads or coverlets, 6 sheets, 12 towels, 4 mattress covers, a bolster and two pillows. A quilt may also have been included."[43] This trousseau freed the new wife from the need to outfit her own household; she then continued the tradition for her own daughters. Note that quilts are not central to the trousseau, the focus being on handwoven blankets, which were almost exclusively woven from *coton jaune.* It is sometimes mentioned that each son received a blanket.

## Research Methodology

The goal of this research was to study as many quilts made with Acadian *cotonnade* as possible, expanding on Dr. Kuttruff's textile analysis of three quilts, and determine whether any patterns could be established. To date the author has examined twenty-four quilts (twenty-three in person and one through photographs), which includes the three quilts in Dr. Kuttruff's study. (Appendix A.) Each quilt was measured and photographed, front and back, along with any unusual materials, patches, damage or other notable features. The author visually identified its fabric, batting and thread content; noted condition, repairs and binding; determined and sometimes sketched construction method; counted the number of pieces in each construction segment; sketched the quilting pattern and measured the stitches per inch and line spacing; and documented any provenance, including exhibition or publication history. In the case of the eight quilts in the Holden collection, thread counts for four representative sample pieces from each quilt were also recorded. The Quilt Index documentation

## Appendix A: Acadian Cotonnade Study Quilts

| Category/Study Name | Location | Date |
|---|---|---|
| **Acadian Format/Clothing Scraps** | | |
| Gallier Summer Spread | Gallier House New Orleans, Acc. #1973.74.1 | ca 1900; by L'Amour de Maman curator |
| Holden #117 | Holden Family Collection | 1st qtr 20th century; by author |
| Holden #118 | Holden Family Collection | 1st qtr 20th century; by author |
| Holden #119 | Holden Family Collection | ca 1920; by L'Amour de Maman curator |
| Holden #124 | Holden Family Collection | 1st qtr 20th century; by author |
| Laf Sci AB6 | Lafayette Science Museum, Acc. #2009.0110 | ca 1950; by museum or collector |
| Laf Sci Thompson | Lafayette Science Museum, Acc. #1985.3 | ca 1930; by author |
| LSM Holden #1 | Louisiana State Museum New Orleans, Acc. #1981.9 | ca 1890; by L'Amour de Maman curator |
| LSM Holden #2 | Louisiana State Museum New Orleans, Acc. #1982.134 | ca 1920; by museum |
| LSU AB5 | LSU Baton Rouge, Acc. #2007.074.001 | 1st qtr 20th century; by author |
| Reaux #1 | Reaux Private Collection | 1st qtr 20th century; by author |
| Whitecloud #2 | Whitecloud Private Collection | 1st qtr 20th century; by author |
| Whitecloud #3 | Whitecloud Private Collection | 1st qtr 20th century; by author |
| Whitecloud #4 | Whitecloud Private Collection | 1st qtr 20th century; by author |
| **Acadian Format / Household Textiles** | | |
| Erath #1 | Acadian Museum Erath, no accession number | 3rd qtr 20th century; by author |
| Gallier Whole cloth | Gallier House New Orleans, Acc. #1973.29 | ca 1900; by L'Amour de Maman curator |
| Laf Sci DesHotels | Lafayette Science Museum, Acc. #1984.20 | 3rd qtr 20th century; by author |
| Miller Whole cloth | Miller Family Collection | ca 1910; by family member |
| Whitecloud #1 | Whitecloud Private Collection | 3rd qtr 20th century; by author |
| **Block Format/Household Textiles** | | |
| Holden #120 | Holden Family Collection | 3rd qtr 20th century; by author |
| Holden #121 | Holden Family Collection | 3rd qtr 20th century; by author |
| Holden #122 | Holden Family Collection | 3rd qtr 20th century; by author |
| Holden #123 | Holden Family Collection | 3rd qtr 20th century; by author |
| Whitecloud #5 | Whitecloud Private Collection | 3rd qtr 20th century; by author |

form was used as a recording tool, and the notes were compiled into an analysis database.[43]

During this time period two *coton jaune* researchers, Sharon Gordon Donnan and Suzanne Chaillot Breaux, released a new documentary in DVD format: *"Coton Jaune*—Acadian Brown Cotton, a Cajun Love Story." The author attended two premieres of this film, both of which included paper presentations and discussions by experts in the field. The author also learned how to weave, taking a class in Acadian weaving at the John C. Campbell Folk School in North Carolina, and learning the basics of two-harness weaving plus the Louisiana Acadian techniques of *cordons, boutons* and *chenilles.*

While Louisiana Acadian weaving is well documented, Acadian quilt-making is not. A search of the literature revealed no publications on Acadian quilts, except Dr. Kuttruff's articles and the author's article for *Blanket Statements.*[45] Requests for information on other studies of Acadian quiltmakers and their quilts consistently received a negative response: Acadian music, food, storytelling and language have all been extensively documented, but not their quilts. Two Louisiana quilt documentation projects have skipped Acadiana, covering only the northern half of the state, the southeastern parishes and the area around New Orleans.[46] Online searches for Louisiana quilts made from homespun fabric in the Quilt Index (which includes the original Louisiana documentation project's quilts) and the International Quilt Study Center's online collection yielded no results.[47]

As noted above, a quilt is sometimes mentioned in the *L'Amour de Maman* trousseau, but its inclusion is parenthetical. The author found only one historic reference to Acadian quilts, in the anonymous Breaux Manuscript mentioned above. The best documentation that Acadian women made quilts exists in the quilts themselves. And the earliest quilts made by the Acadians were probably made from *cotonnade* weaving scraps.

## Acadian Format or Block Format

The most notable feature of the traditional Acadian *cotonnade* quilts in this study is their lack of any standard pieced pattern. Nineteen of the twenty-four quilts in the study fit this description, and the author has chosen a label proposed by American Quilt Study Group member Xenia Cord—Acadian format. In this style, fabric pieces of various sizes and

Fig. 7. Blue Acadian format quilt with fan quilting (Holden #119), c. 1920, 87 x 71 inches, Holden Family Collection. Photograph by Jim and Reni Zeitz.

shapes are joined into long strips, which are combined to make the quilt. This method of construction reflects Acadian frugality of materials and time expenditure.[48] (Fig. 7.)

The strips in the tops of fourteen of the Acadian-format quilts run vertically (along the long axis of the quilt); three of the quilts are con-

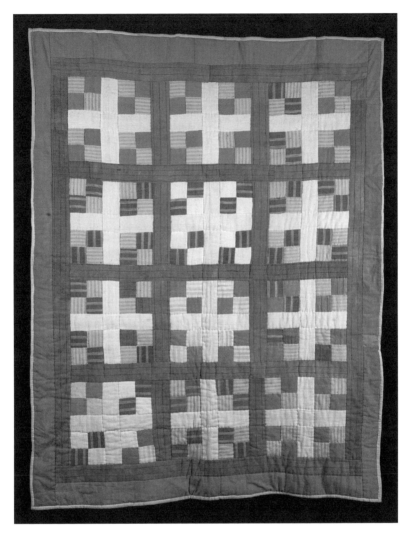

Fig. 8. Block format quilt with cordons in inner and outer sashing (Holden #121), c. 1970, 88 x 69 inches, Holden Family Collection. Photograph by Jim and Reni Zeitz.

structed with horizontal strips, and the piecing method of one quilt could not be determined. The average number of strips per quilt top is five, with a range of two to thirteen; they vary in width from four inches to forty-one inches. Most of the quilt backs are also constructed in vertical strips.[49] The average number of pieces in each top in these Acadian-format quilts

Fig. 9. Acadian format quilt of household fabrics (Erath #1), c. 1970, 62 x 46 inches, Acadian Museum, Erath, Louisiana. Photograph by the author.

is 115, with a range of 41 to 214. This study did not determine the number of unduplicated fabrics in each quilt top, but Dr. Kuttruff's study identified eighty-nine different fabrics in three quilts.[50]

Three pieces in this study have unusual formats. The first, cataloged as a "quilt top" in the *L'Amour de Maman* exhibit catalog, is an Acadian-format summer spread. It is constructed in three vertical strips; the center strip is a loom-width wide, with four pieces of the same fabric and visible selvedges. All seam edges in the spread are hand overcast. Two others could, from their visual appearance, be classified as whole-cloth quilts, being made exclusively of white *cotonnade* fabric, with large pieces of fabric on front and back. Both of these follow the Acadian format of joining pieces into long strips.

The remaining five quilts in the study are block-pieced with simple squares: two are constructed in a checkerboard pattern from two fabrics, one is a Four Patch quilt with inner and outer sashing, and two are Nine Patch quilts with sashing. (Fig. 8.)

## Clothing Scraps or Household Textile Scraps

The twenty-four study quilts can alternatively be grouped by type of *cotonnade* fabric scraps. Fourteen quilts have tops composed mainly of clothing-type *cotonnade* fabrics. Two quilt tops in this group have small amounts of commercial fabrics, two are composed of approximately thirty percent and one of seventy percent commercial fabrics. Interestingly, many of the commercial fabrics in these quilts were woven in traditional Acadian color-and-weave patterns, demonstrating that commercial yardage duplicating Acadian *cotonnade* patterns was being produced and marketed in the area by the early twentieth century.[51] All of these fourteen quilts are in Acadian format; the pieces that comprise the strips are largely rectangles but sometimes are angled, appearing to be clothing remnants from cutting out legs or sleeves. The remaining five Acadian-format quilts and the five block-format quilts are made mostly or exclusively with household textile *cotonnades*. (Fig. 9, color plate 4.)

The backs of four of the clothing scrap quilts are also pieced from clothing-type fabrics. One quilt has a few commercial fabrics on the back, and one has a grey commercial fabric for the majority of the back. The backs of the other twenty quilts are all or predominantly household *cotonnades*, usually solid white.

## Construction Methods

The quilts in this study share many construction methods. All but three are hand-pieced on both sides; one block-format quilt and two Acadian-format quilts with significant amounts of commercial fabrics are machine-pieced. All are self-bound from one side to the other, except for one that has a whip-stitched knife edge finish. All are hand-quilted at two

# Appendix B: Acadian Cotonnade Study Quilt Characteristics

| Study Name/Category | Condition | Oganization | Quilting Pattern | Knots Visible | Shared Fabric |
|---|---|---|---|---|---|
| **Acadian Format/ Clothing Scraps** | | | | | |
| Gallier Summer Spread | Fair/worn | Vertical strips | n/a | n/a | |
| Holden #117 | Fair/worn | Vertical strips | Parallel lines | Yes | X |
| Holden #118 | Fair/worn | Vertical strips | Elbow/fan | Yes | |
| Holden #119 | Very good | Vertical strips | Elbow/fan | Yes | |
| Holden #124 | Very good | Vertical strips | Elbow/fan | Yes | |
| Laf Sci AB6 | Fair/worn | Vertical strips | Elbow/fan | Yes | |
| Laf Sci Thompson | Fair/worn | Vertical strips | Elbow/fan | Yes | |
| LSM Holden #1 | Fair/worn | Horizontal strips | Elbow/fan | Yes | |
| LSM Holden #2 | Fair/worn | Vertical strips | Elbow/fan | Yes | |
| LSU AB5 | Fair/worn | Unable to determine | Parallel lines | Yes | X |
| Reaux #1 | Fair/worn | Horizontal strips | Elbow/fan | Yes | |
| Whitecloud #2 | Fair/worn | Horizontal strips | Parallel lines | No | |
| Whitecloud #3 | Fair/worn | Horizontal strips | Single fans | Yes | |
| Whitecloud #4 | Fair/worn | Vertical strips | Elbow/fan | Yes | |
| **Acadian Format/ Household Textiles** | | | | | |
| Erath #1 | Very good | Vertical strips | Elbow/fan | No | X |
| Gallier Whole cloth | Good | Vertical strips | Elbow/ fan; lines | Yes | |
| Laf Sci DesHotels | Very good | Vertical strips | Ditch | No | X |
| Miller Whole cloth | Good | Vertical strips | Elbow/ fan; lines | Yes | |
| Whitecloud #1 | Very good | Vertical strips | Ditch | No | X |
| **Block Format/ Household Textiles** | | | | | |
| Holden #120 | Very good | Blocks | Ditch | No | X |
| Holden #121 | Very good | Blocks | Ditch | No | X |
| Holden #122 | Very good | Blocks | Ditch | No | |
| Holden #123 | Very good | Blocks | Ditch | No | X |
| Whitecloud #5 | Very good | Blocks | Ditch | No | X |

to three stitches per inch. Batting when visible is cotton; one quilt has a mix of white and *coton jaune* batting.

There are significant differences in quilting pattern between the clothing scrap quilts and the household textile quilts. All in the first group have either elbow/fan or parallel line quilting.[52] In all but one the thread knots are visible on the outside of the quilt. In contrast, seven of the ten household textile quilts are quilted in the ditch around individual pieces, and knots are buried in eight of these ten quilts. The quilting thread in nine of the clothing scrap quilts appears to be either hand spun or un-mercerized white thread; this could indicate a construction date before 1898.[53] One block-format quilt is quilted with monofilament, and the rest appear to be quilted with commercial mercerized thread. Quilting thread is white in all instances but three; two of the household textile quilts are quilted with black thread and one with brown.

Two household textile quilts are small (forty-six by sixty-two inches and forty-eight by fifty-seven inches), probably made for use by children. The other twenty-two quilts average sixty-nine inches wide and eighty-seven inches long.[54]

Condition is dramatically different between the quilts made from clothing scraps and those made from household textiles. All but two in the first group are obviously worn, and most are stained and heavily patched. All of these quilts were repaired after construction, although some fabrics exhibited stains and fading that existed before construction, indicating that the fabrics were from used clothing as well as from construction scraps. In some pieces the *coton jaune* threads were disintegrating, and nearly every instance of dark brown dyed thread was damaged, while the white and indigo *cotonnade* threads exhibited more durability. The repair patches were skillfully applied. In the summer spread two holes in a blue and tan striped fabric were patched with the same fabric; the stripes were matched and the patches were finished on both sides. Some patches were themselves comprised of many small pieces of fabric.

In contrast to the poor condition of the clothing scrap quilts, the quilts constructed of household *cotonnades* are all in good or very good condition. Most have some stains, fading and patches, but repairs were usually made prior to quilt construction, indicating that used household textiles were converted into quilts. An interesting observation found in both groups of quilts is that in general there does not appear to be significant wear from use as bedding. Few stains are found to penetrate from front to back, and there is little wear or discoloration along the short edges

**Appendix C: Acadian Cotonnade Study Quilts with Shared Fabrics**

| SHARED FABRICS | Holden #117 | LSU AB5 | Erath #1 | Laf Sci DesHotels |
|---|---|---|---|---|
| Solid tan | | | X | X |
| Brown with white and blue stripes | | | | |
| Lt tan with blue and white stripes | | | X | |
| Tan with red cordon | | | X | |
| Light tan with three light tan stripes | | | X | |
| Pale tan stripe | | | X | X |
| Medium tan stripe | | | | |
| White with pale blue stripe | | | | |
| White with triple blue stripe | | | X | |
| Yellow/tan with two white stripes | X | | | X |
| Two-tone tan large scale plaid | | | | X |
| Pale tan nubby | | | X | X |
| Light tan with multiple blue and white stripes | X | | | X |
| Red/blue plied | X | X | | |

of the quilts from being handled along these edges.

These quilts exhibit many examples of the weavers' skill. Many clothing *cotonnades* include weft pattern changes, where the weaver used one warping to create a variety of patterns; the transition areas were used in the quilts. The Four Patch quilt includes two sashing fabrics with *cordonné*; the inner white sashes have a pattern of eight cordons while the *coton jaune* outer sashings have single red *cordons*. Dr. Kuttruff noted red/blue and blue/white thread *dublé* plying in one quilt in her study, creating mottled effects.[55] Red/blue *dublé* fabric is also found in one of the Holden Family Collection quilts.

Dating Acadian *cotonnade* quilts is difficult, since normal quilt dating metrics do not apply. Most were purchased from individuals, flea markets or antique shops in the 1970s and 1980s, with no provenance. Museum curators have assigned dates between 1890 and 1950 to seven quilts, and I

| Whitecloud #1 | Holden #120 | Holden #12 | Holden #123 | Whitecloud #5 |
| --- | --- | --- | --- | --- |
| X | X | X | X | X |
|   | X | X |   |   |
|   | X |   |   |   |
|   |   | X |   |   |
| X |   |   |   |   |
|   | X |   |   | X |
| X | X | X | X |   |
| X | X | X | X |   |
|   |   |   | X |   |
| X |   |   |   |   |
|   |   |   |   | X |
| X |   | X | X | X |

have estimated a date of around the turn of the twentieth century for the other clothing-style quilts based on their condition and the phasing out of clothing production in the last half of the nineteenth century. (Appendix A.) But without the normal dating methods of fabric and style analysis, these estimates could be significantly incorrect. In two instances, though, we know who made the quilts, and we can estimate when they were made.

### The Thompson Family Quilts

The Lafayette Science Museum displayed many of its Acadian textiles, including three *cotonnade* quilts, at the premiere of the documentary film "*Coton Jaune*—Acadian Brown Cotton, a Cajun Love Story" held there in September, 2014. Three quilts were included, one with this information on its collection card: "Acadian Patchwork Quilt by Mrs. Evan Thompson of Ville Platte. Fabric threads spun & woven by Mrs. Paulene [Thompson] &

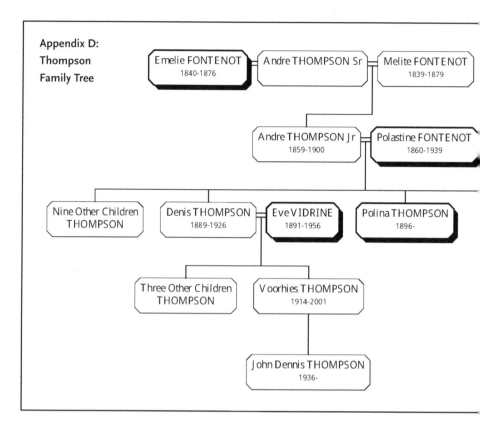

**Appendix D: Thompson Family Tree**

- Emelie FONTENOT 1840-1876 — Andre THOMPSON Sr — Melite FONTENOT 1839-1879
  - Andre THOMPSON Jr 1859-1900 — Polastine FONTENOT 1860-1939
    - Nine Other Children THOMPSON
    - Denis THOMPSON 1889-1926 — Eve VIDRINE 1891-1956
      - Three Other Children THOMPSON
      - Voorhies THOMPSON 1914-2001
        - John Dennis THOMPSON 1936-
    - Polina THOMPSON 1896-

Mrs. Emily Fontenot Thompson. Purchased by the Museum Association from Mrs. Betty Leger of Eunice." (See fig. 1.) The buyer, Betty Leger, connected the author with the Thompson family in Ville Platte. The author determined, from information collected from the family during a visit in 2015 and additional genealogical research, that the maker of the quilt, "Mrs. Evan Thompson," was probably Eve Vidrine Thompson.[56]

Eve Vidrine, daughter of Artemon and Emelie Vidrine, was born in 1891 in St. Landry Parish. She married Denis Thompson (b. 1889), son of André Thompson Jr. and Polastine Fontenot Thompson. André and Polastine had twelve children, including son Denis and daughters Polina and Olina. André's father, André Thompson Sr., married Emelie Fontenot (1840–1876) in 1875 after the death of his first wife Melite in 1874. Emelie and Melite were first cousins.[57] Eve Vidrine and Denis Thompson had four boys between 1912 and 1923: Avie, Voorhies, Curliss and Joseph Aaron. (Appendix D.) Eve made a quilt for each boy, and Voorhies' quilt was

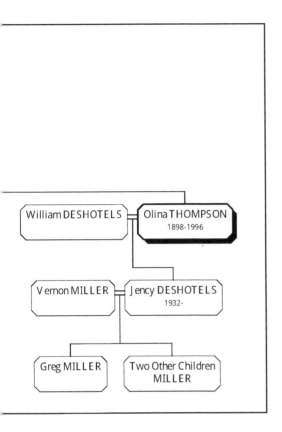

| William DESHOTELS | Olina THOMPSON<br>1898-1996 |
| --- | --- |

| Vernon MILLER | Jency DESHOTELS<br>1932- |
| --- | --- |

| Greg MILLER | Two Other Children<br>MILLER |
| --- | --- |

passed down to his son John Dennis Thompson.[58] Eve died in 1956; Voorhies' quilt was purchased by Betty Leger, and she sold it to the Lafayette Science Museum in 1985.

The Thompson quilt is similar to the other traditional Acadian-format quilts in the study. It is constructed of seven vertical strips with over 150 *coton jaune* and indigo pieces, plus a few pieces of commercial twill fabric. The back is also constructed of vertical strips of indigo and *coton jaune* fabrics; one long blue panel has multiple weft pattern changes, and this panel also has four dark dart shapes along one edge, indicating its possible initial use as clothing. The quilt is quilted in an elbow/fan pattern. It has been well used, with stains, tears and patches. The date of 1950 assigned by the museum is probably late; Eve probably made each boy's quilt for him before he married, and since Voorhies married in 1932 a more accurate date would be around 1930.

This quilt preserves the weaving tradition of the Thompsons and Fontenots. The index card states that the fabrics in the quilt were spun and woven by "Mrs. Paulene [Thompson] & Mrs. Emily Fontenot Thompson." Paulene is probably Polina, Eve's sister-in-law, and Emily Fontenot Thompson is probably André Sr.'s second wife Emelie, who died at the age of thirty-six in 1876. If Emelie did indeed create some of the *cotonnades* in the quilt, they were over fifty years old when they were incorporated into the quilt.

The estate inventory for Emelie Fontenot Thompson in 1876 lists "one flax wheel," and André Thompson Jr.'s estate inventory in 1906 included three spinning wheels, two sewing machines, thirty bed spreads and "1 lot quilts."[59] But neither Artemon Vidrine's estate in 1916 nor Eve Vidrine's estate after her death in 1956 included looms or spinning wheels.[60] This could reflect a difference in the two families—that the Thompsons wove but the Vidrines did not—but it is more likely that it reflects the abandonment of home production of textiles in this time period.

Eve was not the only member of the family to make quilts out of the old *cotonnade* fabrics that had been created by the family. Jency DesHotels Miller, daughter of Olina Thompson DesHotels (1898–1996, sister of Polina Thompson and sister-in-law of Eve Vidrine Thompson), remembers that her mother inherited some of the family's white *cotonnade* textiles and split them with her sister Ude in the 1950s.[61] Jency believes that Polastine Fontenot Thompson, Olina's mother, wove *cotonnade* and that the family still had a loom around the turn of the twentieth century. Olina made two quilts with her *cotonnades*, and Ude quilted those quilts, which remained in Ude's family.

A white quilt now owned by Jency Miller's son is included in this study. This quilt might have been made by Olina, or possibly by Polastine or one of Olina's sisters. It resembles the other Acadian-format quilts in every way: vertical strip piecing, self-binding, and elbow quilting with large stitches and widely spaced rows. It has a few patches, but no staining or other signs of heavy use. (See fig. 2.)

Olina and Jency, who was born in 1932, also made traditional quilts with commercial fabrics. Together they quilted a hexagon quilt top that had been pieced by Olina's mother, Polastine, before she died, when Jency was around six years old. The top was saved for Jency, and taken out and quilted when Jency wed in 1950. Olina often had quilting parties with her sisters, family and friends. She sewed for additional household income, using commercial patterns even though she could not read, and saved the scraps for her own quilts. Jency remembers that her family had *cotonnade* for clothing when she was young but that no new *cotonnade* was being woven. Jency also remembers sleeping under *coton jaune* blankets that had been woven at her grandmother Polastine's house. They valued *coton jaune* blankets as bed coverings, but not *cotonnade* quilts, which were considered old and unimportant and were used for moving and covering things. As an example of this, the white quilt in this study was passed down to Jency's son Greg to use when camping. This attitude toward these quilts could explain the observation about condition noted above—that they appear to not have been used as bedding.[62]

The fact that these *cotonnade* fabrics are still remembered by family members, and that the Thompson quilt's documentation includes the makers of the fabrics, along with the maker of the quilt, emphasizes their importance to these families. These quilts, which preserve the handwoven textiles in a useful form, reinforce the strong family connections found in Acadian families, their ethic of frugality, and the value placed on their *cotonnade* weaving tradition.

### The Nine Patch Quilter

During the analysis phase of this project the author noticed similarities in the household textile quilts. The four Holden Family Collection block-format quilts have strikingly consistent construction and quilting techniques, and the fabrics in the quilts in two different museums are markedly similar. By studying the photographs of each quilt the author has determined that these are more than coincidence: nine quilts in the study share the same fabrics. (Appendix C.) All but one of the shared fabrics are distinctive household *cotonnades*. A solid *coton jaune* fabric with red *cordons* is used in two quilts; a yellowish-tan fabric with two white stripes in three quilts; a dark brown fabric with a specific white and blue stripe pattern in two quilts; and a pale tan fabric with a loose nubby texture in six quilts. At first it appeared that only the household textile quilts were connected, but further examination revealed that a fabric pieced into a household textile quilt is also used to patch an older clothing scrap quilt. This older quilt also has pieces of the mottled red/blue plied thread fabric which is used in the quilt at LSU. (Fig. 10.)

It is certainly possible that multiple weavers were sharing weaving patterns or exchanging fabrics, but attributing all of these fabrics to one individual or family explains other observations about the household textile quilts. Most of these quilts are in very good condition, showing no signs of post-construction use, although most also include fabrics that were used before quilt construction. All of the block-format quilts, except the Holden checkerboard quilt, are included in this pool of nine quilts with shared fabrics; all of the quilts that are quilted in the ditch except that same one are in this group; all of the quilts with buried knots except one clothing scrap quilt are in this group; and all use modern quilting threads. Based on construction method similarities, the Holden checkerboard quilt is probably also part of this group, even though it does not share fabrics with the others. It is also likely that closer examination would reveal other duplicated fabrics between these quilts. All of these weak clues, when taken together, suggest a single quiltmaker.

Fig. 10. Acadian format quilt of clothing fabrics (Holden #117), c. 1910, 87 x 69 inches, Holden Family Collection. Photograph by Jim and Reni Zeitz. This quilt includes a piece of red/blue plied thread fabric also found in a quilt at Louisiana State University (LSU AB5), and has patches of household textile fabric also used to construct a household textile style quilt now at the Lafayette Science Museum (Laf Sci DesHotels).

A likely explanation is that Acadian textiles passed down in a family were repurposed as quilts by an Acadian who had learned current methods of quilt construction. The quiltmaker retained the traditional quilt construction methods found in the earlier quilts: hand piecing, hand quilting, and back-to-front binding. The quiltmaker pieced three of the quilts in Acadian format, and used traditional elbow/fan quilting in one of them. The quiltmaker also used new methods: block-format piecing, ditch quilting, colored quilting thread and buried quilting knots. And the quilt-maker made two of these quilts in a smaller format than was traditional. This conversion of sheets to quilts might have been an attempt to preserve the heritage of a weaving family while also creating useful as well as beautiful objects—very Acadian characteristics.

Some of these quilts may have been made specifically for sale, since in the late 1970s interest in collecting these textiles increased, with more money offered for quilts than for sheets. Whatever the motive for making the quilts, they were sold to multiple collectors and are now found in private and public collections across the area. Based on this analysis, the date of construction for the household textile quilts in this study is probably the third quarter of the twentieth century.

Conclusion

Many quilts made in block format with commercial fabrics are found in public collections in the Acadiana area. An obvious next step in researching Louisiana Acadian quilts is to study these quilts to answer the question: When did Acadian women first start making quilts, and how do *cotonnade* quilts fit into that tradition? Louisiana folklorist Susan Roach asserts that "[t]raditional quiltmaking … is widely practiced by Anglo- and African-American women in the rural areas of the state…. [T]he quilt-making tradition traveled to Louisiana with settlers across the upland South."[64] Is this true for the Acadiana region? Did the influx of Americans to the area after the Louisiana Purchase influence Acadian households and their reliance on blankets for warmth? Or was quiltmaking a later development, influenced by increased literacy and communication options? Did the desire to be "more modern" influence the change? Areas to research include estate inventories, area newspapers, public and private collections and the family traditions of current Acadian quiltmakers.

William Faulkner Rushton asserts: "Weaving is the principal and most accomplished craft of the Cajuns. Outside of Cajun music and the rich Cajun language, weaving is the oldest, and least modified, surviving folk phenomenon of the culture."[65] The quilts in this study document this important heritage by preserving the weaving tradition in a new form. Traditional Acadian-format quilts may have been made for practical reasons from the scraps left over from clothing construction, and they certainly reflect the frugality and self-sufficiency apparent in all aspects of Acadian life. But they also underscore the central importance of the extended family and the continuity of established traditions, and thus cannot be considered simply utilitarian objects. The quilt made by Eve Vidrine for her son Voorhies and the quilt now owned by Jency DesHotels Miller's son from *cotonnade* remnants passed down through this extended family manifest not only love for these sons, but their connection with their ancestors through these textiles. The newer quilts represent a desire to preserve family textiles in a modern format. And all of the quilts record the artistry and creativity of the patterns the Acadian weavers wove as they made their *cotonnades*. They are important cultural artifacts that document and preserve Acadian heritage.

## Acknowledgments

This project would not have been possible without the encouragement of the custodians of these quilts: The Thompson family; Jency, Karen and Greg Miller; Dr. John and Pat Holden; Warren and Mary Perrin; Mercedes Bordelon Whitecloud; Andy Reaux; Deborah Clifton and Blake Lagneaux, Lafayette Science Museum; Wayne Phillips, Louisiana State Museum; Jenna Tedrick Kuttruff, Louisiana State University; and Morgan Pierce, Hermann-Grima & Gallier Historic House. Acadian researcher Judith Rygiel shared her extensive collection of Acadian weaving documentation. I also appreciate the collectors, researchers, and weavers who assisted with this project: Betty Leger; Elaine Bourque; Charlene Quinilty; Melissa Weaver Dunning; Charlotte Lindsay Allison; Yvette Voorhies; Sonya LaComb; Brenda LaLonde; Ray Brassieur, University of Louisiana at Lafayette; and Shane Bernard, McIlhenny Company.

## Notes and References

1. John Mack Faragher, *A Great and Noble Scheme: The Tragic Story of the Expulsion of the French Acadians from Their American Homeland* (New York, NY: W. W. Norton & Co., 2005), 49.
2. Carl Brasseaux, *Scattered to the Wind: Dispersal and Wanderings of the Acadians, 1755–1809* (Lafayette, LA: Center for Louisiana Studies, USL, 1991), 4; Stephen A. White, "The True Number of the Acadians," in *Du Grand Dérangement à la Déportation: Nouvelles Perspectives Historiques,* ed. Ronnie-Gilles LeBlanc (Moncton, New Brunswick: Chaire d'études acadiennes, Université de Moncton, 2005), 56.
3. Brasseaux, *Scattered to the Wind,* 1–3.

4. Ibid., 11–28.

5. Carl Brasseaux, *The Founding of New Acadia: The Beginnings of Acadian Life in Louisiana, 1765–1803* (Baton Rouge, LA: Louisiana State University Press, 1987), 34.

6. Brasseaux, *Scattered to the Wind*, 28–70.

7. Ibid., 67.

8. For the evolution of Acadian customs in Louisiana see Carl Brasseaux, *Acadian to Cajun: Transformation of a People, 1803–1877* (Jackson, MS: University Press of Mississippi, 1992); *The People Called Cajuns: An Introduction to an Ethnohistory* (Lafayette LA: University of Southwestern Louisiana, 1983); and William Faulkner Rushton, *The Cajuns: From Acadia to Louisiana* (New York NY: Farrar Straus Giroux, 1979). Rushton devotes an entire chapter of this book to the Acadian weaving tradition.

9. Faragher, *A Great and Noble Scheme*, 60.

10. Bernard V. LeBlanc and Ronnie-Gilles LeBlanc, "Traditional Material Culture in Acadia," in *Acadia of the Maritimes: Thematic Studies from the Beginning to the Present*, ed. Jean Daigle (Moncton, New Brunswick: Chaire d'études acadiennes, Université de Moncton, 1995), 615.

11. LeBlanc and LeBlanc, "Traditional Material Culture in Acadia", 617–618.

12. Jack D. Holden, H. Parrott Bacot and Cybèle T. Gontar, *Furnishing Louisiana: Creole and Acadian Furniture, 1735–1835* (New Orleans, LA: The Historic New Orleans Collection, 2010), 15.

13. Dorothy K. Burnham, *The Comfortable Arts: Traditional Spinning and Weaving in Canada* (Ottawa, Ontario: National Gallery of Canada, 1981), 54.

14. Ibid. This volume and Harold B. Burnham and Dorothy K. Burnham, *Keep Me Warm One Night: Early Handweaving in Eastern Canada* (Toronto, Ontario: University of Toronto Press, 1972) contain examples of post-expulsion Canadian Acadian two-shaft coverlets. The Burnhams contrast the textile production of the Acadians to that of the colony in Quebec, where "the needs of the colonists were met by materials brought from France," (*Keep Me Warm One Night*, 7). For examples of Louisiana Acadian *couvertures du mariage*, see Dale Drake, "Quest for *Cotonnade*: In Search of a Tradition," *Blanket Statements* 93 (Fall 2008), 1–5, and the exhibition catalog *L'Amour de Maman: La Tradition Acadienne du Tissage en Louisiane* (La Rochelle, France: Musée du Nouveau Monde, 1983). This catalog contains the most comprehensive documentation of Louisiana Acadian weaving traditions, history, tools and textiles to date.

15. Robert E. Smith, "Acadian Weaving," in *Louisiana French Furnishings 1700–1830: Bicentennial Exhibition at the Art Center for Southwestern Louisiana, April 28 through August 31, 1974* (Art Center for Southwestern Louisiana, 1974), 43; Brasseaux, *The Founding of New Acadia*, 128.

16. *L'Amour de Maman*, 29.

17. Brasseaux, *The Founding of New Acadia*, 137–139.

18. Sonya LaComb, "Habillés et déshabillés: Dress and Undress of the Louisiana Acadians/Cajuns, c. 1765–1830," in *L'Acadie au féminin: Un regard multidisciplinaire sur les Acadiennes et les Cadiennes*, ed. Maurice Basque, Isabelle McKee-Allain, Linda Cardinal, Phyllis E. LeBlanc and Janis L. Palllister (Moncton, New Brunswick: Chaire d'études acadiennes, Université de Moncton, 2000), 191. The motion picture *Belizaire the Cajun* (Cote Blanche Productions, 1986) is set in pre-Civil War Louisiana and includes authentic reproduction costuming of the period.

19. The Adams County Quilt Project Committee, *The Hands That Made Them: Quilts of Adams County, Pennsylvania* (Camp Hill, PA: Plank's Suburban Press, 1993), 14; Merikay Waldvogel, "Southern Linsey Quilts of the Nineteenth Century," in *Quiltmaking in America: Beyond the Myths,* ed. Laurel Horton (Nashville TN: Rutledge Hill Press, 1994), 128: "…by the mid-1800s, quiltmakers in the South were able to use fabrics imported from the British Empire."

20. Brasseaux, *Acadian to Cajun,* 24–25.

21. "Excerpts from the Anonymous *Breaux Manuscript* (1840–1901)," www.louisianafolklife.org/LT/Articles_Essays/the_breaux_manuscript.html.

22. Elaine Bourque, telephone communication with the author, February 19, 2016 and Jenna Kuttruff, telephone communication with the author, September 16, 2014.

23. Brenda LaLonde, personal communication with the author, September 28, 2014. Gika Rector, "Gladys Clark: Acadian Spinner," *Spin-Off* (Fall 1996), 38–43.

24. Jenna Tedrick Kuttruff, "Three Louisiana Acadian *Cotonnade* Quilts: Adding Pieces to a Puzzle," in *Uncoverings 1999,* ed. Virginia Gunn (Lincoln, NE: American Quilt Study Group, 1999), 64–67. The piecing and quilting diagrams for the three quilts in this article were particularly valuable in my research. See also Jenna Tedrick Kuttruff, "Pieces of a Puzzle: Acadian *Cotonnade* Quilts," *Louisiana Agriculture* 41, no. 2 (1998), 12–13.

25. *L'Amour de Maman,* 25.

26. See Rushton, *The Cajuns: From Acadia to Louisiana,* 196, for a discussion of indigo in Louisiana, and the methods that Gladys Clark's *grandmère* used to prepare the dye.

27. *L'Amour de Maman,* 21.

28. C. Ray Brassieur PhD, "Acadian Brown Cotton Dynamics in Culture: An Ecological Perspective" (presentation at the screening of "Coton Jaune—Acadian Brown Cotton, a Cajun Love Story," The Historic New Orleans Collection, New Orleans, LA, October 17, 2015).

29. Sally Fox sells Foxfibre® naturally colored cotton products on the website www.vreseis.com.

30. Brassieur, "Acadian Brown Cotton Dynamics in Culture."

31. Beatrice B. Exner, "Acadian Brown Cotton," *Handweaver & Craftsman,* Fall 1960, 23.

32. J. O. Ware, L. I. Benedict and W. H. Rolfe, "A Recessive Naked-Seed Character in Upland Cotton," *Journal of Heredity* 38 (10), 313–32, jhered.oxfordjournals.org.

33. Elaine Bourque, telephone communication with the author, February 19, 2016. Elaine studied spinning and weaving with Gladys Clark, and has extensive documentation on Acadian blankets.

34. Kuttruff, "Three Louisiana Acadian *Cotonnade* Quilts," 67.

35. See Rita J. Adrosko, *Natural Dyes and Home Dyeing* (New York, NY: Dover Publications, 1971), 49; Laurel Thatcher Ulrich, *The Age of Homespun: Objects and Stories in the Creation of an American Myth* (New York: Vintage Books, 2001), 332 and 409; Merikay Waldvogel, "Southern Linsey Quilts of the Nineteenth Century," 128.

36. Jesse Gary, round table discussion at the screening of "*Coton Jaune*—Acadian Brown Cotton, a Cajun Love Story," October 17, 2015.

37. Yvette Voorhies, telephone communication with the author, February 5, 2009.

38. Definition of color-and-weave effect: "An effect that is produced when different coloured warp and weft threads are woven together resulting in distinctive weaves." www.textileglossary.com.

39. *L'Amour de Maman*, 35–41. A modern-day West African woman using a cotton bow is pictured on page 12 of *Indigo Quilts: 30 Quilts from the Poos Collection* by Kay and Lori Lee Triplett (Lafayette, CA: C&T Publishing, 2015); it is intriguing to speculate that both *coton jaune* and cotton bows might have been brought to Louisiana from West Africa.

40. Gayle Begnaud, Elaine Bourque and Jesse Gary (round table discussion at the screening of "*Coton Jaune*—Acadian Brown Cotton, a Cajun Love Story," September 28, 2014).

41. Ibid.

42. Charlotte Lindsay Allison, telephone communication with the author, March 23, 2016. Charlotte learned the art of indigo dyeing from Gladys Clark and documented 150 different weaving patterns from the textile collection of collector Audrey Bernard. Between 2005 and 2011 she organized a project with the Complex Weavers (www.complex-weavers.org) to replicate each of these patterns. Each participant created a swatch for herself and for each of the other participants (similar to a round robin quilt block exchange).

43. *L'Amour de Maman*, 23.

44. "The Quilt Index Documentation Form," quiltindex.org/docs/QI_docform_compfieldsfinal.pdf.

45. Dale Drake, "Quest for *Cotonnade*: In Search of a Tradition," *Blanket Statements* 93 (Fall 2008), 1–5.

46. Susan Roach, communication with the author, November 2, 2010; Elise Schebler Roberts, *The Quilt: A History and Celebration of an American Art Form* (Stillwater, MN: Voyageur Press, 2007), 314.

47. It is possible that there are Louisiana quilts made from handwoven fabrics in these collections, but that the database records are not coded for retrieval by the search engine.

48. Kuttruff, "Three Louisiana Acadian *Cotonnade* Quilts: Adding Pieces to a Puzzle," 65.

49. In many cases it was difficult to determine which side was the top. In most cases "top" was somewhat arbitrarily assigned to the side with the most piecing.

50. Kuttruff, "Three Louisiana Acadian *Cotonnade* Quilts: Adding Pieces to a Puzzle," 83–84.

51. Sonya Lacomb, telephone communication with the author, February 2, 2008; Mercedes Bordelon Whitecloud, personal communication with the author, October 14, 2015.

52. Three excellent line diagrams of this type of quilting pattern are in Kuttruff, "Three Louisiana Acadian *Cotonnade* Quilts: Adding Pieces to a Puzzle".

53. G. S. Cole, *Cole's Encyclopedia of Dry Goods* (Chicago, New York, St. Louis: Root Newspaper Association, 1900), 355.

54. The sizes range from 57.5 to 77 inches in width and 82 to 96 inches in length.

55. Kuttruff, "Three Louisiana Acadian *Cotonnade* Quilts: Adding Pieces to a Puzzle," 71.

56. The following genealogical resources were used in this research: Rev. Donald J. Hébert, *Southwest Louisiana Records (1750–1900)* (Rayne, LA: Hébert Publications, 1975–2001), CD-ROM edition; Ancestry.com; findagrave.com.

57. Mary Ann Thompson, telephone communication with the author, May 24, 2016.

58. Kay Thompson, telephone communication with the author, September 20, 2015.

59. St. Landry Parish, Louisiana. Estate inventory no. 6416 (1906), Andre Thompson Jr., and Estate inventory no. 3888 (1876), Emelie Fontenot Thompson; Clerk of Court, St. Landry Parish, Louisiana.

60. Genealogical researcher Cheryl Myers, telephone communication with the author, March 4, 2016.

61. Jency DesHotels Miller, telephone communications with the author, November 26, 2016.

62. Jency DesHotels Miller, telephone communications with the author, May 21, 2016, November 26, 2016 and January 12, 2017. Interestingly, Jency only knew of white *cotonnade* quilts; she was not aware that these quilts were made in colors other than white.

63. This difference in pricing was confirmed by Dr. Holden in email communication with the author, April 28, 2016.

64. Susan Roach, "Traditional Quiltmaking in Louisiana," Louisiana's Living Traditions, www.louisianafolklife.org/LT/Articles_Essays/creole_art_quiltmaking_tra.html.

65. Rushton, *The Cajuns: From Acadia to Louisiana*, 194.

# Baltimore Album Quilts: New Research

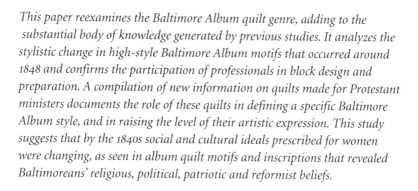

Deborah Cooney and Ronda Harrell McAllen

*This paper reexamines the Baltimore Album quilt genre, adding to the substantial body of knowledge generated by previous studies. It analyzes the stylistic change in high-style Baltimore Album motifs that occurred around 1848 and confirms the participation of professionals in block design and preparation. A compilation of new information on quilts made for Protestant ministers documents the role of these quilts in defining a specific Baltimore Album style, and in raising the level of their artistic expression. This study suggests that by the 1840s social and cultural ideals prescribed for women were changing, as seen in album quilt motifs and inscriptions that revealed Baltimoreans' religious, political, patriotic and reformist beliefs.*

## Reassessment

Baltimore Album quilts continue to rank among the most accomplished creations of women's art ever made.[1] Several major studies of this phenomenon have been published, beginning in 1946 with William Rush Dunton, Jr., followed by Dena Katzenberg, Elly Sienkiewicz, Jennifer Goldsborough, and Nancy Davis. This paper builds on the research of these scholars, reassesses the quilts' stylistic progression, and incorporates information from quilts and genealogical evidence discovered since those works were published.[2]

Considered as a group, Baltimore Album quilts give insight into the families, religions, reforms, and political climate of the city and surrounding areas during the 1840s and 1850s. Researchers now have additional resources with which to study their production. Digital databases, search engines, and expanded computerized technology have allowed fresh insights into the time frame in which the quilts were produced, the social context influencing the city and region, and influence of religious and political affiliations on their makers.

## Emergence

Quiltmaking was in its infancy in the post-Revolutionary period. Fabrics and layouts fashionable in Britain and France influenced styles across the Atlantic for years to come. The European "Romantic" movement came to the U.S. in the early 19th century, promoting a desire for freedom from tyranny, greater self-expression, love of nature, and similar liberating impulses. In this country, Romanticism influenced literature, architecture and dress as well as motivating republican concepts of liberty, individualism, and civic engagement. In popular culture, Romantic ideals including the value of imagination and emotional sensibility, and the pursuit of the divine through nature, persisted through mid-century.[3]

The concept of "republican motherhood" followed from Romantic ideals—the duty of women to teach republican values to their children. After about 1820 a home-grown ideology termed by historians the "cult of domesticity" dovetailed neatly with republicanism and the increased religiosity of the Second Great Awakening revivals. Women, according to the social expectations of the period, were meant to inhabit the private domain of the home rather than the public sphere of men. They were to "cultivate piety, purity, submissiveness, and domesticity in all their relations," according to historian Lucinda MacKethan.[4] Women's roles were to be wives and mothers overseeing their children's education and creating a domestic haven from the world of politics and commerce. These dictates were promoted by men and women through popular magazines, housekeeping manuals, and the sermons of clergymen.

Prescribed behavior for the "true woman" applied largely to Protestant women of the expanding middle class and the elite, not to the poor or to ethnic and racial minorities. While confining in many ways, the home-centered culture allowed women, within limits of propriety, some freedom of thought and activity—given their "natural" gifts of purity and humility. Restrictions were never applied consistently, and receded as women pushed the boundaries.

By the early 1830s, women participated in activities that brought them out of the domestic sphere prescribed for them, and into "public social space."[5] Popular literature and women's private diaries mention their involvement in benevolent societies and charity work. Many women became involved in organizations that provided relief to the poor, founded schools and orphanages, and visited the disabled and sick in their homes. The temperance movement became one the most widespread causes for women in the 1830s and 1840s. Only the bravest advocated for dress reform, the abolition of slavery, or the rights of women.

Women had long been active in their churches, raising money for home and foreign missions, and sewing for the poor. Women's efforts aided the basic functioning of many churches. However, ministers relied on women for more than their labor. Clergy had turned to women to support the theological turn toward a kinder and gentler God in the early nineteenth century.[6] The Protestant religious revival brought a widespread rejection of the old Calvinistic orthodoxies, emphasizing instead mankind's potential for good by their own efforts. Ministers recognized the power of women's "informal" influence within congregations and communities. For example, Methodist minister George C. M. Roberts became known as "the quilting room preacher" in the 1830s when one woman arranged for a reluctant community of local women to meet him during a quilting bee.[7]

All of these trends appear in the quilts of the era. New England mills produced millions of yards of affordable fabric by the early 1830s, and imports supplied more. Quiltmaking was "democratized" as larger numbers of women could buy fabrics dyed and printed mechanically.[8] They began making quilts in large numbers, judging by the legacy of those that survive. While constructed in fashionable patterns and colors, some of these bedcovers revealed the makers' social, religious and political leanings.[9] Quilts were made as tokens of high regard for public figures such as political leaders and ministers; celebrations of life events; and evidence of community needs, such as charity and sobriety. One type of quilt—high-style album quilts made in and near Baltimore around mid-century—particularly manifest the convergence of these trends.

The city of Baltimore lay in the center of the developing nation. Geographically set between North and South, it became a boomtown following the end of the War of 1812. Its port received domestic and international shipments, and canals linked the city to the interior. Baltimore received the first telegraph line and the terminus of the first railroad line. In 1824 President John Quincy Adams called Baltimore the "monumental city" for its memorial tributes to George Washington and a victory over the British in 1814, plus the spires of many churches. Residents took pride in the city's importance in transportation and communications revolutions and in its architectural beauty.[10]

The early decades of the nineteenth century saw rapid population growth and industrial development, especially in cities such as Boston, New York, and Philadelphia. Baltimore moved more slowly into the changing economic and social currents, a transition somewhat softened by its cultural homogeneity. Its population consisted of British and German immigrants, plus a sizable number of free blacks and slaves.

Local women began making album quilts, in which each block was different, in the early 1840s as the style spread beyond its origin in the Philadelphia–southeastern Pennsylvania region.[11] Around Baltimore, the album style integrated with fine appliqué work done with floral chintz cut-outs. Maryland albums used the newer calicos of red and green in the block style; they contained more floral appliqués and fewer Pennsylvania-favored geometrics and paper cut-outs. Many album blocks featured names of donors, Bible verses, lyrics from hymns, and lines of sentimental poetry. The Romantic era seemed obsessed with gardens and with flowers, which appeared in clothing and decorations for the home. The numerous publications on the language and meaning of flowers probably inspired many floral wreaths, bouquets and baskets on album quilts.[12]

Early High Style

In amazingly few years, album quilts in Baltimore and its environs became extraordinary in realistic representation and complex layering of appliqué pieces. Even the early Baltimore Album quilts often included new designs, especially crossed branches, floral wreaths, bouquets in baskets, and three-dimensional flowers. Album blocks appeared that are among the most elaborate and graceful in the long history of American quiltmaking.

By about 1845, one particular style had reached a very high level of excellence. Its blocks depicted eagles with flags and liberty caps; epergnes and cornucopias loaded with flowers and fruits, doves carrying branches, and album books or Bibles. Buildings and memorials also appeared: the U.S. Capitol; Baltimore's Merchant Exchange and its Battle Monument, several Protestant churches, the earliest Baltimore & Ohio Railroad engine. A spectacular quilt top dated 1846 comprises twenty-five blocks all by the same master maker or group of makers (fig. 1, color plate 5).[13] Each square contained multiple, complex elements. Some flowers have up to fifteen pieces set in five or six layers.

Fig. 1. Early Designer I blocks, one dated 1846. Many motifs are composed of multiple pieces in several layers. Cotton, 86 x 84 inches, Daughters of the American Revolution Museum 98.31.

The effect of the combined shapes and colors on the modern viewer is almost visually overwhelming, which may explain why this top is the only one known with all blocks by this designer. Other album quilts put a group of these blocks in the central section, perhaps with one or two in the outer frame.[14]

Many of the same blocks appear in quilts by different makers, suggesting squares produced in kit form.[15] Very similar blocks exist with various elements and fabrics swapped out: bouquets sit in different baskets, epergnes contain different fruits, wreaths have other flowers, and eagles are reversed. The designer or blockmaker apparently customized these squares to suit buyers who appliquéd them with varying skills, which

Fig. 2. Mature Designer I block, motifs of fewer pieces more tightly massed, c. 1850. Cotton and silk, 26 x 26 inches. Authors' collection.

accounts for some having a better effect than others.

This scenario implies a personal interchange between buyer and seller. No records of such transactions have come to light. However, origins of many quilts with these blocks can be traced to Baltimore's inner wards near the port. Many, though not all Baltimore Albums, bear signatures that allow the location of the donors to be found. Quilts with high-style designs had imitators, as these blocks were soon copied in less elaborate form. Simple "cookie-cutter" shaped motifs found in the same quilts as high-style motifs and in the same fabrics suggest that these women worked together, or that the group sold simpler blocks at a lower price.[16]

Fig. 3. Album Quilt, 1848; American; cotton; 100 1/4 x 100 1/4 inches; Saint Louis Art Museum, Gift of Mrs. Stratford Lee Morton 1:1973.

Later High Style

Beginning around 1848, album blocks appeared that took high-style design to yet another level. These squares had even more elaborate wreaths and large baskets filled with tighter groupings of blossoms and more overlapping edges. Especially noteworthy is the woven wicker basket with one edge raised. The basic visual vocabulary remained much the same as in the earlier high style, but the ornamentation became even greater, and near-perfection was achieved in graceful arrangement and draping of all elements. Printed fabrics gave depth and contour to individual motifs, adding almost a third dimension (fig. 2).

By 1848, this designer achieved a breakthrough in the shaping and

Fig. 4. Album quilt made by Maria Williams for Dr. John P. Mackenzie, c. 1850. Mary Simon cut and basted the blocks, according to diarist Hannah Trimble. Cotton and silk, 119 x 120 inches. William Rush Dunton, Jr., Dr. J. P. MacKenzie quilt, 1933. Quilt scrapbook volume IV, page 55, Dunton Quilting Collection, Archives and Manuscripts Collections, The Baltimore Museum of Art. DQ7.55

assembly of individual motifs to produce intricate designs in a more effi-cient way—by reducing the number of fabric pieces needed. A daisy of four or five layers was reduced to one or two. Reverse-appliquéd roses with tiny openings lost their under layer. The earlier reverse-appliquéd tulips became more uncommon. Newer style flowers consisted of two lay-ers of three pieces, the top often a contrasting color and texture, including velvet and silk. All of these changes added up to a more natural and

Fig. 5. Baltimore Presentation quilt, c. 1849. Cotton, 106 ¼ x 103 ¾ inches.
Metropolitan Museum of Art, NY, 1974.24.

refined look that could produce a complex block faster (fig. 3).

Peak production of the high style lasted until the mid-1850s, after which it faded quickly. Baltimore Albums continued to be made until the eve of the Civil War without the best of the older blocks. This surge of creativity that required such laborious enterprise has scant documentation. It continues to defy efforts to identify the originators of the designs and patterns, production and assembly steps, inscribers, and calligraphers, in spite of the best efforts of numerous researchers. Women's assignment to the domestic realm and anonymity still held sway.

Reviews of contemporary publications, newspapers and private diaries have yielded only one short passage, found by Jennifer Goldsborough

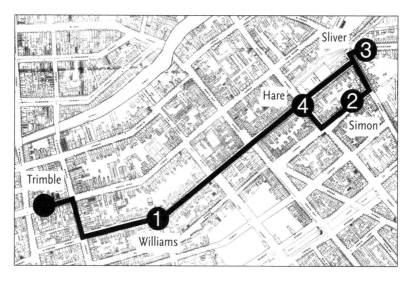

Fig. 6. Route Hannah Trimble walked on February 1, 1850, to view quilts on exhibition and blocks at Mary Simon's home.

during the work for *Lavish Legacies,* her exhibitions and catalogue of Baltimore Album quilts and their history in the early 1990s.[17] A diary entry of Baltimore resident Hannah Mary Trimble for 1 February, 1850 reads:

> "…Aunt S. & myself went to Mrs. Williams in Exeter St. to see a quilt which was being exhibited and intended for Dr. Mackenzie as a tribute of gratitude.... I could not imagine anything of the kind more perfect.... (Fig. 4.)
> …Then out to Mrs. Simon's in Chesnut St., **the lady who cut & basted these handsome quilts—saw some pretty squares.** [emphasis added] Next went to Mrs. Sliver's in Constitution St. and saw some very beautiful quilts, one of which was a decidedly superior one similar to Mrs. Williams...."[18] (Fig. 5, color plate 6; fig. 6.)

Trimble's phrase "saw some pretty squares" suggests that unfinished blocks similar to those on the just-viewed quilts were being offered for sale. This cottage industry production explains the appearance of nearly identical blocks on various album quilts. Goldsborough's research identified Mary Simon as the woman showing the squares; she designated

Simon as **Designer I** of the three major style categories she formulated following her examination of around 300 Baltimore Album quilts for *Lavish Legacies*.[19]

Thus Simon's name has come to be associated with most of the high-style Baltimore Album blocks. She cut and basted quilt blocks, but whether she worked on her own or under someone else's direction is open to question. Recent research has uncovered more information on Simon and two other women, expanding the scope of the Designer I designation.

### Simon's Role

Mary Simon was born Anna Maria Hergenroder in 1808 to Kasper Hergenroder and Maria Eva Sitzmann in Unterleichterbach, Bavaria. Ship records confirm that she arrived in Baltimore in late 1839 with one-year-old Catharina. Why she emigrated, who she knew in the city (if anyone), and how she supported herself are unknown. Philip Simon, a German weaver, arrived in Baltimore on June 7, 1844; sixteen days later he and Anna Maria were married. Perhaps they already knew each other or the union was arranged. Their family would have numbered four, including Philips's seven-year-old son.

Philip Simon is not listed in the 1845 city directory or in the city tax records of 1846, which probably indicates that he had not accumulated enough property to meet the $50 minimum for an assessment. He is listed as a carpet weaver in the 1847 city directory, which means that he and Anna Maria had managed to set up a household of their own. Perhaps at this point Anna Maria, or "Mary" to her American neighbors, had the stability and space in which to cut fabrics and assemble numerous pieces into kits. Goldsborough attributes the most accomplished high-style blocks to Mary Simon. She describes that in contrast with Simon's later work, blocks from this early phase were "more stylized designs using a great deal of brilliant blue rainbow fabric with applied yellow and red accents may represent a slightly more 'folk-y' phase of her work or that of another, similar, very talented designer."[20]

As a German-speaking, Roman Catholic immigrant in an overwhelmingly Protestant city, Simon probably was only dimly aware of pride in local prosperity, the evangelical religious fervor sweeping the city, or the political issues that led to the Mexican War. The designer of the early high style likely was native-born or a long-time Baltimore resident. Several early Designer I album quilts include pieces of chintz from the 1820s, perhaps from a scrap bag of long accumulation.

Nevertheless, by 1848 Mary Simon was producing quilt squares. Her first known work for the Mackenzie and Sliver quilts (mentioned in the above quotation) must have been undertaken by late 1848, as the quilts were finished and ready for exhibition in early 1850. No evidence has yet surfaced to indicate that Simon was involved in the earlier phase. Hannah Trimble's diary credits her with supplying squares for quilts made by others and that people visited her home, presumably to buy similar squares.

Fig. 7 a & b. Early-style rose (a); and mature-style roses (b, probably by Mary Simon). Detail a: cotton, 1846, Daughters of the American Revolution Museum 98.31. Detail b: cotton, c. 1850, authors' collection.

The extent of her involvement beyond these activities is not known.

Goldsborough refers to the second design phase as Simon's "mature" style, which includes "intricately woven red baskets, miniature figures in fully tailored garments," plus landscapes and sailing ships. She believes the mature style flourished between 1850 and 1854 and is epitomized by an album quilt made for Mary Heiner at the Maryland Historical Society (see fig. 11). The spread rose almost defines the mature phase, using what Goldsborough describes as the "characteristic layered leaf or paisley-shaped petal technique."[21] The earlier style of eight to twelve pieces per rose was reduced to five or six pieces (fig. 7a & b).

### Factors in the Transition

Why did the shift in style take place at this point? Women exhibited their handiwork in their homes or shops, presenting opportunities for viewing the latest in what had obviously become a fad for making album quilts.[22] Among the few period references is the Baltimore *Sun's* description of a quilt presented to a minister in 1848: "one of the most elegant and curiously wrought bed quilts ever exhibited in this city."[23] This comment implies that exhibitions had occurred in previous years. By the early 1840s, women exhibited quilts and competed for premiums in local county fairs. County and church fairs were advertised in the local papers, but private exhibitions apparently spread awareness by word of mouth in a small community.

The beginning of the annual fairs of the Maryland Institute for the Promotion of the Mechanical Arts in 1848 gave local women the opportunity to exhibit quilts and needlework to a wider public, which may have spurred greater creativity. Agricultural fairs provided other exhibition venues. Newspapers published lists of the items deposited for display in all categories and the names of the prize winners. Often female entrants shielded their identities by giving only their husband's names, or their last names, which makes them hard to trace.

The desire of women to create presentation quilts, especially for ministers who were admired or were moving to a new church, may have prompted them to buy already basted blocks and borders that could be finished more quickly than the earlier, multi-layered kits. Speed was a relative concept in the making of these albums, especially those with twenty-five to forty-two blocks of very complex motifs. Another possibility is that new figures joined a flourishing block-production trade. Perhaps Mary

Simon and others brought new skills or inspiration to the tasks. To date, no quilts signed by Simon or with provenance attributed to her, are known. She did not enter her work in the Mechanics Institute Fairs and no advertisements of her blocks for sale have been found.

Whatever the case, the new type of high-style block became dominant in the best Baltimore Album quilts made after 1848. The earlier type is seldom seen after 1850, suggesting that the earlier designer or designers stopped working or adopted the newer style. The context in which diarist Hannah Mary Trimble mentioned Simon suggests that she may have worked with or for Mrs. Williams and Mrs. Sliver.[24]

### Other Influences

Mrs. Williams was Maria Bond Wehner Williams (1792–1863), Baltimore-born and one of the first quiltmakers to use early Designer I blocks. She and several family members made two Baltimore Album quilts and contributed to others from about 1846 to 1850. All found to date were made for family members or friends and not for sale. This group may have played a role in making high-style blocks, but other blocks they contributed are not impressive. The Williams family used all mature-style blocks in the quilt for Dr. John Mackenzie, who treated Maria's husband Samuel Williams, a Methodist lay minister, without charge for many years.[25] Their working and/or financial dealings with Simon have yet to be discovered.

A more likely candidate for influence on the development of the mature style is Elizabeth McKenney Sliver (1808–1888). Married to Baltimore widower Abraham Sliver in 1842, Elizabeth exhibited an album similar to Dr. Mackenzie's during Trimble's visit. Quilts in two museum collections fit the description in Trimble's journal entry in February 1850. One at the Metropolitan Museum of Art in New York has the type of binding mentioned, but its dedicatory inscription was removed so it is impossible to be sure if this is the exhibition quilt.[26] The other one is at the Baltimore Museum of Art.[27]

The 1850 federal census recorded four women between the ages of twelve and twenty living with the Slivers who do not appear to be family members. This group may have been a workshop making blocks and quilts. Sliver's husband was a well-to-do manufacturer of soap and candles, thus Elizabeth had the resources to buy the best fabrics and spend time making quilts.

In contrast, Mary and Philip Simon had added two sons to the household by 1850; the census records no real or personal estate. The purchase of the expensive fabrics used in the quantity of mature-style blocks known at present was likely beyond Simon's means. Therefore, someone must have supplied her with needed funds or raw materials. Goldsborough even found socioeconomic differences in those purchasing these blocks; the names she traced on quilts of all-mature blocks "come from a more prosperous segment of the population than those on quilts with only one of her designs."[28]

In the fall of 1850 Trimble saw another album quilt at Sliver's house. This probably was the quilt for which Sliver won first place at the 1855 Maryland Institute fair, described as a "fancy quilt" made for her son William.[29] Like the two quilts described above, this one may have been arranged in the "Sliver formula": a large central basket or eagle surrounded by four double block-sized woven baskets and single block-sized open wreaths. The corners of the outer rows are filled with cornucopias and completed with bouquets, wreaths, trees, birds, trophies of arms or musical instruments. Several others in this configuration, presumably by Simon and Sliver, are located in museum and private collections.

These quilts boast superior artistic skills. The heavily laden elements are laid out in a plain field of negative space, making a bold statement. They suggest designers with knowledge of classical imagery and aesthetic principles, without the crowded compositions of many earlier Baltimore Album quilts or various forms of German folk art. Other quilts of Simon/Sliver-style squares are similarly accomplished, although smaller and laid out in the standard twenty-five single-block arrangement.

No advertisements for Elizabeth Sliver blocks or quilts have been found, but the presence of four unrelated women in her household hints at activities beyond everyday chores. One of them, Margaret McCaddin, was listed as a tailoress in the 1860 federal census. Sliver and her helpers probably made quilts for sale. Perhaps they were commissioned, but no traces of the transactions are known. Several short advertisements did appear in January 1849 in the *Sun* that read, "Miss Chase would inform her friends and customers that she has on hand . . . a few Album Squares for quilts, very handsome."[30] Mary Chase's public notices are the only ones yet found.

Mary Chase was in business for herself. She owned a fancy dry goods and millinery store from around 1842 into the 1850s in northwest Baltimore. Dr. William Rush Dunton, Jr., earliest of the Baltimore Album quilt

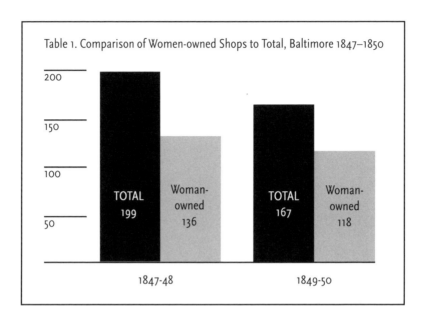

Table 1. Comparison of Women-owned Shops to Total, Baltimore 1847–1850

| | |
|---|---|
| TOTAL 199 | Woman-owned 136 |
| TOTAL 167 | Woman-owned 118 |

1847-48      1849-50

historians, posited that album blocks were "sold at shops," and that such commercial sales were a method of distribution.[31]

Millinery and fancy dry goods shops have a direct connection with album quilts.During the period 1847–1850, seventy percent of the fancy dry goods shops in the city were owned and operated by women.[32] (Table 1). By the 1850s, fancywork had become a commercial enterprise for urban women. Historian Elizabeth White Nelson found that, "A store for fancy goods was an appropriate enterprise for a lady as long as she conducted it in a decorous manner."[33] It is reasonable to assume that such shops sold preassembled quilt squares that were more accomplished than those purchasers had the skills or time to make themselves.

Several milliners incorporated blocks into album quilts and entered them in Maryland Institute fairs. An 1844 album quilt at the Minneapolis Institute of Arts includes a block signed by Baltimore milliners Eleanor Hugg and Rebecca Haswell.[34] In 1850 Ruth Sanks, a milliner at 47 Baltimore Street, won a first prize for her album quilt.[35] The Herget family owned a confectionary and millinery shop at the time of the making of the 1847–1848 Pool-Herget quilt.[36]

Mary Chase was involved with the album blocks as early as 1846 when she contributed a signed block to an album quilt.[37] Again in 1847, she contributed a block as did her brother Wells.[38] Both blocks are quite simple appliqués, nothing like the high-style blocks already available. A recently discovered quilt top includes a block in a different but unremarkable pattern with Chase's name and the date 1849 inscribed.[39] Two of these three quilts are attributed to the Gorsuch family in north Baltimore County, who may have bought their blocks from Chase directly. In 1848, Chase entered two rugs in the Maryland Institute Fair. Baltimore's *Sun* newspaper described them: "These are certainly among the most elegant articles of the kind on exhibition. They are altogether the work of the needle, and cannot, we should think, be easily surpassed."[40] Then in 1849, Chase entered a "fancy quilt" in the Fair, which won a first prize.[41] She might have used high-style blocks such as those found in the Gorsuch family quilts, in order to top the field.[42] The extent of Chase's role in making album quilts is uncertain, but she must have been a talented needle artist. The Gorsuch family was known for its involvement in Methodism.[43] Chase, who was baptized as Associate Reformed Presbyterian, converted to Methodism as an adult in 1847.[44] The Gorsuch/Chase quilting association may have influenced her conversion.

It is very unlikely that one woman could have made the huge number of high-style blocks that are known, all with hundreds of pattern pieces to be pinned, cut out correctly, positioned to overlap other pieces, and basted in place in set schemes. Collaboration must have existed among Mary Simon and probably others as yet unidentified, and quiltmakers such as Maria Williams and Elizabeth Sliver. Evidence of involvement of the Williams household in the design of early high-style blocks is slim, while such a role for the Sliver and her household looks more likely.

Use of later high-style blocks continued into the mid-1850s. More than two dozen of the most complex compositions dated from 1850 to 1856 are known, and others remain to be discovered.

## Pictorial Statements

As a body of work, Baltimore Album quilts are unique in the history of American quiltmaking in several ways. They comprise a very large number of examples—perhaps 350, depending on how the parameters are defined. They were made over a short period of time, just over ten years, in and around one city. Many are signed, allowing their contributors to be identified and their family, social, and religious connections to be traced. Some quilt blocks were enhanced with inked drawings of buildings and symbols that can be recognized and analyzed. These characteristics exist on a significant number that are among the most artistically skilled and elaborately constructed bedcovers known to exist in any location in any era.

Therefore, a large amount of information on these quilts can be understood in the present day. In an age when women's "voices" were a scant part of the historical record, these fabric expressions are invaluable indications of their thinking on private and public matters, their lives, and the world they inhabited.

## Family and Friends

The majority of Baltimore Album quilts inscribed with names and occasionally dates and places seem to fit the general description and conclusions of quilt historians that they were made to acknowledge relationships among families and friends. Album quilts are often described as cloth versions of paper autograph albums, popular from the late eighteenth century. These recordings often included emotional and religious sentiments, drawings, and sometimes political and patriotic statements. Women were the largest participants in these exchanges.

Over the years, curators and historians have studied the names on many of these quilts. In some examples the identity of the signers and the connections among them are discerned through genealogical searches. Both male and female names are present, but females predominate. For his book *Old Quilts,* Dunton studied more than fifty album quilts during the 1920s and 1930s, recording names and the histories provided by owners. At that point, the quilts were still largely held by the original families. His research confirmed much of their information, but he recognized that some of it was fanciful. He provided better dates and interpretations when possible.

Dena Katzenberg studied examples in the collection of the Baltimore Museum of Art and more for her exhibition and catalogue *Baltimore Album Quilts* in the early 1980s. She delved into the family backgrounds of the signers, their kinship ties, religious affiliations, and even the types of penmanship that were present. However, the true history and purpose of many of these quilts may never be known.

Goldsborough's research uncovered the key piece of evidence of a professional designer or group for the high-style blocks. She studied quilts of all skill levels and identified two additional style categories.[45] Her analysis and conclusions remain largely relevant today. The discovery of previously unknown album quilts has brought even more signers' names to light. A good number can be matched with those identified by the earlier historians. Additional community and familial ties are revealed in these newer examples.

## Ministers

Maryland was founded in 1634 as a proprietary colony of the Roman Catholic Calvert family, which created a haven for their co-religionists from the turbulence of sectarian strife in England. (In 1689 the Calverts lost control of their holdings in a Protestant revolt. The new governing body barred Catholics from practicing their religion or holding office.) Maryland became a royal colony in 1691, after which Anglicanism was established as the official religion.[46] Protestantism was not only the norm but enjoyed "quasi-establishment" status, according to historian of religion Michael S. Franch.[47]

The religious revival movement characterized by historians as the "Second Great Awakening" contributed to the dominance of Protestantism in a growing new country. Beginning in the late eighteenth century as the original states disestablished official religions, the Awakening lasted into the 1850s. Revival meetings brought new membership to traditional denominations and newly formed sects in cities and the expanding frontier regions.

Evangelical preachers attempted to turn listeners from sinful ways with an emotional message describing the horrors awaiting the unsaved and the joys of salvation through a newly empathetic God. Historians note that they emphasized individual human initiative, emotional spiritual experience, and egalitarianism, echoing the Romantic impulses that were gaining strength at the same time.[48] Baptists and Methodists were especially active in holding emotion-charged camp meetings, but even more staid Presbyterians and Congregationalists modified their theologies to align with populist enthusiasms. By the 1820s, revivalism became part of mainstream culture. Protestant women, who were the majority of supporters of the movement, were channeled toward domestic duties, as well as toward efforts to save others and ameliorate social ills.[49]

Having ascended to positions of influence over a range of issues, Protestant clergy played large roles in national life in these years. Michael Franch contends, "They were leading carriers and shapers of American culture, expounding on economics, family life, [and] political responsibility" through the pulpit and secular orations, lectures, and literary associations.[50] Baltimore was a center of populist evangelical activity according to William Sutton.[51] By the 1830s, he notes, "Baltimore was unique among American cities in terms of the depth of populist religious influence; contemporaries estimated Methodism to be significantly stronger in Baltimore than in any other urban center."[52]

In competitive efforts, other denominations recruited membership from native-born migrants to the city, immigrants, and—to a lesser extent—free blacks. German churches conducted services in English or German, depending on their origins and membership. Evangelical beliefs influenced the city's workers as they formed craft unions in the 1820s, which became strong and influential in the 1830s. They used the ethics and language of evangelical religions in attempting to mitigate the worst effects of unbridled capitalism.[53] Workers, artisans, shopkeepers, and professionals alike joined in a religious movement that began in the winter of 1839–1840 with a long revival in one Baptist church led by Jacob Knapp, an itinerant revivalist. Other Protestant congregations joined in, creating a city-wide revival of remarkable intensity. It increased religious fervor, brought about numerous conversions, and spurred missionary outreach that continued throughout the 1840s.[54]

Baltimore's evangelical environment made people receptive to the power of such revivals: ". . . most major [Protestant] denominations more than doubled their number of congregations in a city that increased [in population] about 150 percent . . . 64 congregations in 1840, 108 in 1850," and at least 155 in 1860.[55] Baltimoreans founded so many new congregations because they regarded them as necessary for saving souls and regenerating society. The city's religious community was vigorous, and had good clerical leadership in many denominations—Presbyterian, Episcopal, Baptist and Methodist—as well as energetic laymen.[56] However, Methodists increased the most. Revivals and long prayer meetings already were a central part of their practices.[57] Methodism had a large corps of trained lay preachers and exhorters to carry its message to the unchurched through missions and outreach, and to promote and serve new congregations.[58] Methodism became Baltimore's largest denomination in the 1840s and 1850s.[59]

Women participated fully in the evangelical and revival fervor of the time. Women's relationships with their congregations are usually discussed in terms of their spiritual and emotional needs. In Baltimore as elsewhere, they depended on their clergy and fellow church members to withstand the churning that accompanied the turnover of urban congregations and the increasing pluralism of the culture.[60] Franch explains that congregations reinforced "the tie of community." "Whether directly 'religious' or not, the sewing circles, fundraising fairs, and other congregational activities tended to increase the role of the church as the center of its communicants' lives."[61]

Even though shut out of influence on practices and governance, women made large contributions to Baltimore's Protestant congregations and their charities. Franch found that, "Women's societies, sewing circles, benevolent associations and other groups solicited subscriptions, held fairs and teas, and sold the products of their sewing baskets and kitchens to pay for the necessities and amenities of congregational life."[62] They also raised money to pay church debts, support local and foreign missions, build and staff their churches' orphanages, refuges, and Sunday schools. Women thus demonstrated their abilities "to manage enterprises of considerable administrative and financial complexity . . . in an otherwise male-dominated society." Franch concluded.[63]

Despite their enormous contributions, ministers depended more on women's participation than on their labors. Franch's study found that church attendance was more important in the lives of the city's women than men. "Despite an urban population almost evenly divided between the sexes, Baltimore's white Protestant churches, across the denominational and economic spectrum, had nearly three females for every male member."[64] The continued existence of these theocratic organizations, not just their congregational programs, would have been at risk without the support of the female membership.

The loyalty of women apparently was not due entirely to their spiritual yearnings. Attendance at services, prayer meetings, and church-related projects were well known as acceptable reasons for women to leave their homes unescorted. The need to seek social contact outside their domestic duties brought them into these church-sanctioned activities. In fact, Mrs. Franklin Wilson, a Baptist minister's wife, complained in her journal that "women of her congregation were more eager to attend the women's sewing circle than they were to attend women's prayer meetings."[65] Most prayer meetings, especially Methodist class meetings, were segregated by sex. Weekly classes, where women and their spiritual leaders met in churches or private homes, may have provided some of the creative spark for expressions of gratitude and respect.

Baltimore churchwomen made many quilted tributes, often album

Table 2

Quilts made for Clergy in
Baltimore and nearby
communities, 1840–1862.

| | Made for | Date | |
|---|---|---|---|
| 1 | Launcelot B. Minor | 1840 | |
| 2 | Eliza Hay Morris (Rev. John G.) | 1842 | 1844 |
| 3 | Edward McColgan | 1843 | |
| 4 | John Suman & wife Agnes | 1843 | 1847 |
| 5 | Eli Henkle | 1844 | |
| 6 | William G. Eggleston & wife Sarah | 1844 | 1847 |
| 7 | Hezekiah Best* | 1845 | 1847 |
| 8 | Susan D. Morgan (Rev. Lyttleton) | 1846 | |
| 9 | John W. Smith | 1846 | |
| 10 | Thomas Harrison West Monroe | 1846 | 1847 |
| 11 | Isaiah Mercier | 1846 | 1847 |
| 12 | Samuel Williams* (lay) | 1846 | 1847 |
| 13 | Francis M. Mills* | 1846 | 1847 |
| 14 | William Wagner Orwig | 1846 | 1848 |
| 15 | Robert M. Lipscomb & wife Elizabeth* | 1847 | |
| 16 | John G. Smart | 1847 | |
| 17 | Bernard H. Nadal* | 1847 | |
| 18 | Dr. George C.M. Roberts* | 1847 | 1848 |
| 19 | Robert S. Vinton | 1847 | 1848 |
| 20 | George Holtzman* (class leader) | 1847 | 1849 |
| 21 | Thomas McGee | 1848 | |
| 22 | Elias Heiner* | 1848 | |
| 23 | Peter L. Wilson* | 1848 | |
| 24 | Jacob Geiger | 1849 | |
| 25 | John W. Hall (Sunday school leader) | 1849 | |
| 26 | David Thomas (assumed) | 1851 | |
| 27 | Ebenezer Stewart* (supporter) | 1851 | |
| 28 | Mary Heiner* (Rev. Elias) | 1852 | |
| 29 | David H. Laney | 1853 | |
| 30 | William Jenkins | 1853 | |
| 31 | William Finney | 1854 | |
| 32 | John Russell* | 1854 | |
| 33 | Daniel Kreamer* | 1856 | |
| 34 | Joseph Levin Mills | 1862 | |

*High-style design

| Made by | Location | Denomination |
|---------|----------|--------------|
| "Young Ladies of Thorndale Seminary" | Carroll Co., Md | Episcopal |
| Women of the First English Lutheran Church | Baltimore | Lutheran |
| Probably women of St. Peter's Roman Catholic Church | Baltimore | Roman Catholic |
| Family, friends & congregants | | Baltimore/N. Va Lutheran |
| Women of Westminster Station M.P. Church | Carroll Co., Md | Methodist Episcopal |
| Congregants of various churches served | Baltimore/DC/Va | Methodist Episcopal |
| Members of several religious classes | Baltimore | Methodist Episcopal |
| Women of High Street M.E. Church | Baltimore | Methodist Episcopal |
| Supporters of Seamen's Bethel Mission | Baltimore | Methodist Episcopal |
| Congregants of various churches served | Hereford/Baltimore | Methodist Episcopal |
| Sunday School class, Emory M.E. Church | Ellicott City, Md | Methodist Episcopal |
| Family, friends & congregants, Exeter Street, M.E. Church | Baltimore | Methodist Episcopal |
| Class members, probably E. Baltimore Station M.E. Church | Baltimore | Methodist Episcopal |
| Probably women of Evangelical Association Church | Baltimore | Evangelical Association |
| Friends and congregants of High Street M.E. Church | Baltimore | Methodist Episcopal |
| Women of First Presbyterian Church | Baltimore | Presbyterian |
| Women of Columbia Avenue M. E. Church | Baltimore | Methodist Episcopal |
| Class members & friends, several M.E. churches | Baltimore | Methodist Episcopal |
| Women of William Street M.E. Church | Baltimore | Methodist Episcopal |
| Women of Eutaw Street M.E. Church | Baltimore | Methodist Episcopal |
| Women of his [religious] society, Severn Circuit, M.E. | Anne Arundel Co., Md | Methodist Episcopal |
| Women of First German Reformed Church | Baltimore | German Reformed |
| Probably congregants of Greene Street M.P. Church | Baltimore | Methodist Protestant |
| Women of Manchester German Reformed Church | Carroll Co., Md | German Reformed |
| Women teachers of Caroline Street Sunday School #2 | Baltimore | Methodist Episcopal |
| Women of E. Baltimore Station and Caroline St. M.E. Church | Baltimore | Methodist Episcopal |
| Women of Columbia Ave. M.E. Church | Baltimore | Methodist Episcopal |
| Women of First German Reformed Church | Baltimore | German Reformed |
| Women of the Severn Circuit, M.E. | Anne Arundel Co., Md | Methodist Episcopal |
| Women of the Lutheran Church | Baltimore | Lutheran |
| Women of the Churchville Presbyterian Church | Harford Co., Md | Presbyterian |
| Women of Old Otterbein Church | Baltimore | United Brethren |
| Women of Emanuel Church | Baltimore | Evangelical Association |
| Friends in honor of his ordination | Harford Co., Md | Methodist Episcopal |

quilts, for their ministers and class leaders. Whether these often elaborate presentation pieces were made within church sewing circles is unknown, as scant corroboration of this obvious location has been found. Not surprisingly, the largest numbers of these quilts to survive were made for Methodist clergy.

Dena Katzenberg was the first of the scholars to point out the connection between Methodism and Baltimore Album quilts. She identified the Methodist affiliation of many album quilt signers from surviving church class lists. However, the number of quilts she discussed was small. Goldsborough studied many others, determining that most were made by "members of Protestant churches, especially Methodist and German Reformed."[66] Several more have come to light in the last few years, allowing for a wider interpretation.

At least thirty-four surviving quilts and unquilted tops were made for Baltimore-area clergymen, their wives and church supporters between 1840 and about 1862: twenty-six for city residents and eight in nearby communities. (Table 2.) Twenty-eight are floral albums, three are pieced blocks, and two are appliquéd motifs. In terms of denomination, the Catholic, Episcopal, and United Brethren churches are each represented by one quilt. Presbyterian and Evangelical Association have two, while Lutheran and German Reformed are represented by three quilts. The other twenty-one were made for Methodists. Some ministers' quilts were exhibited for public viewing. Several were presented to the recipients in public ceremonies and written up by local newspapers.[67] Quilts given to clergy in other areas are known, but the number in Baltimore appears to be without equal.

The beauty of these quilts, made specifically for presentation, is high; many are among the best examples known. Several factors may account for the number and quality. Evangelical fervor in the city's Protestant sects continued to increase, thanks to the still vibrant revival movement that had begun in 1839–1840. The female majorities of the most active churches were motivated to honor the clergy who tended to their spiritual needs with something of themselves—these quilts manifested the makers' artistic talents in design and fabric selections, and their devotion in the inscriptions of scriptural verses and sentiments.

New and expensive fabrics made up these ministers' quilts.[68] Many women obviously purchased their blocks from one of the many professional kit makers, including Designer I's high-style offerings (see the starred quilts in Table 2). Twenty were made in the years 1845 to 1849. Five included cloth representations of the churches served by the recipient and another includes a small drawing of the building. Production was especially large during the years 1846 to 1848. It appears that a competition among church-going women across Baltimore was underway, as one group learned of the efforts of another. Such motivation might account for the cluster of quilts for clergy in those years. If so, more quilts were made and either did not survive or are still awaiting discovery.

Work on these quilts may actually have helped stimulate the development of the mature-style Designer I blocks, as women showed their willingness to buy blocks with even larger numbers of pieces and more expensive fabrics. The minister's quilts and tops dating from about 1851 to 1856 include quite a number of mature-style blocks but only one church representation; the fad for these presentation pieces appears to have waned. Quilts of high-style blocks were made in the 1850s, many of presentation size, but their purposes seem to be more private.

The larger number of Methodist minister's quilts might be explained partly by the larger number of Methodist congregations, and perhaps by their clergy and laymen's continued efforts in proselytizing, recruiting membership, and building churches. Another factor could have been the church's policy of reassigning ministers to different congregations every two years. As so many of them left their flocks, with the attendant emotional difficulties for them and for the faithful, more parting tributes were needed.

The quilt made for Father Edward McColgan in 1843 is a telling indication of the separation of Catholics from the American mainstream. Catholicism was tolerated: "allowed to exist as a sect but defined by the dominant religion as on the periphery of national culture," historian Franch states.[70] The small, older Catholic population in Baltimore was joined by large tides of immigrants, mostly Irish and Germans, from 1840 to 1860, which soon led to nativist opposition to their growing presence and political power. McColgan's quilt pattern is a Maryland favorite: crossed laurel branches. It is the only one known to have been made for a Catholic priest in this time period. In 1843, the ladies of the congregation held a fair to raise money for the completion of St. Peter's Church. Possibly, the quilt was a gift to McColgan around the time of the dedication.[71]

Baltimore's small Jewish community was closed and generally not receptive to activities outside of Jewish tradition, with the exception of quilting. Goldsborough identified as the work of Designer III, a small but distinct group of Baltimore Album quilts, many of which descended in

Fig. 8. Baltimore Album quilt presented to Rev. Bernard H. Nadal in 1847 by women of his Columbia Avenue congregation. Complex blocks in the center and four compass points are early Designer I style. Cotton, 105 x 105 inches. National Museum of American History, Smithsonian Institution, 1983.0866.01.

Jewish families. Ronda McAllen's 2006 *Uncoverings* paper described their association with Baltimore's German-Jewish community. These quilts were outliers; their motifs were based more on German folk art than the realistic floral designs of early and mature Designer I blocks.

### Religious Expressions

Quilted expressions of religious sympathies did not end with clergy and churchmen. Christian symbols are some of the more recognizable on Baltimore Album quilts. The dove bearing an olive branch is seen often; the Bible is present on several. Lyres and anchors have religious associations. At least one Arc of the Covenant is known, as well as a portrait of John

Fig. 9. Mary E. Gray, Baltimore Album quilt, 1851. Cotton and silk, 114 ½ × 113 ½ inches. Quilt made for Ebenezer Stewart by the same Columbia Avenue congregation. Its center nine blocks probably were created as kits by Mary Simon. Dallas Museum of Art, anonymous gift.

Wesley, founder of Methodism. Many Baltimore Album quilts, including high-style examples, are inscribed with biblical verses, psalms, and lines of hymns by Isaac Watts, an interdenominational favorite.

Three bedcovers made by women of the Columbia Avenue Methodist Church illustrate the changes in high-style quilt blocks in just a few years. The congregation was formed by laboring-class Methodists in the late 1830s. In their rudimentary building they held a "notable" revival in the winter of 1841–1842; by 1844 they had built a meeting house.[72] In 1845, they were assigned the Reverend Bernard H. Nadal (1815–1870), a scholarly

Fig. 10. Baltimore Album quilt made for Rev. Elias Heiner by women of his First German Reformed congregation in 1848. Four elaborate blocks are Designer I early style, the cornucopia in mature style. Cotton, 106 x 106 inches. Courtesy of Elly Sienkiewicz.

man, as their pastor. When he left for another assignment in 1847, he was presented with a Baltimore Album quilt made largely of early-style Designer I blocks almost identical to those on the 1846 DAR Museum top.[74] The quilt must have been quite an effort in money and time for the wives of grocers, shoemakers, a druggist, millwright, butcher, blacksmith and wagoner.[74] (Fig. 8.)

Four years later in 1851, the congregation and some of the same contributors made the "Brickmaker's" quilt and the "All Saints' Day" top. The quilt was created for Ebenezer Stewart, a devoted supporter of the church. He was a brickmaker by trade.[75] A representation of his house appears in

Fig. 11. Baltimore Album quilt made for Mary Heiner in 1852 by members of the same congregation. Entirely Mary Simon-style blocks and border. Cotton and silk, 107 x 105 inches. Maryland Historical Society 91.17.

the central block, hence the quilt's name (fig. 9). Some of the same women made a top honoring their deceased relatives; it was dedicated on November 1, 1851, All Saints' Day.[76] Inscriptions identify those departed. Both pieces are composed mostly of mature-style Designer I blocks of overabundant wreaths, urns, and baskets with the innovative paisley-shaped rose petals. For all reasons suggested previously, the newer high style flourished when the best was called for.

The same shift is seen in two quilts by members of the First German Reformed Church, which operated in German and English. In 1848, church women made an album quilt for their minister, Elias Heiner (1810–1863), who was known across the city and revered for service that stretched almost twenty-eight years.[77] An accurate miniature church building sits in the center surrounded by chintz wreaths, plus four early Designer I blocks (church, urn, compote, double wreath) and one in mature style (cornucopia). Makers were wives of a clerk, druggist, grocer, carpenter, tailor, but also a real estate agent and farm implement manufacturer.[78] Most were Maryland-born, likely of German descent. (Fig. 10, color plate 7.)

In 1852, several members of the Horton family, congregants of the First German Reformed Church, and several other signers of the Reverend Heiner quilt made an album quilt of mature-style blocks and border for Heiner's wife Mary. The unity of style and graceful combination of fabrics, inscriptions, and quilting make this one of the finest dozen Baltimore Album quilts, according to Goldsborough.[79] Contributors to this masterpiece were among the more affluent in the congregation.[80] (Fig. 11.)

## Specific Events

Baltimore Album quilts were made for specific events, according to plausible family history or subsequent research. Four are reliably documented marriage quilts. The most elaborate, the 1849 Sliver wedding quilt (discussed above) is the complete work of Mary Simon and Elizabeth Sliver. Another for Isabella Battee, about 1852, contains ten blocks by the same designer team. Two others from about 1847 have two or three high-style squares accompanied by typical wreath and floral blocks.[81] The modern notion that many Baltimore Albums were made as brides' quilts was disproved by Goldsborough's research.[82]

Two "freedom" quilts are known. Family tradition related that they were made to mark the male recipient's twenty-first birthday and attainment of legal majority. Female friends and relatives of Benjamin Almoney were said to have gathered to celebrate the day and put the quilt together, according to Dunton.[83] Another for Daniel Crowl was made by female relatives.[84]

One of the finest Baltimore Album quilts to survive, the Doctor Mackenzie quilt (described above) was presented in honor of many years of service to his patient. Some of its history was saved, while those of other albums in presentation style have been lost so their recipients and reasons for tribute are unknown. The Samuel Williams quilt likely was made to mark his retirement from more than forty years of Methodist church work.[85] The central square was signed by one of Williams's friends, a lay minister also, who aided Baltimore's poor alongside Williams.

A dramatic, mature-style album quilt was made for Captain George W. Russell in 1852 as a tribute of esteem for his oversight of the construction and appointment as Captain of the steamer *North Carolina*.[86] A top, also in high-style blocks for a Captain Aust, includes a rendering of a three-masted ship likely in recognition of the recipient's profession.[87]

Political

Women could not vote, but their increasing literacy and the explosion in popular publications in the 1830s brought them greater means to understand the political climate in which they lived. Andrew Jackson was a first "man of the people" from the frontier to become a popular favorite. Baltimore was the site of the Democratic Party convention in 1828 that nominated Jackson for president. During the campaign the party made some appeals to women, printing fabrics with Jackson's portrait. Women were paying attention to these political activities. Appliquéd blocks with the Democratic Party symbol, the rooster, are found on at least three album bedcovers.[88] Two of them were made in the Baltimore area in the 1840s.

Alexander I.W. Jackson, a working-class union leader, printer by trade, honored President Andrew Jackson in a block he contributed to a high-style Baltimore Album quilt made 1845–1847.[89] He inscribed a statement attributed to the president, "The Blessings of Government, Like the dew of Heaven, Should be equally dispersed on the Rich and the Poor." The block, a heart-shaped berry wreath, is inscribed "Andrew Jackson's Heart." Although Jackson had died in 1845 he was still considered a champion of working people in their struggle against "monied" interests, especially the Whigs, the Democrats' political rivals.

Another Baltimore Album quilt with a similar wreath is inscribed, "Presented by Miss Mary Ann Grooms/Democracy is my Motto/Baltimore 1847" and "Gen'l Jackson's Heart."[90] Quite a few other Baltimore Album quilts have such wreath blocks.[91] They may indicate approval of Democratic policies or admiration of Andrew Jackson himself.

The Whig Party's presidential candidate in 1840 was William Henry Harrison, a hero of the War of 1812. His nomination was celebrated in Baltimore with two days of parades and rallies in May 1840. Whig campaign organizers encouraged women to attend the main rally, going so far as to build a separate pavilion for them and the clergy, so they would not be jostled by crowds of rowdy men.[92]

Although he was descended from a prominent Virginia plantation-owning family, Harrison's campaign used the image of his humble log cabin home in Ohio to buttress his appeal to both rural and urban voters. Log cabins appeared in political cartoons, on campaign fabric and ribbons and elsewhere, becoming one of the dominant motifs of the 1840 election.[93] Log cabins appeared again in the 1844 presidential campaign, when Henry Clay was nominated in Baltimore in similar fashion to Harrison.

Log cabins, indications of Whig sympathies, began appearing on quilts in the mid-1840s. On the Pool-Herget quilt (mentioned above), made largely in Designer I's early style, the log cabin flanks a flag-bearing eagle and the United States Capitol—three symbols found on Whig campaign banners, ribbons, and other paraphernalia. A similar, elaborate Designer I album quilt of the same years features an eagle block with the bird's wing pointing to the log cabin in an adjacent block.[94] Several other Baltimore Album quilts have log cabin blocks, and in others the log cabin is drawn on.[95] Three high-style albums include blocks depicting the raccoon, the Whig mascot.[96]

Patriotic Expressions

Evidence both of Baltimore women's engagement with and affection for their country are easily read on their album quilts. The eagle is the symbol most used, usually set in the center, accompanied by the star-spangled banner, liberty cap, shield, and/or bugle, all surmounted by floral garlands. The first eagle block appeared on a Baltimore Album around 1845; eagles continued to be seen into the late 1850s.[97] Designer I created the most elaborate eagles, which were copied by both professional and amateur block makers.

Several Baltimore Album quilts are inscribed with patriotic statements and references. A high-style presentation album dated 1848 puts a spread-winged eagle in the center, surrounded by four mature-style baskets and an undulating floral border (see fig. 3).[98] One block was given "from one of the Rough & Ready to the worthy president," a reference to General Zachary Taylor, who was running for president on the Whig ticket. The quilt was presented to an "E. Morrison" by the "Ladies of Baltimore." Katzenberg thought this group was a sewing circle.[99] Newspaper research has revealed that it was a women's group dedicated primarily to honoring the military, supporting troops in wartime, as well as temperance activities.[100] It had many counterparts in other cities. The ladies of Baltimore commissioned flags for militia companies and Baltimore veterans of the War of 1812. They visited militia encampments during summer exercises in 1844 to thank the troops for their service, and they sent flags and supplies to local regiments during the Mexican War in 1846 and 1847.

Baltimore sent a militia regiment to fight in that war and lost two officers, William Watson and Samuel Ringgold in the first few months. Within a year of their deaths, blocks in their honor were produced for album quilts.[101] Several other Baltimore Album quilts are inscribed with tributes to Zachary Taylor and one includes a drawing of him on his horse.[102] "Rough and Ready" quilts were entered at the Maryland Institute fairs and won prizes.[103] References to political figures have not been found on Baltimore Albums in the 1850s. The Whig Party began to collapse after Taylor's death in 1850 and fielded its last candidate for president in 1852. By this time the early Designer I blocks are rarely seen.

Several scholars have suggested that women preferred Whig candidates in presidential contests in the 1840s.[104] They are writing largely about white, Protestant women of the middle class, rather than working class. It is possible that some early high-style Baltimore Albums were associated with quiltmakers of Whig political leanings. The presentation of wreaths and bouquets to political figures, and their frequent depiction in Designer I blocks, may indicate a connection between political sympathies and the popularity of Designer I's output, especially the early blocks made before 1850.

### Expressions of Reform

Among the signs of a maturing nation was the recognition of the need to reform some of its social ills, which became urgent in the 1830s and 1840s. Baltimore had many problems that had to be addressed. Many middle-class Protestant women stepped out of their private roles to help with issues of poverty, hunger, and alcoholism. Religious impulses and the obligations of women's higher nature to transform society led some of the city's women to join reform movements.[105]

The devastating effects of strong drink on men, women, and children were already well known early in the century.[106] Temperance societies led largely by Protestant laymen and clergy began in the 1820s. Temperance, like church work, was one of the few socially acceptable associational activities for women. In Baltimore as elsewhere, men led these efforts; women played supporting roles. However, both men and women attended public meetings, listened to speeches, and advocated for total abstinence to friend and stranger. Among many local groups, the Washington Temperance Society began in Baltimore in 1840 with a populist ethos, combining benevolence and political goals, including banning the sale of alcohol.[107] Jacob Knapp, the revival preacher, promoted temperance and became a major supporter of the Washingtonians; he reflected "the tendency to link temperance to popular evangelism."[108]

In the mid-1840s the Washingtonians were overtaken by a new mutual benefit society, the Sons of Temperance, which grew rapidly in Baltimore and elsewhere. Women were not allowed membership and thus were denied roles they had held in other temperance societies. They were invited to the Sons' elaborate parades and conventions to support male members' resolve.[109]

Through ministers, the Ladies of Baltimore presented Bibles to chapters of the Sons of Temperance at church ceremonies in 1845 and 1847.[110] The Ladies and other supporters included temperance blocks on their album quilts. The triangular emblem of the Sons appeared on a Baltimore Album quilt made for Methodist minister Thomas H. W. Monroe in 1847–1848.[111] Fountains spouting pure water were symbols of several temperance societies. Blocks depicting such fountains, often with eagles hovering above, are seen on several Baltimore Album quilts. Many were made by Designer I in both early and mature styles as well as simpler forms by others. An oversized but unfinished block of Baltimore's City Springs is the best known temperance square in the mature style.[112]

## Odd Fellows

The first American wing of the English Odd Fellows was founded in Baltimore in 1819 as the Washington Lodge no.1. In 1843, the Order broke away to become the Independent Order of Odd Fellows because of the English group's focus on relief, while the Americans included benevolence and moral reform with relief. An Odd Fellow's duty was to visit the sick, relieve the distressed, bury the dead, and educate the orphan. The first great general principal was to care for others, due to the belief that no one has the right to live simply for himself. As a result, Odd Fellows closely aligned themselves with other benevolent societies. In 1851, a fierce battle occurred within the Order over female membership, resulting in the creation of a female branch, the Rebekah Degree. At that time, only wives of 5th Degree or Scarlet members could be appointed.[113]

Odd Fellowship became the working-class alternative to Freemasonry.

Its members were primarily Protestant, due to the Catholics' dislike and distrust of any secular secret society. During the 1830s, anti-Masonic movements swept the nation; a wave of upper-middle-class men joined, bringing an emphasis on moral reform. While Baltimore's male citizens flocked to the Odd Fellow's Hall on Gay Street, their wives, sisters and daughters stitched the Odd Fellows' symbols into their album squares. Blocks containing the triple link chain (symbolizing friendship, love and truth), as well as beehives, arrows and quivers, heart-in-hand, and the all-seeing eye can be found in many of the best album quilts.

An album quilt made by Ann E. Bush has a high-style center block that depicts the 1843 Gothic façade of the Odd Fellows' Hall; thirty-six smaller blocks represent different Odd Fellows symbols.[114] This quilt appears to have been made as a tribute to her husband George H. C. J. Bush's initiation in 1848 into Baltimore's Iris Lodge no. 48. The quilt was displayed in May 1848 at the Mechanics and Manufacturers' Fair and entered into the Maryland Institute fair. Three other known quilts also depict the city's Odd Fellows' Hall façade.[115] At least a dozen Baltimore Album quilts contain a single block showing Odd Fellows insignia.

Squares alluding to abolition of slavery or women's rights are not found on Baltimore Album quilts. Apparently these issues were too controversial for Baltimore women to consider including.

Conclusion

The years 1848 to 1852 represent a peak in excellence of design and in expressions of support for Protestant clergy, the Whig and Democratic Parties, temperance and fraternal organizations, and probably in overall production of Baltimore Album quilts. Fewer pictorial images appear after 1850, as high-style compositions became more complex but largely floral. If the latter contain specific references, their meanings are now lost.

In Maryland, and especially Baltimore, a variety of motives led to a decade of enormous physical and mental effort by hundreds of women to create statements, both public and private, through quilting. Building on a legacy of fine sewing skills, Baltimore women joined with brilliant artists such as Mary Simon, contributing to a popular trend to pay tribute to public figures as well as domestic relationships. The seemingly sudden appearance of elaborate, multi-pieced quilt blocks from modest predecessors may have spurred production beyond ordinary levels. It is also possible that the urge to make special quilts inspired by religious exuberance prompted intuitively gifted or artistically trained persons to new heights of achievement to fill the demand.

Women used album quilts to express their views and indicate what was most meaningful to them. Baltimoreans put high-style squares in their most important quilts, including acknowledgments of family milestones of marriage, coming of age, and departures, and gifts or recognitions of revered clergy and religious leaders, and political and military figures. They showed pride in Baltimore's fine public buildings and monuments, as well as the role of overseas trade and the railroad to its economic power. They recognized the goals of the temperance movement and the work of their husbands' fraternal organizations.

It was a happy coincidence of inspiration from Baltimore women taking larger roles in public life and the presence of highly skilled designers with the ability to create finer work that gave Baltimore Album quilts their unique character.

## Notes and References

1. Jennifer Goldsborough, *Lavish Legacies* (Baltimore: Maryland Historical Society, 1994), 27.

2. William Rush Dunton, Jr., *Old Quilts* (Catonsville, MD: Self-published, 1946); Dena Katzenberg, *Baltimore Album Quilts* (Baltimore: Baltimore Museum of Art, 1981): Elly Sienkiewicz, *Baltimore Album Quilts: Historic Notes and Antique Patterns* (Lafayette, CA: C & T Publishing, 1990); Elly Sienkiewicz, *Baltimore Album Legacy* (Concord, CA: C & T Publishing, 1998); Elly Sienkiewicz, *Baltimore Beauties and Beyond: Studies in Classic Album Quilt Appliqué, Volume Two* (Concord, CA: C & T Publishing, 1991); Elly Sienkiewicz, *Baltimore Album Revival!:Historic Quilts in the Making* (Lafayette, CA: C & T Publishing, 1994); Jennifer Goldsborough, *Lavish Legacies;* and Nancy E. Davis, *The Baltimore Album Quilt Tradition* (Baltimore: Maryland Historical Society, 1999).

3. Lynne Zacek Bassett, *Gothic to Goth: Romantic Era Fashion and its Legacy* (Hartford, CT: Wadsworth Atheneum, 2016), 16–18; "The Romantic Era," www.myholyoke.edu/courses/rschwart/hist255/jkr/romanticism.html.

4. Lucinda MacKethan, "The Cult of Domesticity," National Humanities Center, 2011, http://americainclass.org/the-cult-of-domesticity.

5. Mary P. Ryan, *Women in Public: Between Banners and Ballots, 1823–1880* (Baltimore: Johns Hopkins University Press, 1990), 59.

6. Ann Douglas, *The Feminization of American Culture* (New York: Knopf, 1997), 5–7.

7. Christine Leigh Heyrman, *Southern Cross: The Beginnings of the Bible Belt* (New York: Knopf, 1997), 169.

8. Robert Shaw, *American Quilts: The Democratic Art, 1780–2007* (NewYork: Sterling, 2009), 42–43.

9. Goldsborough, *Lavish Legacies,* 36.

10. William R. Sutton, *Journeymen for Jesus: Evangelical Artisans Confront Capitalism in Jacksonian Baltimore* (University Park, PA: Pennsylvania State University Press, 1998), 11.

11. Shaw, *American Quilts: The Democratic Art,* 58–63; Goldsborough, Lavish Legacies, 4, 7.

12. Bassett, *Gothic to Goth,* 57–58. See Sarah J. Hale's *Flora's Interpreter* (1832 and later) for her Dahlia, which was copied almost exactly for several Baltimore Album blocks.

13. Baltimore Album quilt top, maker unknown, 1846, Daughters of the American Revolution Museum, 98.31.

14. Samuel Williams quilt, (Baltimore Museum of Art 1988.206), Pool-Herget (Yale University), Nadal (Smithsonian 1983.0866), Best, Lipscomb, Wilson (Lovely Lane), Ryder (American Museum in Britain 1964.5) quilts; Chamberlain and Blessings quilts and others in private collections; and several with one or two blocks only.

15. Goldsborough, *Lavish Legacies,* 15–16.

16. Anita Jones, Curator of Textiles, Baltimore Museum of Art, discussion with the authors, July 2015.

17. Goldsborough, *Lavish Legacies,* 16–17.

18. Hannah Mary Trimble Papers 1748–1916, Maryland Historical Society Library, Special Collections, MS. 2517.

19. Goldsborough, *Lavish Legacies,* 14, 22–23, 35.

20. Goldsborough, 22–23.

21. Ibid.

22. "The Clay Quilt," *Sun* (Baltimore, MD), September 18, 1845; "The Clay Quilt," *Sun* (Baltimore, MD), September 19, 1845; *The Adams Sentinel* (Gettysburg, PA), September 29, 1845. A quilt made for Henry Clay was exhibited in a confectionary shop on Charles Street, Baltimore, on Friday, September 19 – 20, 1845. *The Adams Sentinel* reported, "Upwards of eighteen hundred persons went to see the Clay Quilt."

23. "A Handsome Present," "Local Matters," *Sun* (Baltimore, MD), December 9, 1848.

24. Mary Simon did not die in the 1850s as earlier theorized; she lived at 220 Chestnut Street until her death in 1877. Estate inventories of Philip and Mary did not list any quilts or related items. Her entire estate was sold to her daughter-in-law for $32. Although Simon's descendants have been found, unfortunately they know nothing of Simon's involvement with album quilts.

25. Dunton, *Old Quilts,* 41.

26. Baltimore Album quilt, probably made by Elizabeth Sliver, c. 1849, Metropolitan Museum of Art, New York, 1974.24.

27. Baltimore Album quilt, probably made by Elizabeth Sliver, c. 1849, Baltimore Museum of Art, 76.63.

28. Goldsborough, *Lavish Legacies,* 22.

29. "Closing of the Eighth Annual Exhibition of the Maryland Institute, Award of Premiums,) *Sun* (Baltimore, MD), November 6, 1855.

30. Advertisement, *Sun* (Baltimore, MD), January 20, 1849.

31. Dunton, *Old Quilts,* 119.

32. Author's conclusion is based on data collected from *Matchett's Baltimore Directories,* 1847–1850.

33. Elizabeth White Nelson, *Market Sentiments: Middle-Class Market Culture in 19th Century America* (Washington, D.C.: Smithsonian Books, 2010), 140.

34. Baltimore Album quilt, various makers, c. 1844–1845, Minneapolis Institute of Arts, Minneapolis, MN, 75.9.1.

35. "Fair of the Maryland Institute," *American and Commercial Daily Advertiser* (Baltimore, MD), November 6, 1850.

36. Matchett, *Matchett's Baltimore Directory*, 1847–48, 156.

37. Baltimore Album quilt, various makers; c. 1846, Maryland Historical Society, Baltimore, MD, 2006.16.

38. Private collection.

39. Private collection.

40. "The Fair of the Maryland Institute," *Sun* (Baltimore, MD), November 17, 1848.

41. "Fair of the Maryland Institute," *American and Commercial Daily Advertiser* (Baltimore, MD), October 18, 1849.

42. The winner of the second prize that year may be the appliqué quilt pictured in *A Maryland Album* on page 118. Descriptions of quilts were written by male Institute officials, whose knowledge of quilts may have been sketchy.

43. Ruthella Mory Bibbins, *How Methodism Came, The Beginnings of Methodism in England and America*, (Baltimore, MD: The Daily Record Press, 1945), 59; Gordon Pratt Baker, *Those Incredible Methodists, A History of the Baltimore Conference of the United Methodist Church* (Baltimore, MD: Parthenon Press, 1972), 45.

44. "Strawbridge Methodist Church Records, 1843–1954," Maryland Historical Society, Baltimore, MD, MS 1799.

45. Goldsborough, *Lavish Legacies*, 23–24.

46. Robert J. Brugger, *Maryland: A Middle Temperament, 1634–1980* (Baltimore: Johns Hopkins University Press, 1988), 52–55.

47. Michael S. Franch, *Congregation and Community in Baltimore, 1840–1860*, PhD. Dissertation, University of Maryland, 1984, 30, 307. This important study examined the records of all major and most minor denominations with a presence in Baltimore during those years. His research suggested to the authors that religious enthusiasm was a factor in the development of Baltimore Album quilts.

48. Sutton, *Journeymen for Jesus*, 44–45; Bassett, *Gothic to Goth*, 46.

49. Sutton, *Journeymen for Jesus*, 47–49; Bassett, *Gothic to Goth*, 46–47.

50. Franch, *Congregation and Community in Baltimore*, 316–317.

51. Sutton, *Journeymen for Jesus*, 11.

52. Ibid., 79.

53. Ibid., ix–xi.

54. Franch, *Congregation and Community in Baltimore*, 146–150.

55. Ibid., 111–113.

56. Ibid., 140–142.

57. Ibid., 148.

58. Ibid., 141.

59. Ibid., 97, 148.

60. Ibid., 93–94.

61. Ibid., 94.

62. Franch, 30; "Missionary Fair. –The Sewing Society of the Second Presbyterian Church," *Sun* (Baltimore, MD), April 10, 1841; "The Fair," *Sun* (Baltimore, MD), May, 18, 1842; "Ladies' Fair," *Sun* (Baltimore, MD), June 2, 1844; "Ladies' Fair," *Sun* (Baltimore, MD), December 24, 1847.

63. Franch, *Congregation and Community in Baltimore,* 60–61.

64. Ibid., 57.

65. Quoted in Mrs. Franklin Wilson, Journal, various dates 1850–53; Franch, *Congregation and Community in Baltimore,* 106.

66. Goldsborough, *Lavish Legacies,* 14.

67. "A Handsome Present," *Sun* (Baltimore, MD), December 9, 1848; "A Beautiful Present," *Sun* (Baltimore, MD), February 26, 1851.

68. Goldsborough, *Lavish Legacies,* 35.

69. Dunton, *Old Quilts,* 149–151, location unknown.

70. Franch, *Congregation and Community in Baltimore,* 322.

71. "The Ladies Fair," *Sun* (Baltimore, MD), October 2, 1843.

72. Sutton, *Journeymen for Jesus,* 121–122.

73. Daughters of the American Revolution Museum, 98.31.

74. 1850 U.S. Census, Maryland, Baltimore County, population schedule; R. J. Matchett, *Matchett's Baltimore Directory,* Baltimore, MD, 1849–1850.

75. Matchett, *Matchett's Baltimore Directory,* 1849–1850, 377.

76. Davis, *The Baltimore Album Quilt Tradition,* 122.

77. "A Handsome Present," "Local Matters," *Sun* (Baltimore, MD), December 9, 1848.

78. Matchett, *Matchett's Baltimore Directory,* 1845–1850.

79. Goldsborough, *Lavish Legacies,* 60.

80. 1850 U.S. Census, Maryland, Baltimore County, population schedule; *Records of the First Reformed Church of Baltimore, 1768–1899,* (Westminster, MD: Family Like Publications, 1995).

81. Baltimore Album quilt, made for Isabella Battee, c. 1852, Baltimore Museum of Art, 77.30; Baltimore Album quilt, made for Angeline Hoffman, c. 1846–1847, private collection; Baltimore Album quilt, made for Leonora Welch; c. 1847, Maryland Historical Society, Baltimore, MD, 1958.10.1.

82. Goldsborough, *Lavish Legacies,* 26.

83. Dunton, *Old Quilts,* 75–77.

84. Davis, *The Baltimore Album Quilt Tradition,* 54–55.

85. Baltimore Album quilt, friends and family of Samuel Williams, 1846–1847, Baltimore Museum of Art, 1988.206.

86. Baltimore Album quilt, friends and family of Captain George W. Russell, 1852, Baltimore Museum of Art, 1971.36.1; "Local Matters, Tribute of Esteem," *Sun* (Baltimore, MD), December 22, 1852. This information was discovered by Sara Schamerloh as a result of her ongoing research on the Captain Russell quilt.

87. Baltimore Album quilt top, maker unknown, 1852, Maryland Historical Society, 79.29.1.

88. Dunton, *Old Quilts,* 138–139; Baltimore Album quilt, Mrs. John Koch, c. 1850, Baltimore Album quilt top, various makers, 1845–1848, Metropolitan Museum of Art, New York, 2016.172; Album with Rooster, Hannah J. Swin, Bergen County, NJ, 1868, collection of Bill Volkening.

89. Baltimore Album quilt, various makers, c. 1845–1847, Daughters of the American Revolution Museum, Washington D.C., 87.68.

90. This quilt by Mary Ann Grooms was sold by Skinner Auctioneers, Boston, MA, August 15, 2010. Location unknown.

91. Baltimore Album quilt, maker unknown, c. 1849, Maryland Historical Society, 88.8; Baltimore Album quilt, maker unknown, c. 1850, Maryland Historical Society, 60.19.1; Baltimore Album quilt, maker unknown, c. 1847–1850, Baltimore Museum of Art, 46.101; Baltimore Album quilt, maker unknown, c. 1845–1850, Maryland Historical Society, 1994.2*Baltimore Album;* Elly Sienkiewicz, *Baltimore Beauties and Beyond,* 8.

92. Robert G. Gunderson, "The Great Baltimore Whig Convention of 1840," *Maryland Historical Magazine* 46, no. 1 (March 1952): 12.

93. Roger A. Fischer, *Tippecanoe and Trinkets Too: The Material Culture of American Presidential Campaigns, 1828–1984* (Urbana and Chicago: University of Illinois Press, 1988), 29–70.

94. Private collection.

95. Baltimore Album quilt, Mary Celia Hiss Crowl, c. 1845–1848, Maryland Historical Society, 93.1; Shaw, American Quilts, 68–69; Dunton, *Old Quilts,* 147; Rebecca Diggs's Commemorative Appliquéd Quilt Top, maker unknown, c. 1840–1845, National Museum of American History, Washington, D.C., 163105; Presentation album quilt sold at Freeman's Auction, April 19, 2016, Mary Worrall Parry, c. 1847; private collection.

96. Shaw, *American Quilts,* 68–69, Yale University; Baltimore Album quilt, friends and family of Samuel Williams, 1846–1847, Baltimore Museum of Art, 1988.206; Baltimore Album quilt, maker unknown, c. 1849, Winterthur Museum, 2013.0010.

97. Jacqueline M. Atkins & Phyllis A. Tepper, *New York Beauties, Quilts from the Empire State* (New York: Dutton Studio Books, 1992), 82.

98. Friendship quilt, various makers, c. 1848, St. Louis Museum of Art, St. Louis, MO, 1:1973.

99. Katzenberg, *Baltimore Album Quilts,* 65.

100. "Intelligence from the north by tonight's mail," *Daily Union* (Washington, D.C), October 27, 1846; "Celebration of the Fourth of July by the Maryland Volunteers," *Sun* (Baltimore, MD), July 19, 1848; "Handsome Banners," *Sun* (Baltimore, MD), July 4, 1850; "The Ladies of Baltimore, to the New York Fillmore Men," *Sun* (Baltimore, MD), June 26, 1852.

101. Baltimore Album quilt, maker unknown, c. 1849, Maryland Historical Society, 88.8; Baltimore Album quilt, Rachel Meyer Walters, c. 1850, Maryland Historical Society, 70.56.1; Baltimore Album quilt, friends and family of Samuel Williams, c. 1846–1847, Baltimore Museum of Art, 1988.206; Baltimore Album quilt, maker unknown, 1847, IQSCM, 2005.056.0001; Dunton, *Old Quilts,* 29.

102. Brashears Baltimore Album quilt, friends of Ella Knighton, 1848, Virginia Quilt Museum, 1998.005.001.

103. "Local Matters," *American & Commercial Daily Advertiser* (Baltimore, MD), November 22, 1848; Friendship quilt, various makers, c. 1848, St. Louis Museum of Art, St. Louis, MO, 1:1973.

104. Lori D. Ginzberg, *Women and the Work of Benevolent Morality: Politics and Class in the Nineteenth Century United States* (New Haven: Yale University Press, 1990), 54; Ryan, *Women in Public,* 137–141; Elizabeth R. Varon, *We Mean to be Counted* (Chapel Hill, NC: University of North Carolina Press, 1998), 71–101.

105. Ginzberg, *Women in Antebellum Reform,* 8–14.

106. "The Temperance Movement," *United States History,* http://www.u-s-history.com/pages/h1054.html.

107. Varon, *We Mean to be Counted*, 33–34.

108. Sutton, *Journeymen for Jesus*, 270–272.

109. Varon, *We Mean to be Counted*, 35.

110. "Presentation of a Bible," *American and Commercial Daily Advertiser* (Baltimore, MD), November 29, 1845; "Anniversary Meeting—Bible Presentation," *Sun* (Baltimore, MD), February 15, 1847.

111. See Goldsborough, *Lavish Legacies*, 97. Father Edward McColgan, recipient of an album quilt, founded a parochial temperance society for immigrant meatpackers in 1849. Franch, *Congregation and Community in Baltimore*, 360.

112. Unfinished quilt square, probably Mary Simon, c. 1850, Maryland Historical Society, 90.11.1–7.

113. Rev. Aaron B. Grosh, *The Odd-Fellow's Manual* (Philadelphia: H.C. Peck & Theo. Bliss, 1856), 170–171; James L. Ridgely, *History of American Odd Fellowship, The First Decade* (Baltimore, MD: Published by James L. Ridgely, by Authority of the Grand Lodge of the United States I.O.O.F, 1878), 330.

114. Odd Fellows Quilt, Ann E. Bush, 1848, Maryland Historical Society, 2012.24.

115. "Odd Fellow's Hall," Mrs. E. E. Cooke, c. 1850, International Quilt Study Center, Lincoln, NE, 2005,023,0001; "Rare Baltimore Album Quilt Top," maker unknown, Contentment Farm Auction, 2008, Item Number 2218; private collection.

Figure 2. Detail, Album Quilt, Baltimore, Maryland, 1850. International Quilt Study Center & Museum, University of Nebraska-Lincoln, 1997.007.0319.

# Whence Garlands, Swags, Bowknots, and Baskets? Four Neoclassical Design Motifs Found in American Quilts

Anita Loscalzo

*Baskets of flowers, bowknots, garlands, and swags appear frequently as appliqué, pieced, and whitework motifs in American quilts made in the first half of the nineteenth century. The historical use of these motifs as architectural elements and in porcelain, textiles, wallpaper, and furnishings will be explored, as well as possible routes of their assimilation into the general design vocabulary of American quilt makers. Garlands derived from ancient times, first as funerary items in Egypt, and later as decorative elements in Greece and Rome with the addition of bowknots or substitution with drapery swags. Sixteenth-century architects revived these classical motifs, but the greatest revival occurred during the neoclassical period of the mid- to late-eighteenth century. Baskets of fruits or flowers became popular motifs in the decorative arts of Europe in the seventeenth century and gained further prominence in the eighteenth century. European ideas of architecture and decorative arts spread to colonial America, and then to the early federal republic, beginning in the last quarter of the eighteenth century. As a result, examples of the motifs abounded in the everyday surroundings of the populace of the young United States, giving ready examples to needleworkers to copy and adapt for their works.*

## Introduction

Baskets of flowers, bowknots, garlands, and swags appear frequently as appliqué, pieced, and whitework motifs in American quilts made in the first half of the nineteenth century (figs. 1 and 2). These motifs did not spring spontaneously into the imaginations of needleworkers, but were parts of a design vocabulary surrounding them that had evolved over centuries: in architecture, home furnishings and décor, textiles, and items for

Fig. 1. Detail, Medallion Quilt, possibly Maryland, c. 1810–1830. International Quilt Study Center & Museum, University of Nebraska-Lincoln, 1997.007.0634.

everyday use. Was it a Staffordshire creamware teapot decorated with a leafy swag and bow, a Sèvres teacup with an openwork basket of flowers held by a bowknot, a Tucker creamer decorated with a floral garland, or a wall border stenciled with a red and green swag that inspired them?

The relationship between the decorative arts and motifs in bedcovers has been observed and touched upon by others. Lynne Z. Bassett found that the floral motifs on whole cloth quilts and bed rugs in the late eighteenth and early nineteenth century could be traced to baroque and rococo designs appearing in print sources and furnishings.[1] Jennifer Goldsborough traced the many designs found on Baltimore Album quilts to items in the press and in household use, particularly the English transfer-printed dishes in Baltimore homes during the period.[2] Robert Shaw, Lynne Bassett, Amelia Peck, and Elizabeth Warren noted the popularity of stenciling on walls and furnishings and its subsequent use on quilt tops.[3]

The use of baskets of flowers, bowknots, swags, and garlands are manifestations of the neoclassical period in the history of the decorative arts. Lynne Bassett, Linda Baumgarten, Linda Eaton, and Roderick Kiracofe have all commented on the appearance of the neoclassical vocabulary in the design of bedcovers made in the United States.[4]

Neoclassicism generally encompassed the period from the mid eighteenth century to the first quarter of the nineteenth century.[5] Its roots could be found in the fifteenth and sixteenth century Renaissance appreciation of classical Greek and Roman art and architecture, with the first true beginnings in the late seventeenth century in France and the early eighteenth century in Britain. The ancient architectural works of Rome were illustrated with exact measurements in the 1682 publication, *Les Édifices Antiques de Rome*, by the French architect Antoine Desgodetz.[6] The book, dedicated to Jean-Baptiste Colbert, France's Minister of Finance, affected

the development of the classicism of the Louis XIV style. It also was a source for the early-eighteenth-century neoclassical works of the British architect William Kent and later British architects through the English translation published in 1771.

Many architects in England became part of the so-called neo-Palladian movement, based on the architecture and writings of Andrea Palladio (1508–80). His *I Quattro Libri di Architettura* appeared in 1570 and later editions, one of which was owned by the seventeenth-century British architect Inigo Jones, who had spent time in Italy. Palladio's work was published in an English translation in 1715–20 and in 1738. Around 1744 the 1733 English version translated by Godfrey Richards was the first edition to appear in the American colonies.[7]

The discoveries at Herculaneum in 1738 and Pompeii in 1748 gave further impetus to the neoclassical movement. Engravings of the discoveries appeared in nine volumes in intervals throughout the latter half of the eighteenth century.[8] Artists and architects, particularly the British, guided by their knowledge of classic literature, flocked to ancient sites in Italy on their "grand tours" of Europe.[9] The neoclassical style eventually encompassed architecture, interior design, furniture, and all types of decorative objects in Europe and, later, the fledgling United States. Neoclassical motifs permeated the design vocabulary of American needleworkers, beginning as early as the late eighteenth century until this day. The discussion of the motifs' prevalence will begin with garlands, swags, and bowknots found in American quilts.

### Garlands, Swags, & Bowknots in Quilts in the United States

The first cluster of American-made quilts incorporating these motifs appeared during the height of the Federal period of the United States, such as one with lace-effect swags documented as a North Carolina quilt and another with swags held by bowknots from Maryland, both dating

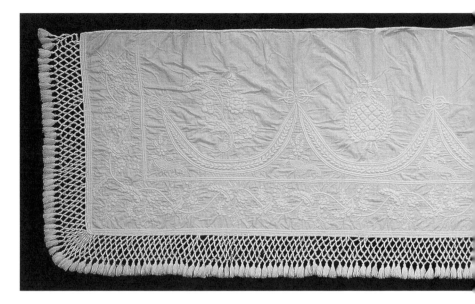

Figure 3. Valance, 1815–1817, Warwick, Rhode Island. Winterthur Museum, Museum purchase, 1957.67.6.

from around 1800.[10] Garlands or swags with and without bowknots appeared frequently in center medallion-style and whitework quilts, counterpanes, and bed hangings of the early Federal period, echoing the prominent features of neoclassical architecture (fig. 3).[11]

Most of the early cut-out chintz appliqué quilts with the motifs were made in Maryland and Virginia, while the few whitework examples with provenance were made in New York and Rhode Island. The motifs were much more prevalent in the period between 1840 and 1860 as borders for red and green repeat-block and album quilts as far west as Missouri. Fewer quilts with the motifs appear between 1875 and 1900, probably due to the popularity of crazy quilts and red work during that period.[12]

A look to the past occurred during the twentieth-century Colonial Revival. The swags bordering Marie Webster's 1908 American Beauty Rose are tricolor and held by rosebuds like those bordering a Rose of Sharon made in 1857.[13] Rose Kretsinger's New Rose Tree of 1929 has a swag, bow, and tassels border, while Hannah Headlee used stylized swags held by irises instead of bowknots for the border of her Iris Garland.[14] Mary McElwain offered two quilt top kits with swag borders for sale in her 1936

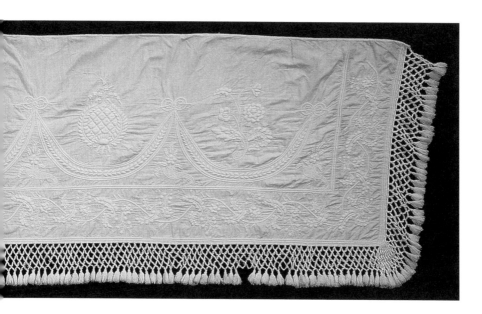

catalog: a Double Irish Chain and an Ohio Rose, both with swags held by flowers rather than bowknots.[15] Similar border treatments are presented in two Mountain Mist patterns for 1935, Painted Poppies and Orange Blossoms, while in 1952, a thin ribbon-like swag held by bowknots borders Sunburst.[16] Over 150 years since first appearing in American needlework, these neoclassical elements retained their hold on the imagination of quilt makers, as has the basket motif, to which we will next turn.

### Baskets in Bedcovers in the United States

Basket motifs became a ubiquitous element of whitework, appliqué, and pieced bedcovers produced in the United States in the nineteenth century. The basket of flowers (and sometimes fruit) became a particular favorite for accomplished needle-wielding ladies in quilted and candlewick-embroidered whitework pieces in the early nineteenth century. In her preliminary study of over 200 surviving candlewick-embroidered bed covers, Gail Bakkom found that forty-one percent of them have a basket as the center medallion motif.[17] Conversely, it appears that far fewer colored-wool embroidered bedcovers incorporated baskets in their designs.[18]

In June of 1831, *The Lady's Book* (later known as *Godey's Lady's Book*) published a pattern for a paper card receiver in the form of an openwork woven basket (fig. 4). The basket in the center of a circa 1840 quilt in the

Figure 4. Detail, Basket
Card Receiver Pattern,
*Godey's Lady's Book,*
June 1831.

**WHAT-NOTS, OR CARD RECEIVERS.**

What-nots, or card receivers, may be made
in a variety of shapes. To construct a card

10                          11

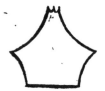

receiver in the shape of Fig. 10, cut a piece of
card-board for the back; (Fig. 11) bind the edge
of the upper part with gold paper; and paste
dead gold paper, on the sides, shading it according to taste; the lower part should be bound with
coloured ribbon; the front is to be formed in the
same shape as the lower part of the back, and
bound with ribbon; it may also be ornamented

12              with diamond figures, (as
 fig. 12,) in the following
                manner: Cut another piece
                of pasteboard the same size,
                and paste them together,
                first cutting the diamonds
in the outer, or front one; gum small circular
pieces of gold paper on the intersections, or diamonds, and lightly shade the intervening spaces.

Philadelphia Museum of Art bears a striking resemblance to this form, but
also has several slatted baskets included as well (fig. 5, color plate 8).[19]
Not all quilters were so proficient in appliqué and, hence, one of them in-
vented the familiar pieced version around 1840 composed of alternating
triangles in a manner similar to a circa 1810 checkered-diamond-pattern
yarn-sewn rug.[20]

The highly accomplished needleworkers of appliquéd baskets exhibited their skills primarily in the genre of album quilts, and particularly
those made in Baltimore between 1845 and 1855. A Mary Simon-style
album quilt in the Metropolitan Museum of Art includes five finely
wrought baskets: three with openwork slats, one with woven openwork,
and one with closed slats. Less-skilled needleworkers abstracted their
baskets, as in the Harper Baltimore album quilt in the DAR Museum.[21]

Over 300 pieced basket quilts appear in the Quilt Index for the last
forty years of the nineteenth century, consisting of a mix of triangle-

Figure 5. Botanical Album Quilt, made by Cinthia Arsworth, Baltimore, Maryland, 1840–1845. Philadelphia Museum of Art, Gift of Mr. and Mrs. Percival Armitage, 1942-4-1.

pieced and solid-pieced bodies for the baskets and only two quilts with openwork slatted baskets. Another three hundred pieced basket quilts are listed for the first thirty years of the twentieth century and over 400, with the vast majority pieced, for the period between 1930 and 1949.[22]

In the 1920s and 1930s era of the Colonial Revival, some patterns were published for appliqué openwork woven baskets, such as the Needle Art Guild kit #3577 Floral Basket, and  and the St. Louis Fancy Work Company of St. Louis, Missouri French Basket, Design No. 1212, marketed as a "Martha Washington Patchwork Quilt Design."[23] The November 1934 issue of *Needlecraft, The Home Arts Magazine* advertised the Basket of Happiness Quilt as a kit for purchase that included sheeting for the top stamped

Figure 6. Baltimore Album Quilt, made by Beatrice S. Utley, Connecticut, 1990. New England Quilt Museum, Lowell, MA, Gift of William T. Utley, Sr., 2003.01. Photograph by Meghan Moore.

with appliqué and quilting lines and all the pre-stamped fabric necessary to complete the appliqué flowers and openwork woven baskets.[24]

The openwork basket, woven or slatted, resurfaced as an appliqué motif beginning in the late 1980s with the revival of the Baltimore Album genre, championed by Elly Sienkiewicz.[25] While it is not indicated in the Quilt Index (due to date parameters set by most documentation projects), anecdotally, hundreds were made. Many included the ubiquitous openwork slatted baskets seen on the originals, as well as bowknots and garlands (fig. 6).

### Antecedents of the Neoclassical Motifs—Garlands, Swags, & Bowknots

What were the historical antecedents of the neoclassical motifs? Garlands, also known as festoons, derive from ancient times. Egyptians placed garlands of flowers on their dead; Greeks used them liberally as decoration in home and civic life. The early Romans hung loops of real fruit and flowers held together by ribbons and leaves around the friezes of temples to celebrate festive days. Later, these motifs were transformed into sculptural reliefs on Roman buildings and depicted on wall paintings.[26] Swags are a variant when fabric is depicted. Roman mosaics and wall paintings including garlands appeared as early as the second century B.C.E.[27] Travelers to Italy would have seen sculpted garlands on the Ara Pacis (Altar of Augustus, 9 B.C.E.), the Arch of the Goldsmiths (A.D. 204) and the Temple of Fortuna Virilis (c. 100 B.C.E.) in Rome, and the Temple of Vesta at Tivoli (c. 100 B.C.E.) (the latter three appear in aforementioned Desgodetz publication).[28] Bowknots tie the ends of the garlands on the Arch of the Goldsmiths.

Architects and artisans began to incorporate classical motifs in their works in the sixteenth century. Sansovino's Biblioteca Marciana in Venice, begun in 1536, features garlands of fruits and flowers. Garlands and swags appeared on majolica wares produced in Italy and distributed to all parts of Europe in the late sixteenth century.[29] Palladio gave examples of the use of garlands and swags held by bowknots in his 1570 publication.[30]

The seventeenth century saw an increased use of classical elements such as garlands or swags held by bowknots. In Britain, Inigo Jones featured them in the Somerset House Chapel, as did Webb on the Wilton House ceiling, and Pratt in the Coleshill House stairway. Grinling Gibbons was noted for his intricate carvings of fruit and flower garlands, at times held by bowknots.[31] In Europe, the Belgian priest Daniel Seghers produced many paintings of garlands of flowers commissioned by the Jesuit order and presented to the royalty of Orange-Nassau, Sweden, and England.[32]

However, in the latter half of the eighteenth century the greatest dissemination of neoclassical motifs occurred in France under the aegis of Louis XIV. Jean-Baptiste Monnoyer specialized in flower paintings, of which Louis XIV owned about sixty. Monnoyer included garlands of flowers and swags in his designs for Gobelins tapestries, as well as painted garlands in the Queen's apartment at the château in Vincennes.[33] In the last quarter of the eighteenth century, Charles Le Brun undertook the design of the decoration of the Palace of Versailles, incorporating classical motifs, including garlands held by bowknots, on wall panels and torchères in the Hall of Mirrors, frames in the Diana Salon, and wall panels in the Bull's Eye Salon. Le Brun was also the director of Gobelins Royal tapestry manufacture, where several of his designs featured luxurious garlands of flowers.[34] In 1674 Jean Berain I became the principal designer of costumes, scenery, stage productions, festivals, ships, and furnishings incorporating neoclassical motifs and themes for Louis XIV. Berain's designs found wide circulation, as in the series of prints Ornemens Inventez par J. Berain (1710) and the Oeuvre de Jean Berain (1711).[35]

Daniel Marot, a Huguenot born and trained as an artist in France, found refuge after the Revocation of the Edict of Nantes in the court of William of Orange, and became Royal Architect when William became King of Great Britain. Marot's designs, published in a series of engravings during his lifetime, encompassed all aspects of the decorative arts and architecture, including elaborate swag and bowknot designs for draperies and bed hangings. His engravings set examples for interior decoration for English designers of the early eighteenth century.[36]

### Garlands, Swags, & Bowknots—Eighteenth Century

The classical elements were well incorporated into British architecture by the early eighteenth century, as evidenced by James Thornhill's designs for the Saloon at Blenheim of 1714.[37] The neo-Palladian classical style in England received its greatest emphasis with the publication of Vitruvius Britannicus by Colen Campbell in 1715. The book included the works of British architects of the day and Campbell's designs for Wanstead House, built for the third Earl of Burlington, promoter of Campbell and others of the neo-Palladian movement.[38] Lord Burlington and the architects William Kent and James Gibbs all spent extensive time in Italy.[39] The 1720s witnessed the increased use of garlands, swags, and bowknots by Campbell, Gibbs, and Kent, making the motifs ubiquitous elements in the decoration of interiors and exteriors of great houses and public buildings.[40]

In 1745, Abraham Swan published his design book, The British Architect, with the common craftsman, rather than the elite architect, in mind. It includes illustrations of three chimneypieces, each with garlands. Batty Langley's, *The City and Country Builder's and Workman's Treasury of Designs* (1740), features a Tuscan altarpiece with drapery swags and bowknots. Langley's book greatly influenced British and American architects and builders, first appearing in the colonies in 1754.[41]

After spending two years studying in Rome, the architect Robert Adam returned to England in 1758 where he specialized in classical interiors of country houses. Garlands held by bowknots adorn the interior and the façade of Kedleston Hall (1765–70) and numerous interiors for his other wealthy patrons' homes in the third quarter of the eighteenth century, as well as a public building, the Theatre Royal Drury Lane (1775). The "Adam Style" carried into furnishings, as well. The interiors, furniture, and elevations and plans of the principal works of Robert and his brother James were published in several volumes between 1773 and 1779, with one posthumous volume appearing in 1822.[42]

In the last quarter of the eighteenth century, George Hepplewhite adopted the Adam style for his neoclassical furniture designs by simplifying the elements, as in chair backs and bed hangings. His designs reached the American colonies through his 1788 publication, *The Cabinet-Maker & Upholsterer's Guide,* which influenced the work of Samuel McIntire of Salem, Massachusetts, and others.[43]

In France, the lighter and more curvaceous Rococo style that relied on the realistic representation of flowers supplanted the formal classic style of Louis XIV. The romantic use of flowers carried into the Louis XVI period, with an overlay of the neoclassical. The textile designers Philippe de Lasalle and Jean Pillement utilized bouquets and garlands tied by ribbon bowknots in their designs.[44] French cabinetmakers of the Louis XV and Louis XVI periods adorned their works with brass swag and garland mounts, producing ornate pieces for the French and English aristocracy.[45]

Tapestries replaced carvings in the paneled areas of great houses. The tapestries of the Gobelins and Aubusson factories featured ever-more abundant floral garlands into the last quarter of the eighteenth century, with and without bowknots, both for patrons in France and England.[46] The last quarter of the eighteenth century brought a lighter look to swags and garlands in printed and woven textiles.[47] Indian palampores and household textiles produced for the European trade featured garlands as early as the mid eighteenth century and bowknots by the last quarter of the eighteenth century.[48]

Swags and garlands carried into fashion. A circa 1730 painting of the dancer Madame de Camargo by Nicholas Lancret shows the ballerina in a costume bedecked with flower garlands.[49] The polonaise skirt of the late 1770s featured a back consisting of three swags of fabric held by bows over a straight skirt.[50] A continuous series of large swags held by bows encircles the skirt and borders the train of a court robe said to have been made in the 1780s for Marie-Antoinette by Marie-Jean Rose Bertin.[51]English quilted petticoats incorporated swags in their designs from the mid eighteenth century onward, often made by professionals for trade in England and the American colonies (fig. 7).[52]

Wallpaper, while not inexpensive, came to replace tapestries for filling wall panels in the great homes of France in the late eighteenth century. The designs of the French manufacturers and Jean-Baptiste Réveillon in particular featured garlands like those seen on Gobelins tapestries and silk textiles.[53] Others imitated festooned drapery, such as an example from the former home of the Marquis de Taulignan or those that Thomas Jefferson imported from Paris in 1790.[54]

Porcelain exhibited the motifs by the second quarter of the eighteenth century. The swag and bow designs of Jean Berain decorate a French serv-

Figure 7. Petticoat, 1760–1780, American or European. Silk and wool. Winterthur Museum, Bequest of Henry Francis du Pont, 1967.1482.

ing platter from the Clérissy pottery works made around 1730.[55] Fine porcelain offered by the German Meissen and the French Sèvres factories in the 1760s featured garlands held by bows.[56] The Chinese potters of the last quarter of the eighteenth century adapted French designs in wares for the export market (fig. 8)[57] By the late eighteenth century, neoclassical motifs were fully established into the design vocabulary of Europe, with inroads into North America.

### Garlands, Swags, & Bowknots – Colonial and Federal America

Classical elements appeared early in the North American colonies. Swags held by rosettes surround a 1732 carved urn in Independence Hall in Philadelphia and a painted swag with tassels borders the ceiling of a home in southeastern Massachusetts built in the early eighteenth century.[58] It was primarily through the importation of goods and design books from Europe, particularly from England and France, that the neoclassical style made its mark on the arts of the English colonies and, later, Federal United States.

By the 1760s the major east coast port cities became centers for the export of commodities to Europe and the West Indies: Boston for fish and timber products, Philadelphia and New York for agricultural products, Baltimore for wheat and tobacco, and Charleston for rice and indigo.[59]

Figure 8. Plate, Chinese, for export, c. 1780. Porcelain. Philadelphia Museum of Art, Bequest of Henrietta Dallas Pepper, 1935-11-6f.

The value of colonial commodities exported to England rose five-fold in the period from 1700 to 1770, while the importation of items from England increased at a higher rate. While the wealthy colonists imitated the English aristocracy, in time even the less wealthy came to consume previously non-essential items, such as ceramic tea cups and fine cloth for dresses and coats. Former Puritan Boston's middle and lower classes turned to the consumption of luxury items, particularly those of English taste. Goods flowed into the Atlantic ports, some up the Connecticut rivers into western Massachusetts; from New York to Albany and beyond; from Philadelphia west on the wagon roads, then south through Virginia to North Carolina along the Great Wagon Road; and from Charleston west to the upland plantations. Peddlers traveled with their wares far into the interior, as well.[60]

Yet the neoclassical styles prevalent in England and France during the last quarter of the eighteenth century did not fully take hold in America until after the American Revolution. The neoclassical symbols and motifs fit the ideals of the new republic that was turning from the extravagant luxury and corrupt power of royalty to rational governance and conduct. Greek and Roman motifs, filtered through the design books and commodities of neoclassical Europe, began to dominate post-Revolutionary architecture, furnishings, and decorative arts. Not only was there a revival of importation of European furniture after the war, but also a wave of European craftsmen steeped in the neoclassical style coming to the new republic.[61]

The majority of furniture and architectural design books published in England and in English translation during the eighteenth century could be found in America. By the end of the 1760s, London booksellers had set up shop in New York, Boston, Charleston, and Philadelphia. The design books of Palladio, Desgodetz, Gibbs, Langley, Adam, Swan, Pain, Chippendale, Hepplewhite, Sheraton, and others appeared in the personal and institutional libraries of the Federal period. Also, *The Ladies Amusement,* a compilation of decorative design elements gleaned from French and English sources for craftsmen, was issued in several editions between 1758 and 1762 and had wide distribution in England and America.[62] All of the aforementioned included designs incorporating garlands or swags and bowknots.

Charles Bulfinch, the first native-born professional American architect, studied the works of the Roman architect Vitruvius, Andrea Palladio, and the English architects Isaac Ware, William Kent, William Chambers, and Robert Adam. He saw some of the English architects' works while on the Grand Tour in 1786–87, but was most inspired by the decorative designs of Adam. In 1791–92, he designed the Joseph Coolidge, Sr. House in Boston, his earliest neoclassical work. Its Adamesque façade included a garland and bowknot relief above the second-story Palladian window. Bulfinch used the decorative motif in and on other private homes, and notably on two public buildings (the State House in 1795–97 and Faneuil Hall in 1805–06, both in Boston), where all could view it (fig. 9).[63]

Bulfinch's contemporary, Samuel McIntire of Salem had access to many design books, and not only designed decorative elements, but also carved them. He furnished wealthy clients with chairs, such as the set with a drapery motif that he carved for Elias Hasket Derby (c. 1795), based on plate two of Hepplewhite's 1788 edition of *The Cabinetmaker and Upholsterer's Guide.* His carved interiors often featured garlands held by bowknots, as on a mantelpiece in the parlor of the Peirce-Nichols House in Salem, Massachusetts (c. 1800). McIntire employed drapery and bowknots on the decoration for exteriors of the E.H. Derby summer house in 1794, the E.H. Derby House in 1798, and Hamilton Hall in 1805, all with open views to the public.[64]

In his 1797 architectural design book, the first published in America, Asher Benjamin included two designs for mantels decorated with festoons held by bowknots. In a later publication, he advises the architect to ornament drawing rooms with "foliage, wreaths, festoons, or baskets of flowers . . . displayed with taste, and in a lively manner."[65] He also includes illustrations of the suggested elements for frieze, ceiling, and doorway ornamentation.

Figure 9. Detail of interior, Faneuil Hall, Boston, Massachusetts, designed by Charles Bulfinch, 1805–1806. Photograph by the author.

The decorative motifs appeared in interiors of the wealthy in other states. Stucco and plaster renditions of swags and garlands of bellflowers adorned the mantels and doorways of several houses built in Baltimore in the late eighteenth century.[66] In Charleston, the Manigault House (1803), features garlands on its parlor, dining room, and study mantels and dining room frieze. Bowknots hold the garlands on the stairwell ceiling.[67] The motifs traveled to the carvers in the interior United States, as seen on garlands on a wooden mantel made in Carlisle, Pennsylvania (c. 1815) and swags on the portico of Boscobel House (1804–08) on the Hudson River, sixty miles north of New York City.[68]

Items for daily living exhibited garlands and swags as well. With the taste for English goods so prevalent before the Revolution, it is likely that Staffordshire creamware decorated with neoclassical decoration appeared on the tables of the colonists.[69] Chinese export and French porcelain wares appeared in America shortly after the Revolution, bearing floral garland borders in the French style. In 1782, the Count de Custine-Sarreck presented Martha Washington with a Niderviller porcelain tea and coffee service decorated with flower garlands and Washington's arms and monogram. French-style garlands decorate a circa 1794 Chinese export porcelain service made for Moses Brown of Providence.[70]

The Boston silversmith Paul Revere adopted the neoclassical forms, engraving items with stylized swags and tassels, as did the Philadelphia silversmiths, Joseph and Nathaniel Richardson.[71] Bohemian wine glasses, exported in great quantities to the United States in the late eighteenth and early nineteenth centuries, appear to be the models for early-nineteenth-century American-made glassware incised with swags and bowknots.[72] The first truly American porcelain manufacturer, William Tucker (later Tucker and Hemphill) of Philadelphia, specialized in neoclassical forms and decoration. The firm's works often closely copied the styles of French Sèvres porcelain; indeed, from around 1832, the firm employed artists and artisans from France, in time to feed the vogue for French floral ornamentation.[73] Textiles produced in England for the American market reflected the fashion for floral garlands of the 1830s (fig. 10).[74] Duncan Phyfe's furniture also embodied the neoclassical style in the mode of Adam with his carved swags, tassels, and bowknot elements. His furniture gained great cachet, with his customers hailing from New York, Philadelphia, New Jersey, Charleston, and the southern plantations.[75]

Wendy Cooper noted that beginning around 1800 the neoclassical style reached beyond the elites to the middle class.[76] In America, the wealthy began using wallpapers in the first quarter of the eighteenth century, choosing expensive English and French papers. By the 1740s, American manufacturers started to produce less costly papers and wallpaper came into general use by the economic elite, while imports of English and French papers continued well into the nineteenth century.[77] Moses Grant of Boston produced a variant of a French design for the walls of General Henry Knox's home in 1795, while Appleton Prentiss, also of Boston, printed a garland border paper around the same time. A newspaper advertisement featuring a swag and tassel for Thomas S. Webb in the *Providence Gazette* dated August 4, 1804, boasts having "A very large assortment of PAPER-HANGINGS, suitable for Parlours, Keeping Rooms, Entries, Halls, &c. with Festoon, Patch, Lace and Fruit Borders, of various widths . . ."[78] Wallpaper's use was not confined to walls; inventive decorators covered

Figure 10. Detail, wholecloth quilt, 1830–1850, American. Cotton. Winterthur Museum, Bequest of Henry Francis du Pont, 1969.3830.

bandboxes and other decorative boxes with drapery swag and garland border papers.[79]

Beginning around the 1790s, largely in New England, the imitation of wallpaper by means of freehand painting and stenciling provided a less expensive means of wall decoration. Itinerant craftsmen traveled up and down the Connecticut River and from eastern Massachusetts throughout New England. Swags and garlands appeared as border motifs in homes and taverns from Massachusetts north to Vermont, New Hampshire, and Maine; and south to Rhode Island and Connecticut. In the first quarter of the nineteenth century, wall stenciling spread to eastern New York State and its western reaches following the shifts in population from eastern New England. Similarly, stenciling motifs found their way to Kentucky and Tennessee via the Shenandoah Valley trail through Virginia from the south and through New York and Pennsylvania from the north. Two Tennessee and Kentucky homes, circa 1830 and before 1840, respectively, and with their locations separated by 390 miles, have walls decorated with an identical swag and tassel border, probably by the same itinerant artist working in the region. Of particular note for the relationship of wall stenciling to quilting, the most popular color scheme was red and green stenciled onto white or light gray walls.[80] Quilters adopted this color scheme readily into their design vocabulary as part of the fashion for red and green quilts in the 1840s to the 1860s (fig. 11, color plate 9).

### Antecedents of the Neoclassical Motifs—Baskets in Architecture & Furnishings

While the basket motif served as a secular motif on American quilts and textiles (fig. 12), early in history the basket was entwined in religious ritual. In ancient Greece, *kanephoroi,* maidens in the period just before their marriage, carried baskets containing items used for ritual sacrifice on their heads to the altar. Syrian sun-worshipers viewed the basket as the container for the soul in their tomb reliefs, while early Christians depicted baskets full of loaves as symbols of the Eucharist in catacomb paintings. The secular still life appeared in first century A.D. Roman villas in Pompeii that included wall frescos displaying the bounty of nature, with some items in baskets.[81]

In the late sixteenth and early seventeenth century, the still life became a popular genre, with baskets of fruit and other objects shown as symbols of an ideal Christian life in some instances, and as plain abundance in others. The taste for still life paintings flourished in the merchant

Figure 11. Mariner's Compass quilt, probably American, circa 1840–1860. International Quilt Study Center & Museum, University of Nebraska-Lincoln, 2008.040.0193.

class of the seventeenth-century Dutch Republic with baskets and vases of flowers appearing in profusion.[82] In France, Jean-Baptiste Monnoyer produced a series of prints of baskets of flowers in a book published in the second half of the seventeenth century, as well as paintings based on the drawings.[83] "October" from the series of plates in the *Twelve Months of Fruits* published by Robert Furber in 1732 and based on the work of another Flemish artist, Pieter Casteels, features an open-work basket overflowing with fruit. The prints were sold in colored and uncolored versions in England at varying prices, making them available to a wide range of consumers.[84]

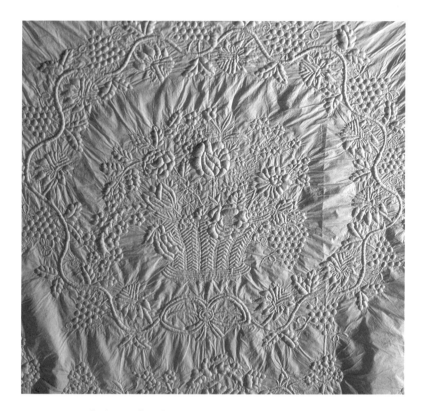

Figure 12. Detail, whitework quilt, 1825–1840, American. Cotton and linen.
Winterthur Museum, Gift of Felicia Krygier, 1989.27.

In the realm of architecture, baskets appeared on a decorative panel in
Certosa di Pavia (circa 1490) and on a pilaster on Santa Maria dei Mira-
coli, Venice (1481).[85] Quite probably, these were seen by seventeenth- and
eighteenth century travelers on the Grand Tour. Baskets appeared as decorative elements on newel posts in mid-seventeenth century England at
Ham House, Thorpe Hall, and Tyttenhanger.[86] By the mid eighteenth century, architects included reliefs of baskets of flowers on chimney pieces
and mantels of great houses, with some based on designs by Batty Langley
and others by Robert Adam.[87] As early as 1749, an example of the openwork basket in an English whitework coverlet mirrored the designs seen in
decorative interiors.[88]

The basket found its way into the design vocabulary of American
colonial artisans. Trained in England and influenced by Chippendale,

Thomas Elfe became the pre-eminent furniture maker in Charleston, incorporating neoclassical elements in his works, such as the use of the basket as a pediment decoration.[89] The early eighteenth-century Boston furniture carver John Welch possibly influenced Samuel McIntire's use of the basket in his carvings for the mantels, cornices, and furnishings commissioned by McIntire's well-to-do patrons; it is a ubiquitous feature of McIntire's carvings. Both woven and openwork baskets, some held by bowknots, adorned the mantels and cornices of the interior of the Oak Hill, the country house of Elizabeth Derby West and Nathaniel West (circa 1800) in Peabody, Massachusetts.[90]

### Baskets in Porcelain

Porcelain depictions of baskets abounded in Europe. In accord with the popular Dutch still life genre, a circa 1690 Delftware figure depicts Queen Mary II of England, wife of the Dutch-born William III, holding a woven basket meant to be used as a vessel for real flowers. The French Sèvres and German Meissen factories produced actual openwork porcelain baskets beginning in the mid eighteenth century.[91] The painted basket motif began to appear on porcelain made by the Meissen factory in the second quarter of the eighteenth century, overlapping with the fashion for the *chinoiserie*.[92] Basket motifs (also known as *corbeilles),* both woven and openwork, and refined by Sèvres porcelain painters such as Bouillat, Parpette, and Xhrouet, became fixtures in French decorative design in the second half of the eighteenth century. The wealthy of France were privileged to have elaborate furniture created that included Sèvres porcelain plaques with basket motifs, on vases, and on dinnerware.[93] Some French cabinetmakers chose marquetry to pattern their creations with the same designs utilized by the porcelain painters.[94]

Perhaps some of these pieces came to America in the 1790s with the French exiles from the Haitian slave revolt or the French Revolution who settled in Charleston, Baltimore, Philadelphia, and New York. These exiles were gentry, artisans, and craftsmen, both bringing their refinement and manners, and a demand and taste for French luxury goods of the neoclassical taste that affected the native citizens of the cities they inhabited. The Binghams of Philadelphia imported coffee cups "with a design similar to those used by the Queen," while the Morrises owned a table made from Sèvres porcelain.[95]

As early as the mid-seventeenth century, the basket motif appeared on a carpet produced by the Savonnerie Manufactory during the early reign of Louis XIV.[96] Eighteenth-century silk designers incorporated baskets in their works in both Spitalfields, England, and Lyons, France, as did the French wallpaper designer, Reveillon.[97] A circa 1760 indigo resist panel of baskets of flowers thought to have been made in India for the American market appears to have been based on a Monnoyer engraving from the late seventeenth century.[98] The aforementioned *The Ladies Amusement,* which received wide circulation in America after its publication in 1760, served as a guide for designs for needleworkers and included several examples for woven baskets of flowers. Sarah Hinchman in 1768 and Susanna Meyer in 1787, both of Philadelphia, adapted the woven basket of flowers in their designs for needlework samplers.[99]

A British textile designer adopted the basket motif in cotton textiles by the last quarter of the eighteenth century, but most appeared in the first quarter of the nineteenth century.[100] An openwork basket in the French style held by a bowknot is featured on a drab-style textile incorporated into an English-made counterpane finished in 1817, while numerous American-made quilts and counterpanes of the first and second quarters of the nineteenth century incorporated the circa 1815 English openwork basket of fruit printed panel based on the Furber/Casteels "October" print.[101] The woven basket also appears on circa 1815 English textiles. English designers returned to the motif for furnishing fabrics in the 1820s and 1830s, including a basket in a draped window and a pillar print from England, available in four colorways.[102] The post-War of 1812 influx of fine cotton textiles to United States from England, whether because of excess capacity or an attempt to destroy the nascent American textile industry, provided needleworkers with ample examples of textiles in the neoclassical taste.

## Baskets in Other American Decorative Arts

The basket permeated all aspects of the decorative arts in the first half of the nineteenth century. The maker of a circa 1810 sewn rug previously mentioned transformed the woven basket into a checkered diamond pattern.[103] Theorem painting on velvet, which relied on the use of stencils, became a necessary skill for young cultivated ladies beginning around 1800 and remained in vogue until the 1840s. Still life portrayals of baskets of fruit or flowers were the most common subjects.[104] Hitchcock chairs stenciled in the fashion of theorem paintings flooded the American market at the rate of 15,000 per year from about 1825 to the early 1840s.[105] Stenciling on textiles also occurred during this period, including on quilts and other bedcovers, particularly in the northeastern United States.[106] Meanwhile, the Tucker porcelain factory of Philadelphia continued its imitation of fine French porcelain, producing openwork fruit baskets and scent bottles decorated with woven baskets of flowers.[107]

## Conclusion

What made these neoclassical motifs so appealing to needleworkers in America? European ideas about and examples of architecture and decorative arts spread to colonial America, and then to the early federal republic, beginning in the last quarter of the eighteenth century. To own refined decorative objects denoted taste, fed by the dual tendencies of Anglophilia and Francophilia in the elite of the early republic, whose influence spread to provincial parts of the nation.[108] The desire to emulate the ideals of the ancients or the tastes of the wealthy had some part in the adoption of the neoclassical motifs, but surely their visual appeal and ubiquity in the makers' surroundings also played a great part in their use.

Surrounded by an abundance of architectural, furnishing, and decorative items bearing fashionable neoclassical motifs, it is natural that needleworkers would incorporate them into their quilts and counterpanes. Elegant baskets of flowers seen on porcelain and furnishings were translated into whitework and appliqué masterpieces and adapted for piecing by those less skilled in, or with less patience for appliqué. Stenciled borders on walls of red and green swags inspired their translation to fabric borders for numerous quilts and counterpanes. With the rise of agricultural fairs beginning in the 1810s that included prizes for the textile items produced by women, the spread of these motifs naturally would have occurred.[109] The motifs remained as design elements in appliqué and pieced bedcovers into the early 1950s, with a revival in the 1980s that continues to this day.

## Notes and References

1. Lynne Zacek Bassett, "Inspired Fantasy: Design Sources for New England's Whole-Cloth Wool Quilts," *The Magazine Antiques,* September 2005, 122–24.
2. Jennifer Faulds Goldsborough and Barbara K. Weeks, *Lavish Legacies: Baltimore Album*

and Related Quilts in the Collection of the Maryland Historical Society (Baltimore, MD: Maryland Historical Society, 1994), 27–34; Jennifer F. Goldsborough, "An Album of Baltimore Album Quilt Studies," in Uncoverings 1994, ed. Virginia Gunn (San Francisco: American Quilt Study Group, 1994), 101–05.

3. Robert Shaw, American Quilts: The Democratic Art, 1780–2007 (New York: Sterling Publishing, 2009), 34-35; Lynne Zacek Bassett, "Stenciled Bedcovers," The Magazine Antiques 163 (2003): 72; Amelia Peck and Cynthia V.A. Schaffner, American Quilts & Coverlets in the Metropolitan Museum of Art, new ed. (New York: MQ Publications USA, 2007), 134; Elizabeth V. Warren, Quilts: Masterworks from the American Folk Art Museum (New York: Rizzoli International Publications, 2010), 21.

4. Lynne Z. Bassett and Jack Larkin, Northern Comfort: New England's Early Quilts (Nashville, TN: Rutledge Hill Press, 1998), 8, 85–86; Linda Baumgarten and Kimberley Smith Ivey, Four Centuries of Quilts: The Colonial Williamsburg Collection (New Haven, CT: Yale University Press, 2014), 52,77; Linda Eaton, Quilts in a Material World: Selections from the Winterthur Collection (New York: Abrams, 2007), 22; Roderick Kiracofe, The American Quilt: A History of Cloth and Comfort, 1750–1950 (New York: Clarkson Potter, 1993), 64.

5. "Neo-Classicism," in Encyclopedia of Interior Design, ed. Joanna Banham (London: Fitzroy Dearborn Publishers, 1997), 863.

6. Antoine Desgodetz, Les Édifices Antiques de Rome Dessinés et Mesurés Très Exactement (Paris: Jean Baptiste Coignard, 1682); Philippa Lewis and Gillian Darley, Dictionary of Ornament (New York: Pantheon Books, 1986), 107.

7. Ibid., 225–226.

8. Ibid., 157.

9. Jeremy Black, The British Abroad: The Grand Tour in the Eighteenth Century (Phoenix Mill, UK: Sutton Publishing, 2003), 305–308.

10. Appliquéd Quilt, Perquimmons County, NC, c. 1800, Museum of Early Southern Decorative Art, 2636; Chintz Appliquéd Quilt, Maryland, c. 1800, Metropolitan Museum of Art 1971.180.123.

11. Eaton, Quilts in a Material World, 22–23.

12. Identified by consulting the Quilt Index and online and published collections from major American museums with quilt collections not included in the Quilt Index.

13. Marie Webster, "American Beauty Rose," 1908, Indianapolis Museum of Art 78.287; Gillie P. and Margaret E. Wright, "Rose of Sharon," Monroe County, Missouri, 1857, Los Angeles County Museum of Art (LACMA) 30.1.

14. Rose Kretsinger, "New Rose Tree," 1929, Spencer Museum of Art 1971.0103; Hannah Headlee, "Iris Garland," 1930-39, Kansas Historical Society 1990.55.1.

15. Mary A. McElwain, The Romance of the Village Quilts, 2014 reprint ed. (Walworth, WI: Mary A. McElwain Quilt Shop, 1936), 5,10.

16. Mountain Mist Catalog of Classic Quilt Patterns, (Cincinnati, OH: Stearns Technical Textiles, c. 2000), 32,33,59. The dates are documented in Vickie Paullus and Linda Pumphrey, Mountain Mist Blue Book of Quilts (Cincinnati, OH: Stearns Technical Textiles, 1996), 55–56.

17. Information presented in a Study Center at the American Quilt Study Group 2013 Annual Seminar, Charleston, SC. Her subsequent publication groups baskets with vases, urns, and sprays. See Gail Bakkom, "'Candlewicks': White Embroidered Counterpanes in

America 1790–1880," in *Uncoverings* 2015, ed. Lynne Zacek Bassett (Lincoln, NE: American Quilt Study Group, 2015), 72.

18. The author was only able to identify five examples by consulting the Quilt Index and online and published collections from major American museums with quilt collections not included in the Quilt Index.

19. "The Ornamental Artist," *Godey's Lady's Book,* June 1831; Philadelphia Museum of Art 1942-4-1.

20. Jan Whitlock, *American Sewn Rugs: Their History with Exceptional Examples* (New York: Jan Whitlock, 2012), 24; the author identified eighteen pieced basket quilts made between 1840 and 1860 and one purported to have been made around 1825 by consulting the Quilt Index and online and published collections from major American museums with quilt collections not included in the Quilt Index.

21. Presentation-Style Quilt, Baltimore, c. 1849, Metropolitan Museum of Art 1974.24; Baltimore Album Quilt, made for Betsy Hobbs Harper and William Harper, c.1848, DAR Museum 87-68.

22. www.quiltindex.org.

23. "Floral Basket," c. 1932, International Quilt Study Center & Museum 1997.007.0791; Waldvogel Archival Collection in Quilt Index, Ephemera Record: 5B-AA-19, www.quiltindex.org.

24. Michigan State University Museum ACC. #6119.44.21, Ephemera Record: 1E-A3-6CF, www.quiltindex.org.

25. Elly Sienkiewicz, *Baltimore Beauties and Beyond,* vol. 1, *Studies in Classic Album Quilt Appliqué* (Lafayette, CA: C&T Publishing, 1989).

26. "Garland," *Encyclopedia Britannica Online* (2012), www.britannica.com/EBchecked/topic/226011/garland.

27. See the mosaic floor from a Roman altar at the Athens Acropolis, c. 150 B.C.E. (Pergamon Museum, Mos. 71) and a wall painting from the villa of P. Fannius Synistor at Boscoreale, c. 50-40 B.C.E. (Metropolitan Museum of Art, 03.14.4).

28. Desgodetz, Les Édifices Antiques de Rome, 93, 102, 219.

29. See Maiolica Plate, Urbino, Italy, Philadelphia Museum of Art 1999-99-11.

30. Andrea Palladio, *The First Book of Architecture by Andrea Palladio,* trans. Godfrey Richards (London: A. Bettesworth & C. Hitch, 1733), pl.139,61.

31. Isaac Ware, *Designs of Inigo Jones and Others* (London: I. Ware, c. 1731), pl.29; Charles Saumarez Smith, *Eighteenth-Century Decoration: Design and the Domestic Interior in England* (New York: Henry N. Abrams, 1993), pl.3; Peter Kidson, Peter Murray, and Paul Thompson, *A History of English Architecture* (Harmondsworth, England: Penguin Books, 1965), 184; Grinling Gibbons, Overmantel, c. 1675, Metropolitan Museum of Art 16.88a.

32. Irene Haberland, "Seghers, Daniel," *Grove Art Online,* www.oxfordartonline.com; an example of his work in the Brussels Royal Museum of Fine Arts features a garland of spring blooms held in place by bowknots at each end, Musées Royals des Beaux-Arts de Belgique, Inv.183.

33. Lesley Stevenson, "Monnoyer, Jean Baptiste," Grove Art Online, www.oxfordartonline.com; Morgane Mouillade, "Versanel, Monnoyer, Blin De Fontenay: Les Artistes De La Premiere Tenture Chinoise," moeblu.fr/2013/12/20/guy-louis-vernansal-jean-baptiste-monnoyer-jean-baptiste-blin-fontenay-part-respective-trois-artistes-realisation-premiere-tenture-chinoise/.

34. Claire Constans, "Le Brun, Charles," *Grove Art Online*, www.oxfordartonline.com. See "Portière des Renommés," Metropolitan Museum of Art 53.57.

35. Jerome de la Gorce, "Berain, Jean, I," *Grove Art Online*, www.oxfordartonline.com; Roger-Armand Weigert, Textiles En Europe sous Louis XV (Fribourg: Office du Livre, 1964), figs.28,36. See also Christie's auction sale 5324, Lot 4.

36. P. Jessen, Das Ornamentwerk des Daniel Marot: In 264 Lichtdrucken Nachgebildet, (Berlin: Wasmuth, 1892), [ii],157, digi.ub.uni-heidelberg.de/diglit/marot1892; Saumarez Smith, *Eighteenth-Century Decoration*, pl.6.

37. Ibid., pl.31.

38. Michael Snodin and John Styles, *Design & the Decorative Arts, Britain 1500–1900* (London: V&A Publications, 2001), 3. For an interior view showing ceiling garlands, see William Hogarth's "Assembly at Wanstead House," Philadelphia Museum of Art M1928-1-13.

39. Ibid., 220; Michael I. Wilson, *William Kent: Architect, Designer, Painter, Gardener, 1685–1748* (London: Toutledge & Kegan Paul, 1984), 52; Terry Friedman, James Gibbs (New Haven, CT: Yale University Press, 1984), 5.

40. Saumarez Smith, *Eighteenth-Century Decoration*, pl. 46, 48, 49, 58; see Charles Philips, "The Strong Family," 1732, Metropolitan Museum of Art 44.159 and Gibbs' King's College façade, Cambridge, 1724.

41. Abraham Swan, *The British Architect: Or the Builders Treasury of Stair-Cases* (London: Robert Sayer, 1745), pl. 48, 51, 54; Batty Langley, *The City and Country Builder's and Workman's Treasury of Designs*, (London: S. Harding, 1756), pl. CVIII, digital.library.wisc.edu/1711.dl/DLDecArts.CityCtryLang; Lewis and Darley, *Dictionary of Ornament*, 184.

42. Saumarez Smith, *Eighteenth-Century Decoration*, 215–221, pl. 216; Damie Stillman, *The Decorative Work of Robert Adam* (London: Academy Editions, 1973), pl.3; Kidson, Murray, and Thompson, *A History of English Architecture*, 239; Lansdowne House Dining Room, Metropolitan Museum of Art 32.12; Croome Court Tapestry Room, Metropolitan Museum of Art 58.75.1; *The Works in Architecture of Robert & James Adam,* (New York: Dover Publications, 1980), pl. 66, 79; Eileen Harris, *The Furniture of Robert Adam* (London: Alec Tiranti, 1963), pl. 24; Lewis and Darley, *Dictionary of Ornament*, 22.

43. George Hepplewhite, *The Cabinet-Maker & Upholsterer's Guide*, 3rd ed. (London: I. & J. Taylor, 1794; repr., London: B.T. Batsford, 1894), pl. 12, 95, 98; Lewis and Darley, *Dictionary of Ornament*, 153–54.

44. Belle McCullough Borland, *Philippe de Lasalle: His Contribution to the Textile Industry of Lyons* (Chicago: University of Chicago Press, 1936), 8, 12, 30. For a design attributed to Pillemont, see Metropolitan Museum of Art 1970.736.41.

45. See Pierre Langlois, Commode with Drawers, c.1766–67, Fitzwilliam Museum M/F.11-1938; Martin Carlin, Drop-front Secrétaire, c. 1780, Louvre OA11176.

46. Croome Court tapestries, 1763–1771, Metropolitan Museum of Art, 58.75.1-22; Fables de La Fontaine, c. 1775–1780, Musée Nissim de Camondo 114; and an Aubusson upholstered settee, c. 1785, Musée Nissim de Camondo 135.

47. Judith Straeten, *Toiles de Jouy* (Salt Lake City: Gibbs Smith, 2002), 17; Mary Schoeser and Kathleen Dejardin, *French Textiles from 1760 to the Present* (Singapore: Laurence King, 1991), 43; Josette Brédif, *Printed French Fabrics: Toiles de Jouy* (New York: Rizzoli, 1989), 137.

48. John Irwin and Katherine B. Brett, *Origins of Chintz; with a Catalogue of Indo-European Paintings in the Victoria and Albert Museum, London, and the Royal Ontario*

*Museum, Toronto* (London: Her Majesty's Stationery Office, 1970), pl. 31, 93.

49. Nicholas Lancret, *Madame Camargo Dancing,* c. 1730, The Wallace Collection P393.

50. Kendra Van Cleave and Brooke Welborn, "'Very Much the Taste and Various are the Makes': Reconsidering the Late-Eighteenth Century Robe à la Polonaise," *Dress 39,* no. 1 (2013): fig.1.

51. Marie-Antoinette's Court Gown, Royal Ontario Museum 925.18.3.A.

52. See quilted petticoats from the second half of the eighteenth century: Colonial Williamsburg Foundation 1996-291, 1941-211.

53. Françoise Teynac, Pierre Nolot, and Jean Denis Vivien, *Wallpaper: A History,* trans. Conway Lloyd Morgen (New York: Rizzoli, 1981), 87, 89; Lesley Hoskins, ed. *The Papered Wall: The History, Patterns and Techniques of Wallpaper,* 2nd ed. (London: Thames & Hudson, 2005), 61. See also a French wallpaper in the style of tapestry, c. 1795, Musée les Arts Décoratifs 2008.10.1.

54. Wallpaper fragment, c. 1800, V&A E.1042-1925; Beatrice B. Garvan, *Federal Philadelphia: The Athens of the Western World* (Philadephia: Philadelphia Museum of Art, 1987), 62.

55. Grand Plat de Monstre, Fabrique Clérissy, c. 1730, Musée Les Arts Décoratifs 2122.

56. Plates, Meissen, c. 1765, Philadelphia Museum of Art 1882-1773, 1774; Pot-pourri Vase & Cover, Sèvres, c. 1765, V&A 4340&A-1857.

57. Plate, Chinese, for export, Philadelphia Museum of Art 1935-11-6f; Elinor Gordon, *Collecting Chinese Export Porcelain* (Pittstown, NJ: The Main Street Press, 1984), 43, fig. 39.

58. Alexander Speltz, *Styles of Ornament* (New York: Bruno Hessling, 1906), pl. 335(4); Ann Eckert Brown, *American Wall Stenciling, 1790–1840* (Hanover, NH: University Press of New England, 2003), 1.

59. "The Economies of the British North American Colonies in 1763," American Husbandry (1775), www.sjsu.edu/faculty/watkins/colonies1763.htm; Blaine A. Brownell and David R. Goldfield, eds., *The City in Southern History: The Growth of Urban Civilization in the South* (Port Washington, NY: Kennikat Press, 1977), 38, 48.

60. T.H. Breen, "An Empire of Goods: The Anglicization of Colonial America, 1690–1776," *Journal of British Studies* 25 (1986): 485, 487–490, 493–494; Carrie Rebora et al., *John Singleton Copley in America* (New York: The Metropolitan Museum of Art, 1995), 32.

61. Jules David Prown, "Style in American Art: 1750–1800," in *American Art: 1750–1800 Towards Independence,* ed. Charles F. Montgomery and Patricia E. Kane (Boston: New York Graphic Society, 1976), 37; "Style as Evidence," *Winterthur Portfolio* 15 (1980): 207–208; Rosemary Troy Krill and Pauline K. Eversmann, *Early American Decorative Arts, 1620–1860: A Handbook for Interpreters* (Lanham, MD: Altamira Press, 1992), 102–103.

62. Morrison H. Heckscher, "English Furniture Pattern Books in Eighteenth-Century America," in *American Furniture 1994,* ed. Luke Beckerdite (Hanover, NH: University Press of New England, 1994), 172–205; William Bainter O'Neal, *Jefferson's Fine Arts Library* (Charlottesville, VA: University of Virginia Press, 1976); Catalogue of the Books in the Boston Athenaeum, (Boston: Boston Athenaeum, 1810), cdm.bostonathenaeum.org/cdm/search/searchterm/BA_Catalogue_1810.pdf; Charles Over Cornelius, *Furniture Masterpieces of Duncan Phyfe* (New York: Doubleday, Page & Co., 1922), 43; *The Ladies Amusement, or Whole Art of Japanning Made Easy,* facsimile ed. (London: Robert Sayer, 1760), preface, pls.10,137

63. Harold Kirker, *The Architecture of Charles Bulfinch* (Cambridge, MA: Harvard Univer-

sity Press, 1969), 4–5, 9–12, pls. 14, 55, 65.

64. Dean T. Lahikainen, *Samuel McIntire: Carving an American Style* (Hanover, NH: University Press of New England, 2007), 37, Figs. 4-75, 4-84, 4-91; Art Institute of Chicago 1938.1321; Dean T. Lahikainen, "A McIntire Restoration: The East Parlor in the Peirce-Nichols House, Salem, Massachusetts," *The Magazine Antiques*, Dec. 2007, 81.

65. Asher Benjamin, *The Country Builder's Assistant* (Bedford, MA: Applewood Books reprint, orig. published 1797), pls. 19, 20; *The American Builder's Companion* (Charlestown: Etheridge and Bliss, 1806), 47, pls. 25, 27, 29.

66. Rodris Roth, "Interior Decoration of City Houses in Baltimore: The Federal Period," *Winterthur Portfolio* 5 (1969): Figs. 9–14.

67. "Joseph Manigault House," www.charlestonmuseum.org/joseph-manigault-house.

68. See Robert Wellford, Mantel from Beltzhoover House, Carlisle, Pennsylvania, c. 1815, Metropolitan Museum of Art 18.119.1; "Boscobel House and Gardens," www.boscobel.org/history/.

69. Rebora et al., *John Singleton Copley in America*, 32. See Staffordshire Cream-colored Earthenware Teapot & Cover, England, c. 1770, Skinner Auction 2663B, Lot 1179.

70. Susan Gray Detweiler, *George Washington's Chinaware* (New York: Henry N. Abrams, 1982), 67–68, 72; Herbert Schiffer, Peter Schiffer, and Nancy Schiffer, China for America: *Export Porcelain of the 18th and 19th Centuries* (Exton, PA: Schiffer Publishing, 1980), 78, 111.

71. Paul Revere, Sugar Bowl & Creampot, Boston, c.1795, Metropolitan Museum of Art 33.120.546 & 547; Joseph & Nathaniel Richardson, Cream Pot, Philadelphia, 1781–1790, Philadelphia Museum of Art, 1940-16-701.

72. Wineglass, Bohemia, 1790–1810, Winterthur 1957.18.38; Covered Sugar, Pennsylvania, c.1820, Wheaton Glass Museum.

73. Edwin A. Barber, "The Tucker and Hemphill Hard Porcelain Manufactory, Philadelphia, 1825–38," *Bulletin of the Pennsylvania Museum* 14, no. 4 (1906): 17, 22. See Tucker Porcelain Factory, Pitcher, 1828/35, Metropolitan Museum of Art 2002.279.

74. See textiles used for two whole cloth quilts, Winterthur Museum 1969.3830 and 1969.3924.

75. Cornelius, *Furniture Masterpieces of Duncan Phyfe*, 48 inset; Duncan Phyfe, "Sofa," c. 1820, Museum of Fine Arts Boston 39.114; "Duncan Phyfe," *Grove Art Online*, www.oxfordartonline.com.

76. Wendy A. Cooper, *Classical Taste in America 1800–1840* (New York: Abbeville Press Publishers, 1993), 22.

77. Teynac, Nolot, and Vivien, *Wallpaper*, 120–121; Roth, "Interior Decoration of City Houses in Baltimore: The Federal Period," 70; Phyllis Ackerman, *Wallpaper: Its History, Design and Use* (New York: Frederick A. Stokes, 1923), 68–69; Brown, American Wall Stenciling, 3.

78. Wallpaper, General Henry Knox Museum, Thomaston, Maine (compare to Réveillon, Wallpaper, Winterthur Museum 1970.1431.001); Wallpaper, Appleton Prentiss Manuf., U.S., 1790–1815, Historic New England 1972.113c; Richard C. Nylander, *Wallpaper in New England* (Boston: Society for the Preservation of New England Antiquities, 1986), fig. I-22.

79. Lilian Baker Carlisle, *Hat Boxes and Bandboxes at Shelburne Museum* (Shelburne, VT: The Shelburne Museum, 1960), 100-101, 62-63.

80. Brown, *American Wall Stenciling*, 15, 90, 140, 143, 150, 169, 196, 206, 209, 218, 228–229.

81. Linda Jones Roccos, "The Kanephoros and Her Festival Mantle in Greek Art," *American Journal of Archaeology* 99, no. 4 (1995): 641–642; William Romaine Newbold, "The Eagle and the Basket on the Chalice of Antioch," *American Journal of Archaeology* 29 (1925): 360, 366; Sybille Ebert-Schifferer, *Still Life: A History,* trans. Russell Stockman (New York: Henry N. Abrams, 1999), 20.

82. Ibid., 38, 41, 48, 93–102.

83. Jean-Baptiste Monnoyer, *Livre de Plusieurs Corbeilles de Fleurs Dessiné et Gravé par Baptiste Monnoyer* (Paris: N de Poilly, 1660–1690?); Metropolitan Museum of Art 20.61.2(13-16); Monnoyer, "Basket of Flowers," c. 1692, Versailles.

84. Furber, Robert, "October," 1732, facsimile, http://www.allposters.com/-sp/Twelve-Months-of-Fruits-1732-October-Posters_i375895_.htm; Stanley H. Johnston, Jr., ed., *The Cleveland Herbal, Botanical, and Horticultural Collections* (Kent, OH, Kent State University Press, 1992), 343, https://books.google.com/books?isbn=0873384334.

85. Owen Jones, *The Grammar of Ornament* (London: Day & Son, 1856; repr., New York, DK Publishing, 2001), 350, 353, 356.

86. Lewis and Darley, *Dictionary of Ornament,* 50.

87. Stillman, *The Decorative Work of Robert Adam,* pls. 97, 100; "Room from Wrightington Hall," Philadelphia Museum of Art 1928-62-1; "Mantel," Chesterfield House, Metropolitan Museum of Art 56.234.4.

88. Knotted Whitework Coverlet, English, 1749, in Cora Ginsburg 2002 catalogue, 8.

89. Samuel A. Humphrey, *Thomas Elfe, Cabinetmaker* (Charleston, SC: Wyrick, 1995), 3; Thomas Elfe, Library Case, Heyward-Washington House, Charleston, SC, c.1770.

90. Lahikainen, *Samuel McIntire,* 146–147, 149, figs. 4-99 & 4-02; Museum of Fine Arts, Boston 22.805, 22.807, 22.809, 22.811.

91. Bouquetière, Delft, c. 1690, Aronson Antiquairs advertisement, *The Magazine Antiques* May/June 2014, 15; Meissen Basket, c.1774–1800, Metropolitan Museum of Art 66.40; Sèvres Fruit Basket, 1756 in Svend Eriksen and Geoffrey de Bellaigue, *Sèvres Porcelain: Vincennes and Sèvres, 1740–1800* (Boston: Faber and Faber, 1987), pl. 116.

92. Meissen plate, c. 1740, Metropolitan Museum of Art 1995.268.196.

93. *Sèvres: Porcelain from the Royal Collection: [Exhibition] the Queen's Gallery, Buckingham Palace, 1979–1980,* (London: [s.n.], 1979), 45, 50, 100–101; Linda Paredes, *Sèvres Then and Now* (Washington, DC: Hillwood Museum and Gardens Foundation, 2009), fig.5; Sèvres Cup & Saucer, 1770–75, Musée National Céramique 22997. Edmé-François Brouillat (active 1758–1810), Philippe Parpette (1738–1808), and Philippe Xhrouet (1725–1775) were pre-eminent porcelain painters for the Sèvres manufactory.

94. *French Cabinetmakers of the Eighteenth Century,* (Paris: Hachette, 1963), 146, 215.

95. Francois Furstenberg, *When the United States Spoke French* (New York: Penguin Press, 2014), 102–104, 132.

96. *Carpet (Tapis),* Savonnerie Manufactory, mid-seventeenth century, Metropolitan Museum of Art 1976.155.111.

97. Natalie Rothstein, Silk Designs of the Eighteenth Century in the Collection of the Victoria and Albert Museum, London (London: Thames and Hudson, 1990), pl.102; Marianne Carlano and Larry Salmon, eds., *French Textiles from the Middle Ages through the Second Empire* (Hartford, CT: Wadsworth Athenaeum, 1985), fig. 3, 34; Henri Clouzot, *Le Histoire du Papier Peint en France* (Paris: C. Moreau, 1935), color plate [n.p.].

98. Amelia Peck, ed. *Interwoven Globe: The Worldwide Textile Trade, 1500–1800* (New York:

Metropolitan Museum of Art, 2013), 113–114, figs. 03 & 04.

99. *The Ladies Amusement,* 6, 10, 11, 18; Betty Ring, *Girlhood Embroidery: American Samplers & Pictorial Needlework 1650–1850,* 2 vols. (New York: Alfred A. Knopf, 1993), 352, 357.

100. Linda Eaton, *Printed Textiles: British and American Cottons and Linens 1700–1850* (New York: Monacelli Press, 2014), 211.

101. See New England Quilt Museum 2010.21; Winterthur Museum 2010.0038; Maciver Percival, *The Chintz Book* (New York: Frederick A. Stokes [1924]), frontispiece; Merikay Waldvogel, "Printed Panels for Chintz Quilts: Their Origin and Use," in *Uncoverings* 2013, ed. Lynne Zacek Bassett (Lincoln, NE: American Quilt Study Group, 2013):, 124, panel 5.

102. Mary Schoeser and Celia Rufey, *English and American Textiles from 1790 to the Present* (London: Thames and Hudson, 1989), 58; Eaton, *Printed Textiles,* 276, 292, 293. The "basket in a draped window" textile in red was used as an alternate block for a c. 1830 stars quilt documented by the Massachusetts Documentation Project (MQ 7043).

103. Whitlock, *American Sewn Rugs,* 24.

104. "The Fine Arts: Painting on Velvet," *The Balance, & New York State Journal,* Sept. 4, 1810; Sumpter Priddy, *American Fancy: Exuberance in the Arts, 1790–1840* (Milwaukee: Chipstone Foundation, 2004), fig. 345; "Yellow Basket with Flowers," c. 1825, Colonial Williamsburg Foundation 1931.403.17.

105. John Tarrant Kenney, *The Hitchcock Chair* (New York: Clarkson N. Potter, 1971), 96; Priddy, *American Fancy,* fig. 265; "Rocking Chair," c. 1832–1843, Brooklyn Museum of Art 76.35.

106. Bassett, "Stenciled Bedcovers," 72. Plate III shows an example of a basket motif stenciled on a quilt made in Reading, New York, in 1834 (Winterthur Museum 1959.0022.08).

107. "Fruit Basket," Tucker Factory, 1826–1831, Philadelphia Museum of Art 1892-65; "Scent Bottle," Tucker Factory, 1826–1831, Philadelphia Museum of Art 1988-27-38.

108. Catherine E. Kelly, *Republic of Taste: Art, Politics, and Everyday Life in Early America* (Philadelphia: University of Pennsylvania Press, 2016), 5–6; Garvan, Federal Philadelphia, 23; Richard L. Bushman, *The Refinement of America: Persons, Houses, Cities* (New York, Alfred A. Knopf, 1982), 403, 411.

109. Virginia Gunn, "Quilts at Nineteenth State and County Fairs: An Ohio Study," in *Uncoverings* 1988, ed. Laurel Horton (San Francisco: American Quilt Study Group, 1988): 105–106; Aimee E. Newell, "Agricultural Fairs and Quilts," in *Massachusetts Quilts: Our Common Wealth,* ed. Lynne Zacek Bassett (Hanover, NH: University Press of New England, 2009), 99, 181.

# The Mystery of the Harlequin Star Quilts: Finding and Naming a Previously Unidentified Regional Design

Kathleen L. Moore

*Could two strikingly similar quilts found by chance in Texas and Georgia state quilt documentation books and identified as belonging to two different families have been made by the same maker? Research on these two quilts found separate journeys but amazing coincidences in their histories. Investigation into state documentation projects and the Quilt Index uncovered several more quilts of similar design. The study of these quilts revealed a previously unknown cluster of unique quilt block designs narrowly confined in origin to the southeastern corner of Tennessee and northwestern corner of Georgia in the third and fourth quarters of the nineteenth century. This case study of regional tastes and design aesthetics additionally illustrates historical truths of nineteenth-century American quilt survival and migration, as the quilts traveled with their owners—possibly crossing paths in post-Civil War Texas.*

## Discovery

Sometime in 2010, while methodically scanning a stack of quilt documentation books for patterns based on a now-forgotten theme, the discovery was made of two nearly identical quilts documented in separate states, one on the east coast and one in the middle of the country. One quilt was well documented, with a picture of the maker and a bit of her life story. It remains in the hands of the quiltmaker's descendants. The second quilt was very poorly documented, but examination of photographs of the two quilts side-by-side gave a strong impression that both quilts might have come from the same quilter or family of quilters. The nearly identical Mariner's Compass blocks were very distinctive and technically difficult to construct. Indeed, the quiltmaker had added an element to increase the level of difficulty: she pieced some of the radiating star points from minute fragments of red and white fabrics to create a checkerboard or harlequin pattern. Additionally, the vining border was pieced rather than appliquéd. The result is visually stunning.

### Gone to Texas—Sally Lewellin's Sunburst Quilt

The discovery in the state documentation book, *Lone Stars: A Legacy of Texas Quilts, 1836–1936,* of a unique version of a pieced and appliquéd Mariner's Compass quilt which was documented as having been made in Texas by Sally Beaird Lewellin led to a compelling and years-long search for others like it.[1] Family history suggests that Sarah Louisa (Beaird) Lewellin, known as "Sally," moved from Georgia to Texas sometime in the late 1870s or very early 1880s.[2] (Fig. 1.) Sally was born September 22, 1852 in Walker County, Georgia, very near the site of the days-long and brutal Civil War battle of Chickamauga. According to her granddaughter, Sally "was a child in Georgia during the Civil War and used to tell of being 'afraid of the Northern soldiers who came through the country burning barns and driving off our mules and cows.'"[3] The war experience had a lasting effect on Sally and may have influenced her choice to leave Georgia when, as a young woman, the opportunity presented itself.

Fig. 1. Sally Beaird Lewellin, Elkins Community, Brown County, Texas, prior to 1932. Photographer unknown.

Sally's birthplace in Walker County is located in the far northwest corner of the state of Georgia. The area was first settled by Creek and Cherokee Indians, who farmed their lands and peacefully co-existed with each other and their European immigrant neighbors. The discovery of gold deposits in the early nineteenth century led to a highly partisan states-rights campaign in state and federal courts over the land rights of Native Americans.[4] By the 1830s, primarily during the administration of President Andrew Jackson, the Native Americans living in north Georgia were dispossessed of their land and moved to Oklahoma territory.[5] Immigrants and Americans of European heritage quickly acquired the vacated farm-steads and resumed the agricultural activities that had existed there for generations.

The economy of the South, and particularly the Beaird family's existence, from then until well into the twentieth century was primarily based on agriculture. Given its location in a geologically mountainous region, Walker County, Georgia, was not populated by large or wealthy plantations. Property tax records indicate that Sarah's father, Elbert Beaird, was a middle class yeoman farmer growing crops on his 160 acres of land and raising a small herd of livestock.[6] As might be expected, Elbert's military record shows that he enlisted in the 9th Infantry of the Confederate Army in 1865.[7] It is interesting to note that this is more than a year after the horrific Chickamauga Campaign (August 21 to September 20, 1863) which was, as noted, fought in the geographic area that includes Walker County.[8] It is not without good reasons that Sally had nightmares about marauding bands of militia stealing their livestock and ransacking their farmstead. Soldiers on both sides were guilty of such depredations.

How and when the opportunity presented itself for Sally and her family to leave Georgia for Texas is unknown. There are no surviving letters or diaries. There are no extant documents to tell us how she traveled to Texas or with whom. According to census records, she was living with her parents and siblings in Walker County, Georgia, in 1870 at age 17, a marriageable age, but given the realities of casualty rates during the Civil War, there may not have been many marriage opportunities for Sally. That census says she was "attending school."[9] The census of 1880 no longer lists Sally as living with her parents in Georgia.[10] But, she does appear in the 1880 Brown County, Texas, census. At that time, she was living with her brother, whose name is given as Monroe Beard (also known as James Marion Beaird), and his wife Maggie. In this instance, Sally was listed by the census taker as Lula Beard (not Beaird).[11] This is the only time that her name appears as Lula in available records.

By 1885 Sally and Monroe's father, Elbert A. Beaird, had moved to Texas and was a land owner living with his children and family in Brown County, Texas.[12] Given this data, it would seem that the Beaird family moved in stages to Brown County in the early 1880s, a fairly common practice during that era. Elbert died in Elkins, Brown County, Texas, in 1918, and is buried in the Elkins cemetery.[13]

Sally married Gabrel (or Gabriel) B. Lewellin, a rancher in Brown County, Texas.[14] According to state marriage records, their actual marriage date is given as 1 August 1883.[15] There are tax records related to Gabrel's ownership of property in Brown County sporadically from 1877–1892, but images of these records are not available online.[16] Without more specific details regarding his status in the community, it is difficult to speculate when and how he came to be in Elkins. Having been born in 1850, he was a child during the Civil War— consequently, there are no military records related to him. Sally's granddaughter, Murl Lewellin Dobbs, inherited Sally's quilts and is responsible for registering them with the Texas Quilt Search in the mid-1980s. She reported that Sally "came to Texas with her parents," where "they settled in the Elkins Community."[17] Based on the available census data, it appears that Sally actually migrated to Texas with her brother and his wife a few years before her parents and some siblings joined them in central Texas.

What can be discerned about the reasons for the Beaird family's move and establishment in Brown County, Texas, must rely on Sally and her family's appearance in census records. The evidence there suggests some possible explanations about the Beaird family's situation in Georgia and their subsequent move to Texas. Since the early 1830s, a steady stream of settlers from the middle and lower South had been moving west to Texas. In central Texas they found land they could farm and, with luck, they could prosper.[18] Very few Georgians moved to Texas before the Civil War, primarily because land was readily available in Georgia. But by the time the Civil War was over, the economic value and productivity of agricultural land in Georgia had declined to the point that Georgians, with an interest in looking for more fertile fields, were willing to take a chance on a move to Texas. Even though it was farther away and plagued with rumors of Indian depredations and general lawlessness, many immigrants skipped over already populated Alabama and Mississippi in favor of Texas, basing their decisions on successful promotions by railroads and real estate speculators.[19]

Once married, Sally and Gabrel built a house of stone quarried from a mountain (or more likely a hill full of limestone rocks) on their homestead in the little community of Elkins.[20] They raised four children there: Hettee B., Carl A., Bertie A., and Jessie M., all born between 1885 and 1891.[21] Sally died at Elkins on May 27, 1941 and is buried in the Elkins cemetery.[22]

For us, the important part of Sally's story is that while living in Brown County she is credited by her granddaughter, Murl Dobbs, as having made a couple of outstanding and unique quilts. As noted above, her Sunburst

Fig. 2. Sunburst quilt by Sally Beaird Lewellin, Elkins Community, Brown County, Texas, c. 1885, 62 x 78 inches, private collection. Photograph by Matthew Lawrence McCoy.

quilt, a tour de force of piecing and appliqué work, is pictured and described in the first volume of *Lone Stars: A Legacy of Texas Quilts, 1835–1935.* (Fig. 2, color plate 10.) It was assumed that Sally's Sunburst was made as a part of her wedding "trousseau of thirteen quilts."[23] Whether or not it was a trousseau quilt, the maker was clearly a skilled and gifted quiltmaker

Fig. 3. Sunburst quilt, Orange and Green version, by Sally Lewellin, c. 1885, 61 x 81 inches, Museum of Texas Tech University, TTU-H2015-011-001. Image courtesy of Museum of Texas Tech University.

with an eye for color and balance that one might be surprised to find in an isolated farming community in the middle of Texas in the late 1800s. At the time this quilt was documented, a second, matching, quilt assumed to have been made by Sally was documented by Karey Bresenhan, who described it as being "executed in different color combinations . . . primarily red and teal with gold and green accents."[24] (Fig. 3, color plate 11.) Bresen-han also noted that, "The gold in both quilts has proved unstable through the years and is sporadically fading to pale yellow."[25] This second quilt was not included in the Texas documentation book.

Both of Sally's Sunburst quilts are striking and complex, with unique design elements based on what we now know as a Mariner's Compass pattern. The pattern requires a skilled quiltmaker who has mastered the challenges of geometry and who can successfully translate those challenges to drafting and piecing small fabric triangles arrayed in a circle. Indeed, in their description of this quilt, Bresenhan and Puentes commented that "These long slender patches, tiny pieces, and sharp points are postgraduate work for any quilter. Mathematical precision and well-chosen colors make this quilt a particularly fine example of excellence in needlework."[26]

Further knowledge about the second quilt was provided by the wife of one of Sally's great-grandsons, who reported the family's belief that Sally planned on making one for each season of the year.[27] This information is consistent with data on The Quilt Index, which states that, "This quilt is one of a pair of matching quilts made by Sally Lewellin, each with designs in different color combinations. The mate to this quilt is predominantly green and gold."[28]

At some point when the family was in financial difficulties, the green and gold quilt was sold and knowledge of its location was temporarily lost. Thankfully, in February 2016, this lost quilt resurfaced. It had been donated by its new owner to the Museum of Texas Tech University sometime in 2015 and has since been included in the catalog for the quilt exhibit, *Legacy of a Thousand Stitches: Quilts of Texas Tech University,* curated by Dr. Marian Ann Montgomery.[29] The quilt is, indeed, as Bresenhan described it: a duplicate of the red, green and gold quilt pictured in *Lone Stars: A Legacy of Texas Quilts, 1836–1936.*

Sally's descendants did not know of the existence of any more quilts she might have made. Surprisingly, then, two more of Sally's quilts were discovered in a 1986 exhibition catalog from the National Ranching Heritage Center of Texas Tech University.[30] One or both of the quilts were likely stitched at the time of or shortly after Sally's migration to Texas. One is an Oak Leaf and Acorn quilt (fig. 4), dated between 1885 and 1895. The second, a Chimney Sweep quilt (fig. 5), was probably made around 1880, the year in which research first places Sally in Texas.

These other two examples of quilts made by Sally look nothing like her challenging and superbly made Sunburst quilts. They are typical of

Fig. 4. Sally Beaird Lewellin, Oak Leaf and Acorn quilt, Elkins Community, Brown County, Texas, c. 1885–1895, 74 x 82 inches, owner and current location unknown. Photographer unknown. Published in *Quilts of the Texas South Plains: A Sesquicentennial Exhibition October 19, 1986–March 8, 1987.*

their day and could be found in many quilters' repertoire. Though they are utilitarian and a bit ordinary in comparison, they may have been a welcome relief from the challenges posed by the Sunburst quilts. Sally's Oak Leaf and Acorn quilt was described in the catalog as being a "formal appliquéd arrangement of nine large blocks" made with a cotton muslin background and a green fabric for the leaves and acorn shells. The dye was described as being fugitive in nature. The "lining" or backing fabric was

Fig. 5. Sally Beaird Lewellin, Chimney Sweep quilt, Brown County, Texas, c. 1880, 74 x 84 inches, owner unknown. Published in *Quilts of the Texas South Plains: A Sesqui-centennial Exhibition October 19, 1986–March 8, 1987.*

identified as "coarse muslin." The quilting was described as "an allover shell pattern...evenly quilted with ecru thread."[31]

The second of Sally's quilts, the Chimney Sweep quilt, was made of cotton prints "in pink, rose, reddish brown, tan and gray" on muslin. The Garden Maze setting includes solids and prints "of green with yellow and black, and a solid orange fabric...."[32] It is bound with a green print and "a piped cording of the orange fabric."[33] The current whereabouts of these two quilts is not known.

Fig. 6. Maker unknown, Mariner's Compass Variation, possibly Georgia, c. 1860, 87 ¾ x 78 ¾ inches, collection of the Bartow History Center, 1988.56.1. Courtesy of Bartow History Center.

For Sally and her family, life in Brown County in the last quarter of the nineteenth century could not have been easy.[34] Brown County is located right in the middle of the state in a triangle created by Fort Worth to the north, San Angelo to the southwest, and Austin to the southeast. For most of the eighteenth and nineteenth centuries, this location was a part of well-established Indian Territory known as the Comancheria. As a matter of fact, it was at the very end of Native American dominance in that area that the little community of Gholson was "developed on two early Comanche Indian trails."[35] The Gholson name was changed to Elkins around 1900, "after a family who owned and operated a mercantile store in the area."[36]

It appears the little community was never very prosperous. It did not have a post office until 1901 and that was gone by 1906. In 1947, the population was counted at twenty-five people, but by 1949 there were no population figures available. This is probably because the community was "displaced" by the establishment in 1939 or 1940 of a very large military training installation—Camp Bowie—that trained soldiers for battle and also housed German prisoners of war during World War II.[37] The camp was decommissioned after the war in 1946.[38] The federal government still maintains some of the original property and currently a National Guard training center is there, on a portion of what was the original camp.

We can only guess at the joys and difficulties Sally experienced in her new life in Texas. We can be fairly confident that she did not experience the terror of a Comanche raid, but it is entirely possible that she heard stories of the horrors experienced by others, particularly from the Civil War years when military presence was thin to non-existent and Comanche raids were frequent and ferocious. We do know she married a rancher in 1883 and lived the rest of her days in Elkins. Sally died of heart disease on May 27, 1941 at age 88 years, 8 months, and 5 days.[39] She was survived by three daughters and a number of grandchildren—and at least four quilts, two of which are stunning Sunburst designs.[40] But where did Sally get the idea for her intricate and unusual block design? There are no surviving drawings or instructions to tell us how she developed her patterns. Thankfully, the historical record is not blank, but a considerable degree of inference is required to find some answers.

### Left in Gratitude—Elizabeth Mosteller Parham

A second—and strikingly similar—quilt was found in the Georgia quilt documentation book, *Georgia Quilts: Piecing Together a History.*[41] The citation for this quilt refers to it as a Mariner's Compass Variation and notes that the quilt's maker and origins are unknown. (Fig. 6.) It further states that the quilt resides in the Bartow History Center, a gift to the center from Elizabeth Mosteller Parham.[42] The block setting for this quilt is much simpler and straight-forward, with each "compass" or roundel set in a dark blue field. The blocks are simply sashed with red-white-red strips. There is no border on this quilt.

The striking thing about this Georgia quilt is that its Mariner's Compass blocks are identical in every detail, except their colors, to the Lewellin quilts from Texas. There are twenty-four primary star points in each block of this Mariner's Compass, just as there are in the Lewellin quilt. Twelve of the star points emanating from each roundel in the nine compass blocks are pieced from tiny eye-catching red-and-white diamonds similar to a harlequin pattern. All the little diamond pieces are no larger than a dime and their production is consistent across all three quilts. There are also twelve small red pointers and twelve dark blue or green pointers and a yellow/gold roundel in the center of each block of the Georgia quilt, just as there are in the Lewellin quilts from Texas. An even more striking characteristic is that the points of all the star points and pieced diamonds of each compass in this quilt are, as in the other Lewellin quilts, sharp and crisp. The aesthetic effect and stunningly successful construction of the star points of these Mariner's Compasses are amazing to behold on each quilt.

These quilts had to have been made by an experienced quiltmaker who understood how to make many small triangular pieces fit together successfully and to lie flat once pieced. Such specific evidence and a lack of comparable examples hint at the possibility of the same maker or family of makers for the three quilts. There is at least one problem with this assumption. Two quilts are documented in Texas and the other in Georgia.

Information from the museum in Bartow County, Georgia, which owns the Mosteller family quilt, provides some intriguing details. According to the museum's donor files, the Mosteller family lived near Adairsville, Bartow County, Georgia, for most of the nineteenth century. The museum record states, "During the Civil War, a refugee family from north of Bartow County passed the Mosteller home and stopped for food and shelter." The Mostellers fed the family. The refugee family had no money but wanted to pay the Mostellers for their kindness, so they gave the quilt as payment. The Mosteller family accepted the quilt and has passed it down through succeeding generations."[43] Walker County, where Sally Beaird Lewellin's family lived, is north and a bit west of Bartow County. It is hard by the Tennessee state line.

Could members of the Beaird family have been the refugees who passed through and left the quilt? The evidence is very tempting but circumstantial and problematic. We know that Sally did not leave Georgia until around 1880. Is it possible that the Mosteller family's story is off by a few years, or that their quilt came from a different refugee family? Importantly, if it did come from another family, the Mosteller quilt becomes an unrelated and additional example of this quilt block design having been made in the northwest corner of Georgia in the nineteenth century.

The Bartow History Center's donor record provides another tantalizing detail about the Mosteller quilt's past. At the time the quilt was donated in 1988, the donor lived in Mineral Wells, Texas. The museum
attempted to contact this family in 1995 but mail was returned with no
forwarding address. Mineral Wells, Texas, is approximately 110 miles north
of Brown County, Texas. When and how the donor, Elizabeth Mosteller
Parham, or her branch of the Mosteller family relocated to Texas is not
known, but its proximity to the community of Elkins in Brown County
adds a compelling coincidental aspect to the story.[44]

Even though it has proven difficult to connect the two sources of the
Texas and Georgia Sunburst quilts through family or friendship, the fact
that these two quilts made similar journeys and were owned within 110
miles of each other is interesting for what it says about migration and settlement in America in the nineteenth and twentieth centuries. Their
provenance and their continued existence are evidence of the social and
cultural upheavals that occurred within families and geographic regions of
the post-Civil War era in the United States. In this sense, the quilts become historical documents as real and telling as a diary or a collection of
letters from family members scattered across the continent.

There is yet another example of this block design which may point to
the origin of the design choices Sally made for her Mariner's Compass
blocks. The Quilt Index has a Starburst quilt with blocks very similar to
Sally Lewellin's Mariner's Compass blocks.[45] It was identified through the
Quilts of Tennessee documentation project as having been made by Polly
Elkins of Loudon County, Tennessee, between 1850 and 1875. Polly's date of
birth is given as 1803. The image available on the Quilt Index website
shows a series of nine Mariner's Compass blocks on a white background.
Just like those on Sally Lewellin's quilt, there are twenty-four star points
on each of Polly Elkins' blocks. The star points are identical in color and
arrangement to those on Sally's quilt. Additionally, the construction of the
central roundel of each block is identical on both Polly's and Sally's quilts.

Whether Polly Elkins' Starburst/Sunburst quilt was made sometime in
the 1850s or later, it seems possible that either Polly's block inspired Sally's
later quilt or Sally's block inspired Polly later than that early 1850 date.
Could it even be possible that they worked together on these blocks? Side-
by-side visual and technical examination might reveal some answers, but
at the time Polly Elkin's quilt was documented, it was in private hands. It
needs to be located and secured for research and investigation. A search

for Polly Elkins in April, 2015, on Ancestry.com was fruitless. There is too little information on the Quilt Index about Polly Elkins to track her or locate her descendants.

There are yet other possible examples of this quilt block design that were seen in Tennessee but not documented, and their current locations are unknown. In corresponding with Merikay Waldvogel in 2012 about Polly Elkins' Sunburst quilt, Waldvogel stated that there was a notation from Bets Ramsey in the documentation file commenting on the fact that she (Ramsey) had photographed a similar quilt at the home of Creed Bates on Signal Mountain, Tennessee.[46] Her reference to this event can be found in her footnoted comment stating that Ramsey "first saw this Sunburst pattern on Lookout Mountain in 1972 at the home of Phenie McGuffey. The quilt had been made about 1870 by Sallie Boyles from a pattern she had acquired in a fortuitous way. A quilt like it had dropped in the road in front of her house when it fell from a passing wagon filled with the belongings of a family moving to a new location." Ramsey also noted that there was a second Sunburst quilt in the possession of Creed Bates of Signal Mountain.[47] It is important to note that Signal Mountain, Tennessee, is about forty miles north of Walker County, Georgia. Lookout Mountain, Tennessee, straddles the border between Tennessee and Georgia and is about thirty miles north of Walker County.[48]

Yet another quilt using this basic design is pictured in *The Quilts of Tennessee: Images of Domestic Life Prior to 1930* by Ramsey and Waldvogel.[49] It was signed by the maker, "Mary Hutton May 20, 1850, Bedford County." The authors cite the maker as Mary Hutton Rankin and it was owned at the time of documentation by her great-great-grandson, Arthur Rankin, Jr. This quilt is a red, green and white Mariner's Compass on a white background. It is not as complex a block as Sally's and the star points are fewer in number at eighteen. That means the harlequin star points would have been larger and a little easier to piece than were Sally's star points. Mary Hutton's central "compass" is much simpler in construction, also. Her harlequin star points are the only element in these Mariner's Compass pieces that resemble Sally Lewellin's compasses. But this quilt, with its date and location inscribed on the quilt, give us a date much earlier than Sally's quilts. Given that date, we can say that the concept of piecing a harlequin star point for a mariner's compass quilt block dates at least to Mary Hutton's dated quilt from 1850 and possibly Polly Elkins' quilt with an early estimated date from approximately 1850.

Mary Hutton's home in Bedford County, Tennessee, is within 120 miles of Walker County, Georgia. Even more interesting, it is within 100 miles of Lookout Mountain and Signal Mountain, in Hamilton County, Tennessee. Given the information we have from Bets Ramsey's experience, the quilts from these two mountain communities were likely made twenty to twenty-five years later than Mary Hutton's quilt. We do not have enough information at this time to surmise how this pattern moved east and slightly south from Bedford County to the Lookout and Signal Mountain and Walker County, Georgia, areas, but they all appear to have been made within a narrowly defined geographic area and it is clear that sharing of the pattern could very likely have happened between 1850 and the 1870s.

The question becomes, did Sally Lewellin see Mary Hutton's, Creed Bates, or someone else's quilts featuring the harlequin star points and copy the idea, then add her own personal refinements in design and construction? Furthermore, if Sally didn't get the idea from one of the Tennessee quilts, where else could she have gotten this challenging quilt block pattern? Are there more quilts out there with this unique feature awaiting discovery?

Ultimately, if Sally Lewellin did make the Bartow County quilt before leaving Georgia, and, considering the Texas documentation that identifies her as the maker of the two Texas quilts, it would seem that she came close to completing her goal of a quilt for each season made from the same challenging pattern. It also begs the question: Could there be a fourth quilt of this design waiting to be discovered?

Sally Lewellin's quilts and their story are significant because it and the citing of similar quilts in the general area of southeastern Tennessee and northwestern Georgia point to the occurrence in a specific and limited geographic location and time period of a unique and difficult-to-execute quilt block design. It is one of a very small cluster of similar quilts with specific and unique characteristics. The fact that dates of occurrence of this design are within an approximate forty-year span of time between 1850 and 1890, and the makers of this quilt block pattern lived within a small geographical radius in the area encompassed by Bedford County to Hamilton County, Tennessee, and Walker County, Georgia, strongly suggests the pattern originated in that area. While some early quilt patterns are known to have been published early in the nineteenth century by periodicals like *Godey's Lady's Book,* quilt patterns were not standardized, syndicated and widely distributed across the country until late in the nineteenth century.[50]

Given the current information, this pattern does not seem to have been published and distributed. A search in Brackman's *Encyclopedia of Pieced Quilt Patterns* revealed a number of block patterns based on the mariner's compass concept, but none match the design Sally used in her quilts. Somehow or somewhere, probably in the southeast Tennessee area or northwest Georgia, Sally saw this pattern and adapted the design to suit her personal preferences. The technical challenges of executing this design did not dissuade her. Indeed, her pieced vining sashes and border and small appliquéd star cornerstones are not only unique in their own right, but had to have been a challenge to construct. The finished quilt tops are a joyous exhibition of design and execution.

## Facts and Interpretations

In summary, there is a substantial body of circumstantial evidence and documentation that Sally Lewellin's beautiful and unique Mariner's Compass quilt block design was being made as early as 1850 in south central Tennessee by Mary Hutton, who signed and dated her quilt, and possibly by Polly Elkins who very well could have made hers that early. Approximately twenty-five years later, a quilt of similar unusual design can be located in Bartow County, Georgia, a distance of about 120 miles from Mary Hutton's location. The similarity of fabric, colors, and construction of the Mariner's Compass blocks, the dating of events and quilt construction estimates to within the time frame of the Civil War or post-Civil War period, and Sally Lewellin's subsequent move to Texas suggest the possibility that either Sally or a close relative made the Georgia quilt and it was given to or found by the Mostellers. But this cannot be proven and seems problematic in clarifying its provenance. Bets Ramsey's story about a similar Sunburst quilt made by Sally Boyles in Tennessee in approximately 1870 having been inspired by a quilt that fell from a wagon in front of her house lends credence to the belief that this pattern existed in the approximate geographic area through which Sally Lewellin might have traveled.

Sally's two quilts, made around 1870 to 1880, are based on the same basic pattern and design used by Mary Hutton around 1850. There is even the possibility that one or both of these quilts could have been made before she left Georgia and brought by her to Texas. Their extravagant and brightly colorful detailing exhibit a high degree of technical and aesthetic skill in all aspects of quilt design and construction. Her dedication to this unique design and the border construction on both quilts seem to have become Sally's magnificent obsession. She couldn't stop making them once she perfected her technique and her design.

Making and using those two quilts would have brightened her days while living in an isolated rural community in the late nineteenth century—days that must have been defined by hard work and long hours. She married at age thirty in Texas. Her four children were born between 1885 and 1891, so she would have had considerable childrearing responsibilities added to her routine household duties during those years, but her mother and father, who arrived in Brown County about 1885, lived nearby and survived into old age. Sarah's mother, Susan (born in about 1830 in Georgia), would likely have been of considerable help to her and may have even contributed fabrics and needle time to the making of Sally's quilts.[51] There is even the tantalizing but unprovable possibility that it was actually Sally's mother, Susan, who made these quilts.[52] They are elegant creations and telling evidence of the skill and determination of the maker to decorate her surroundings and to leave something of herself for her heirs.

Ultimately the many coincidences in this story are far too compelling to be dismissed as serendipity. It is too difficult a pattern to have been attempted by a novice quiltmaker. The difficulty of drafting and piecing this design so that it would keep its shape and remain flat would be as intimidating to most quilters in the late nineteenth century as it is today.

In testimony to that specific issue, a very skilled and knowledgeable Texas quilter, Kathleen McCrady, drafted a pattern for this block in the early 1980s, just about 100 years after Sally did the same.[53] In her memoir, Kathleen noted, "Piecing the 24-pointed star is not for the faint hearted, and she [Sally Lewellin] added another challenge by piecing half of them with sixteen diamonds. The more I worked on the quilt, the more it challenged me. I thought if someone could draft and piece this star in 1885, surely I could do it one hundred years later. I found it was indeed a challenging project, enough so that I chose only to piece one block!"[54]

The basic Mariner's Compass block that Sally modified to fit her own design aesthetic had been drafted and/or made in the United States for a number of decades. Early in the development of American quiltmaking history, American women must have been teaching themselves and others how to draft this pattern. Privileged young women may have learned the basics of drafting this pattern in young ladies' academies in the early nineteenth century. Tellingly, Lynne Bassett found an example of a Mariner's Compass design from 1798 made by a New England schoolgirl.[55] Additionally, in her book, *American Patchwork Quilts,* published in 1980, Lenice Ingram Bacon cites a reference in Florence Peto's, *Historic Quilts,* which describes a Mariner's Compass made by the daughter of "Captain James Darling of Smithtown, Long Island, who drew his Compass Star pattern for the quilt to be made by his daughter while he was away on a long sea voyage."[56] Peto and Bacon's undated description suggests Captain Darling drafted his assignment for his daughter during the time when whaling ships and long transoceanic voyages were being made on wooden sailing ships such as would have been used in the eighteenth and nineteenth centuries.

Sally's story and the existence of similar Mariner's Compass quilts testifies that this was a pattern favored by skilled quiltmakers who enjoyed the challenge and—even in isolated circumstances—were moved to make a statement, as well as something beautiful for themselves and their homes. If Sally's life is any example, it must have been a very satisfying exercise and have given her and her contemporaries a feeling of accomplishment in the midst of long days of domestic hard work.

Summary

The appearance of regional preferences in the production of material artifacts like quilts has long been used as a tool for documenting the evolution and dissemination of cultural traits in any society, whether it be a clan, a city-state, or a country. The items human beings make and use and their conditions and the context in which they are found can tell us much about the individual(s) who made them, as well as the culture from which they come. Not only can we discern much about the culture's aesthetic priorities and their very real worldly circumstances, but we can learn much about the individual maker's preferences and possibly their standing in their community. By comparing an item to a larger sample of similar items, both in context and across time, we can tease out the existence of aesthetic and fabrication preferences by region. Much of this discernment comes from both comparison of real artifacts and a good degree of supposition, but the closer the items come to belonging in our contemporary times, the easier it is to verify our suppositions with known historical facts, especially when comparing to other items in like and kind.[57]

This is certainly the case when studying nineteenth-century quilts. We have access to much of the historical record of our country's development and growth since its inception. Our research has context thanks to the breadth of technology's reach into the records of our ancestral past and a practice among our cultural historians to compare and contrast our material cultural artifacts. We researchers like to publish and discuss our findings and suppositions and theories. Since the publication of state quilt documentation books and articles began, we have been accumulating an ever-growing and ever-refined collection of images and data to help us identify the growth and spread of the aesthetics and technical aspects of quiltmaking in America and abroad. Our own publication, *Uncoverings,* is but one of those publications dedicated to the collection, refinement and dissemination of the information we keep "uncovering."

Utilizing the many state documentation books, online databases, and articles about quilts that have accumulated to date is a daunting task and has limitations, including the amount of time it takes to survey and organize the findings on spreadsheets and yet more databases. Another limitation in analysis is the bias of survival. The fact that the quilt being studied has survived when an unknown number have not, makes it difficult to evaluate its relationship to the unknown universe of its contemporaries. As cultural historian Jules D. Prown has noted, its value and relationships can get skewed by the mere fact of its survival.[58]

Keeping in mind the precautions of material culture scholars and critics about the intricacies and limitations of material culture analysis, we must forge ahead with the resources at hand to reach some conclusions about the value offered by Sally's quilts in answering the question of regionalism in the making of this Mariner's Compass composition. An informal search through approximately twenty state quilt documentation books, along with a search of The Quilt Index and the International Quilt Study Center online databases, found that the many variations on Mariner's Compass block patterns fall into three general descriptive categories. Names for these general categories have been authoritatively cataloged by Barbara Brackman in her *Encyclopedia of Pieced Quilt Patterns.* They are variously and commonly known as Sunflower, Sunburst, Starburst, or Mariner's Compass.[59]

Using these names, limited occurrences of these patterns were found in state documentation books and online databases. An experienced quiltmaker can understand why this would be the case. Even with the tools and equipment available to twenty-first-century quilters, the pattern is challenging to piece and requires a degree of precision known only to the most intentional and adventuresome quiltmaker. Given such a high degree of construction and creative difficulty, it is not surprising that a preliminary survey of published sources found that these designs were limited, not exclusively, but predominantly to the states of Connecticut, Illinois, Indiana, Kentucky, Massachusetts, New Jersey, New York, Ohio, Pennsylvania, Tennessee and West Virginia in the nineteenth century. More specifically, of all the quilt patterns documented within the sample, the Mariner's Compass pattern appeared with the least frequency. Quantifying and identifying the number of examples on the databases consulted proved problematic due to wide variation in data entry, pattern naming, dates and locations of examples, and the number of duplications of a variety of examples. Consequently, that data was used more as a way to validate general findings from the somewhat informal sampling of published sources.

After viewing so many examples, it became obvious that even though Sally named her quilt "Sunburst," it is the Mariner's Compass pattern that most accurately describes her design. Brackman's pattern #3400 comes closest to illustrating the design Sally used. Interestingly, Brackman also offers the names Sunburst, the name Sally chose for her quilts, as well as Chips and Whetstones. Mariner's Compass is a very early pattern and one of a select few whose name we can actually trace to a given date (1798, as mentioned previously).[60]

The quilts found in Tennessee, Georgia and Texas all have one defining aesthetic and construction characteristic that sets them apart from all other examples found. It is the insertion of the compass points that are pieced from tiny red and white diamonds in the harlequin pattern. Only in the examples found in these three southern states does this element occur. The date of 1850 for Mary Rankin's Tennessee quilt establishes the beginning of the occurrence of this improvisation in the pattern. Bets Ramsey's experience in Tennessee, where she saw two examples from the 1870s of this variation on the Mariner's Compass, provides verification that this design had been adopted and employed by a few other regional quiltmakers. Finally, the appearance of Sally Lewellin's two quilts from the 1870s and 1880s further validate that this pattern was of more than passing interest to some quilters in a restricted geographic region of the Deep South in a definable period of time in the nineteenth century. In putting together the many pieces of the story of Sally's Sunburst quilts and other such examples, the evidence points to the conclusion that her Mariner's Compass variation was inspired by a regional pattern that came from Tennessee/Georgia connections and was brought to Texas. There is no evidence that it spread further and there is only one known attempt to reproduce the pattern, that having been done approximately 100 years later.

Finally, the story of the Beaird/Lewellin family's immigration from Georgia to Texas with the quilts or quilt block designs in tow illustrates a common story of life in the United States in a time of war, upheaval and westward movement. Ultimately, whether the quilts were made by Sally or by her mother, Susan, the survival of these quilts and their life stories shines a light on the conditions and shared experiences of ordinary nineteenth-century women making quilts of stunning beauty and technical proficiency, all while living in obscurity and isolation on the sparsely settled and somewhat dangerous frontier. As Linda Eaton has noted, "historic quilts are often the only evidence that survives of the maker's skill, artistry, or existence. It is unusual for a quilt to survive with enough primary documentation to inform us of the significance of the object within the life of the maker or the context of her community."[61] I would only add that without Sally's quilts, we would likely never have been able to identify this regional improvisation and no one outside her family would ever have reason to know that she existed.

## Notes and References

1. Karoline Patterson Bresenhan and Nancy O'Bryant Puentes, *Lone Stars: A Legacy of Texas Quilts, 1835–1935* (Austin, TX: University of Texas Press, 1986), 96–97.

2. Sarah is identified as Sally in the 1930 United States Federal Census for Gabe B. Lewellin. http://interactive.ancestry.com. According to the documentation data from the family, Sarah/Sally migrated to Texas with her family early in the 1880s. See: Bresenhan and Puentes, *Lone Stars*, 96–97.

3. Bresenhan and Puentes, *Lone Stars*, 96–97.

4. H. W. Brands, *Andrew Jackson: His Life and Times* (Anchor Books/Random House, Inc: New York, NY, 2006), 488–492, 536. The gold discoveries in Georgia were minimal in comparison to that of the California gold fields found in 1848. It is likely that for this reason, few general history books mention the existence of gold in Georgia and the role it played in Georgia's early history. B. J. Ramage, "Georgia and the Cherokees," *The American Historical Magazine and Tennessee Historical Society Quarterly* 7, no. 3 (1902): 199–208. Ramage describes in greater detail the interest white settlers took in acquiring Native American property held by members of the Cherokee tribe of Georgia. Agricultural land and the discovery of gold deposits figure prominently as motives. He describes in detail how, despite the best efforts to resist by the Cherokee land owners, state and federal politicians and officials were successful in dispossessing the original land owners and driving them from the state in the 1830s. Jon Meacham, *American Lion: Andrew Jackson in the White House* (New York: Random House, 2008), 91–97, 151–153, 203–205, 317–218. Meacham provides clear and objective narrative on Jackson's involvement in the effort to

dispossess and move the Cherokee from the state of Georgia. He makes clear that Jackson's motives had to do with national security and his view that the Cherokee needed to be removed for their own protection.

5. We know it as the "Trail of Tears," because of the consequential deaths and destitution of so many Native Americans.

6. According to the Georgia Property Tax Digests, 1878–1882, Elbert A. Beaird and family were living in Walker County, Georgia in the 871 Georgia Militia District and owned 160 acres of land valued at $600. A detailed listing shows that the aggregate value of their entire property was $1,164, including livestock and household goods. The range of property values on page 26 of this digest started at $30 for twenty acres and went as high as $1,800 for 300 acres. This suggests that the Beairds were likely closer to what we would now consider to be the middle class. They would have been among the yeomen farming class (middle class) of the Old South as described by Frank L. Owsley in *Plain Folk of the Old South,* which became a groundbreaking report on the agricultural and economic stratification of southern people before and after the Civil War. His work clarified and defined the yeomen farm class of the Old South and differentiated it from the poor and rich classes. See: Frank L. Owsley, *Plain Folk of the Old South* (Baton Rouge: Louisiana State University Press, 1949).

7. National Archives and Records Administration (NARA); *Carded Records Showing Military Service of Soldiers Who Fought in Confederate Organizations, compiled 1903–1927, documenting the period 1861–1865;* Catalog ID: 586957; Record Group #: 109; Roll #: 238.

8. Walker County is now included in the Chickamauga and Chattanooga National Military Park. See http://www.aboutnorthgeorgia.com/ang/Chickamauga_Battlefield.

9. Found in 1870 United States Federal Census for Elbert A. Beard (misspelling of Beaird), accessed through http://interactive.ancestry.com.

10. Found in 1880 United States Federal Census for Elbert Bayard (misspelling of Beaird/Beard) accessed through ancestry.com.

11. Found in 1880 United States Federal Census for Monroe Beard accessed through ancestry.com and 1880 United States Federal Census for Lula Beard; Year: 1880; Census Place: Precinct 1, Brown, Texas; Roll 1292; Family History Film: 1255292; Page: 366C; Enumeration District: 023. Accessed through ancestry.com. On this census record an alternative name for Monroe Beard is given as James Marion Beaird and Lula Beard is shown as a female member of the household, age twenty-six, which matches up with Sally's 1862 birth date. Lula's record from the 1880 census corroborates this, showing that she is living in Monroe Beard's household. Given all the evidence in these records, it is not a far stretch to imagine the name "Lula" to be a diminutive for the name Louisa, which was one of Sally's given names. Consequently, the author assumes that Lula and Sally Louise are the same person.

12. Texas, County Tax Rolls, 1846–1910, index and images, FamilySearch https://familysearch.org/pal:/MM9.1.1/VB9Q-GP1, E. A. Beaird, 1885.

13. Ancestry.com. Texas, Death Certificates, 1903–1982 [database online]. Provo, UT, USA: Ancestry.com Operations, Inc., 2013. Original data: Texas Department of State Health Services. Texas Death Certificates, 1903–1982. iArchives, Orem, Utah.

14. Bresenhan and Puentes, *Lone Stars,* 96.

15. Ancestry.com. Texas, Select County Marriage Index, 1837–1965 (database online).

16. Ancestry.com. Texas, County Tax Rolls, 1846–1910 (database online).

17. Prairie Windmill Quilt History and Research Chapter of the National Quilting Association, *Quilts of the Texas South Plains: A Sesquicentennial Exhibition, October 19, 1986–March 8, 1987* (The Ranching Heritage Center, The Museum, Texas Tech University: Lubbock, TX), 18.

18. T. R. Fehrenbach, *Lone Star: A History of Texas and the Texans,* (New York: MacMillan Publishing Company, 1968), 287.

19. R. Marshall Smith, "Migration of Georgians to Texas, 1820–1870," *The Georgia Historical Quarterly* 20 (Dec. 1936): 307–325, http://www.jstor.org/stable/40576460. Smith's article explains that the expulsion of Cherokee Indians from Georgia after the 1835 treaty ceding their lands to the U.S. government and their agreement to migrate to the west resulted in large tracts of land in Georgia available for settlement. This settlement activity continued in Georgia until just prior to the Civil War. Consequently, a very small number of Georgian individuals participated in immigration traffic to Texas. The 1845 annexation of Texas to the United States as the 28th state included some unique and confusing homesteading laws influenced by Spanish and Mexican laws, which had precedence and were more liberal particularly to women, especially widows of land owners. Thus, Texas became a desirable option for some potential Georgia immigrants. Financial panics in the 1870s were also a driving force in the decision to immigrate. See: Barbara J. Rozek, *Come to Texas: Attracting Immigrants, 1865–1915* (College Station, TX: Texas A&M Press, 2003). Rozek describes a variety of published documents promoting Texas as a good place to immigrate to. She describes and identifies articles and letters and "enticement literature" that were published in newspapers, almanacs, company pamphlets, real estate and railroad company promotional literature, and a number of other documents.

20. *Quilts of the Texas South Plains,* 18.

21. Year: 1900, Census Place: Justice Precinct 4, Brown, Texas, Roll: 1650; Page 8A, Enumeration District 0008; FHL microfilm: 1241615.

22. Sarah L. Lewellin. Austin, TX, USA: Texas Department of Health, State Vital Statistics Unit, Certificate number 21289, Found on Ancestry.com, *Texas Death Index, 1903–2000.*

23. Bresenhan and Puentes, *Lone Stars,* 96.

24. Ibid. In an email to the author dated April 8, 2015, Karey Bresenhan emphatically stated that she "saw two of these quilts with my own eyes! One is in the book, the other was in greens and golds."

25. Email from Bresenhan, April 8, 2015.

26. Bresenhan and Puentes, *Lone Stars,* 96.

27. Conversation with Sally Lewellin's great-grandson and his wife, Ronald and Gayle Dobbs, New Braunfels, TX, July 6, 2010.

28. Sally Beaird Lewellin, Sunburst. c. 1885. From Briscoe Center for American History, University of Texas at Austin, Texas Sesquicentennial Quilt Association, Texas Quilt Search. Published in *The Quilt Index,* http://www.quiltindex.org/fulldisplay.php?kid=4F-88-FA.

29. Marian Ann J. Montgomery, Ph.D., *Legacy of a Thousand Stitches: Quilts of the Museum of Texas Tech University* (Lubbock, TX: Museum of Texas Tech University, 2016), 40–41.

30. Prairie Windmill Quilt History and Research Chapter, National Quilting Association, *Quilts of the Texas South Plains: A Sesquicentennial Exhibition, October 19, 1986–March 8, 1987* (Lubbock, TX: Ranching Heritage Center, The Museum of Texas Tech University, 1987), 18.

31. *Quilts of the Texas South Plains*, 18.

32. The author of the narrative in *Quilts of the Texas South Plains* specified "agrimony orange" in describing the color. A search of the internet for "agrimony" used as a dye was not successful, but did find a number of sites specifying agrimony as an herb that "grows extensively throughout Europe, Canada and the United States." Several sites of use: www.webmd.com; www.mountainroseherbs.com; www.altnature.com. It is possible that the author of that quilt description may have been referring to antimony, a chemical used from antiquity to produce a variety of colors; in certain combinations it is toxic. Barbara Brackman, in her *Clues in the Calico,* refers to antimony orange and chrome orange both of which were available from the 1840s throughout the nineteenth century. She specifies that antimony orange was "discovered in 1817," and she gives a general range of 1840–1890 for purposes of dating antimony orange fabric. Barbara Brackman, *Clues in the Calico* (Charlottesville, VA: Howell Press, 1989), 69.

33. *Quilts of the Texas South Plains*, 18.

34. Florence C. Gould and Patricia N. Pando, "Women Homesteaders," *Handbook of Texas Online* (http://www:tshaonline.org/handbook/online/articles/pww05). Uploaded on June 15, 2010. Published by the Texas State Historical Association. This article focuses on women homesteaders in Texas and it details the difficulties women homesteaders faced. It also notes that "For women and men alike, making a livelihood from 160 acres or less would never have been easy," and that "larger tracts were usually needed for successful farming."

35. Rachel Jenkins, "Elkins, TX (Brown County," *Handbook of Texas Online* (http://www.tshaonline.org/handbook/online/articles/hve19). Published by the Texas State Historical Association.

36. "Elkins Cemetery in Brown County" (http://browncountyhistory.org/elkinsC.html), 4.

37. Ibid.

38. Lorene Bishop, "History of Camp Bowie," (www.brownwoodtexas.gov/323/History-of-Camp-Bowie) The only remaining evidence that the Community of Elkins existed is the Elkins Cemetery, which was established in 1876 and operated until 1939 when Camp Bowie was created. According to a citation describing the Elkins Cemetery, the cemetery dates to the establishment of the Live Oak Church in 1876. Burials were suspended between 1939 and 1946 when Camp Bowie was commissioned and built. Once decommissioned in 1946 some people returned to the community and the cemetery was reopened. (www.browncountyhistory.org/elkinsC.html)

39. Texas Department of Health, Bureau of Vital Statistictics, Standard Certificate of Death found at www.browncountytexasgenealogy.com.

40. The son, Archie Carl (or—inexplicably—"Carl A."), died in 1901 at age 14 and is buried in the Elkins Cemetery. In the 1900 Federal Census he is listed as Carl A Lewellin, age 13. Year:1900; Census Place: *Justice Precinct 4, Brown, Texas;* Roll: 1650; Page 8A; Enumeration District 0008; FHL microfilm: 1241615. The Find A Grave citation lists him as Archie Carl Lewellen with a death date of March 22, 1901. Ancestry.com. U.S., Find A Grave Index, 1600s–Current [database on-line]. Provo, UT, USA: Ancestry.com Operations, Inc., 2012.

41. Anita Zaleski Weinraub, ed., *Georgia Quilts: Piecing Together a History* (Athens, GA: The University of Georgia Press, 2006), 93. The museum collection accession number for this quilt is BHM 1988.56.1.

42. Ibid., 92. The accession number of the quilt is 1988.56.1.

43. Email from Tina Shadden, Registrar, Bartow History Museum, May 11, 2010, to Kathy Moore.

44. Attempts to locate Ms. Parham have had limited results. She was born Carrie Elizabeth Mosteller in 1929 in Cartersville, Bartow County, Georgia, to Joe A. Mosteller and Nannie L. Randolph Mosteller. She was still listed in Social Security records as Carrie Elizabeth Mosteller in 1943, but in January 1957 her name is listed in the records as Elizabeth M. Parham. She donated the quilt to the museum in Bartow County, Georgia, in 1988 when she was living in Mineral Wells, Texas. Available Social Security records indicate that she was still living in Mineral Wells in 1993, but in 1994 her address is listed in Birmingham, Alabama. She died December 4, 1997 and was buried in Oak Hill Cemetery, Cartersville, Bartow County, Georgia. Because of legal restrictions on access to census records before 1950, no census records are currently available for Elizabeth M. Parham, under that or any other name, making it impossible to find records of her husband or offspring. Therefore, it is not possible at this time to track her whereabouts or that of relatives during the years before she donated her quilt to the Bartow County Museum.

45. Polly Elkins, Starburst, c. 1850. Published in *The Quilt Index,* http://www.quiltindex. org/fulldisplay.php?kid=4C-83-1E2. Notes made by Bets Ramsey on a Quilts of Tennessee documentation form in October, 1984, cite Polly Elkins (born 1803) as the quiltmaker and the date made as circa 1850. Interestingly, her notes indicate that she originally estimated the date as circa 1870–1880, then upon reflection changed it to c. 1850, which makes sense given the maker's potential age in 1880. Ramsey further notes that "this quilt is like one I photographed at the home of Creed Bates, Signal Mt., TN." Copy of this documentation is in possession of the author and is available on the Quilt Index.

46. Email correspondence from Merikay Waldvogel to Kathy Moore, May 30, 2012.

47. Bets Ramsey and Merikay Waldvogel, *The Quilts of Tennessee: Images of Domestic Life Prior to 1930* (Nashville, TN: Rutledge Hill Press, 1986), 76. See footnote 28.

48. Current mileages by modern highways found on Google Maps.

49. Ramsey and Waldvogel, *The Quilts of Tennessee,* 69.

50. Lynne Z. Bassett and Jack Larkin, *Northern Comfort: New England's Early Quilts, 1780–1850* (Nashville, TN: Rutledge Hill Press, 1998), 61–62.

51. Year: 1910; Census Place: Justice Precinct 4, Brown, Texas; Roll T624_1535; Page 2A; Enumeration District: 0104; FHL microfilm:1375548.

52. Sally's father, Elbert A. Beaird, died April 26, 1918. Ancestry.com. U.S., Find a Grave Index, 1600s–Current (online database). Sally's mother, Susan A. Beaird, died December 28, 1922. Ancestry.com. U.S., Find a Grave Index, 1600s–Current (online database).

53. Kathleen McCrady, interview by Kathleen L. Moore, Austin, Texas, May 27, 2015. See also, Bresenhan and Puentes, dedication page. This book, *Lone Stars: A Legacy of Texas Quilts, 1836-1936,* is "the official catalog for the Texas Sesquicentennial Quilt Association's traveling exhibition."

54. Kathleen H. McCrady, *My Journey with Quilts* (Austin, TX: McCrady Enterprises, 2005), 29.

55. Lynne Z. Bassett, *Telltale Textiles: Quilts from the Historic Deerfield Collection* (Deerfield, Massachusetts: Historic Deerfield, Inc., 2003), 37, 62.

56. Lenice Ingram Bacon, *American Patchwork Quilts* (New York: Bonanza Books, 1980), 122.

57. Kenneth L. Ames, "The Stuff of Everyday Life: American Decorative Arts and House-hold Furnishings," in *Material Culture: A Research Guide,* ed. Thomas J. Schlereth (Lawrence, KS: University Press of Kansas), 79–112. Ames makes the point on page 80 that "things constitute one of the most significant classes of human behavior and accomplish-ment, and, therefore, one of the most valuable kinds of historical document." In this article, he also notes on page 87 that "objects reflect cultural values." Jules D. Prown notes that "objects made or modified by man reflect, consciously or unconsciously, directly or indirectly, the beliefs of individuals who made, commissioned, purchased, or used them, and by extension the beliefs of the larger society in which they belonged." Jules D. Prown, "Mind in Matter: An Introduction to Material Culture Theory and Method" in *Material Life in America, 1600–1860*, ed. Robert Blair St. George (Boston: Northeastern University Press, 1988), 1.

58. Prown discusses how the bias of survival can skew its value in the mind of the evalua-tor. He also warns against the dangers of letting our change in values and taste—what he refers to as a "degree-of-sophistication scale"—from one culture or generation to another to weight, or skew, our evaluation of the artifact. See: Prown, "Mind in Matter," 4.

59. Barbara Brackman. *Encyclopedia of Pieced Quilt Patterns* (Paducah, KY: American Quilter's Society, 1993), 410–421.

60. Bassett and Larkin, *Northern Comfort,* 61.

61.Linda Eaton, *Quilts in a Material World: Selections from the Winterthur Collection* (NY: Abrams, 2007), 10.

# Contributors

Lynne Zacek Bassett is an award-winning independent scholar specializing in historic costume and textiles. Among her recent quilt publications are *Massachusetts Quilts: Our Common Wealth* (2009), for which she was editor and primary author, and *Homefront & Battlefield: Quilts & Context in the Civil War* (2012), co-authored with Madelyn Shaw. Forthcoming is the International Quilt Study Center & Museum's *American Quilts in the Industrial Age, 1760–1870* (2017), for which Bassett wrote twenty-seven essays. Bassett holds a B.A. in American studies from Mount Holyoke College and an M.A. in costume and textile history from the University of Connecticut. She has been the guest (now adjunct) curator of costume & textiles for the Wadsworth Atheneum Museum of Art in Hartford, Connecticut, since 2007.

Dana Fobes Bowne is an independent textile researcher in Spokane, Washington. She was a contributor to *Quilts of Alaska: A Textile Album of the Last Frontier* (2001). Dana is a retired elementary school teacher who lived for many years in Fairbanks, Alaska. She has a B.A. in Spanish from the University of Washington, an M.Ed. in Curriculum and Instruction from the University of Alaska Fairbanks, and a graduate certificate in quilt studies from the University of Nebraska-Lincoln.

Deborah Cooney is a quilt historian, writer, and lecturer. She has made presentations at DAR Museum and Colonial Williamsburg symposia, and spoken on various topics of quilt history. She has contributed to several publications, including the DAR's *Eye on Elegance* exhibition catalogue and *Blanket Statements.* Debby worked on several quilt documentation projects in Pennsylvania and Virginia, and served six years on the AQSG board of directors. She did her graduate work at the University of Wisconsin, Madison.

Dale Drake is an independent quilt researcher and holds a B.S. in computer technology from Purdue University. She has been active in local history, serving as Morgan County (Indiana) Historian and writing a local news-paper column. She co-edited An *Index to Records of the Indiana Soldiers' and Sailors' Children's Home in the Indiana State Archives,* and continues to research Indiana families as a professional genealogist. She began quilting in the early 1990s, and joined AQSG and the Midwest Fabric Study Group in 2004. She serves as Collections Chair of the Quilters Hall of Fame, restores quilts, teaches hand quiltmaking techniques and tatting, and lectures on quilt history and vintage quilt care.

Anita B. Loscalzo, an independent quilt historian and exhibition curator, is the former curator of the New England Quilt Museum in Lowell, Massa-chusetts. She received her B.A. in art history from the University of Penn-sylvania, an M.S. in library science from Drexel University, and an M.A. in textiles, quilt & museum studies from the University of Nebraska-Lincoln. Prior to her career switch in 2004, Ms. Loscalzo worked for thirty years as a librarian in art and medical libraries and rare book collections. As well as being a member of AQSG and having served on its Board, she is a member of the Quilt Alliance, the British Quilt Study Group, and the Costume Society of America. Loscalzo has published previously in *Uncoverings* and *Quilt Studies.*

Rachel May is the author of three books, including *Quilting with a Modern Slant,* a Library Journal and Amazon.com Best Book of 2014. Her forth-coming book, *Stitches in Time,* is a work of creative nonfiction that tells the story of the Crouch-Cushman family and the people they enslaved. She is an Assistant Professor of English at Northern Michigan University.

Ronda Harrell McAllen is an independent quilt scholar and genealogist specializing in Baltimore Album quilts and Maryland history. She has presented at Colonial Williamsburg, the DAR symposium, as well as the American Quilt Study Group. Her paper "Jewish Baltimore Album Quilts" was published in *Uncoverings* 2006. McAllen has worked with numerous authors and quilt scholars on the origins and understanding of early American quilts and their makers.

Kathy Moore received an M.A. in textile history with an emphasis on quilt studies from the University of Nebraska-Lincoln in 2005. She is a researcher and lecturer, and co-author of *Home on the Plains: Quilts and the Sod House Experience* (2011). Since retiring and moving to central Texas, Moore has been a volunteer in collections care and conservation for the quilt collection at the Briscoe Center for American History at the University of Texas, Austin. She is a long-standing member of AQSG, having just completed two terms of office on the Board of Directors. She is the program chairperson for the Lone Star Quilt Study group and was selected as the Faith P. and Charles L. Bybee Foundation and Texas Quilt Museum's Bybee Scholar for 2016.

Linda Welters is Professor of Textiles, Fashion Merchandising and Design at the University of Rhode Island. She has published articles and books on fashion, European folk dress, archaeological textiles, and American quilts. She directed the Rhode Island Quilt Documentation Project and co-edited *Down by the Old Mill Stream: Quilts in Rhode Island* with Margaret Ordoñez. Dr. Welters has received a number of honors, including a Legacy Society Award from the University of Minnesota, and the University of Rhode Island Foundation Scholarly Excellence Award. She was named a Fellow of the Costume Society of America in 2004 and the International Textile and Apparel Association's Distinguished Scholar in 2002. She both makes and collects quilts.

# Index

St. Louis Fancy Work Company 149
Surinam 42, 55, 66
Sweden/Swedish 151
Syria/Syrian 160

Taylor, Zachary 132, 133
Temperance Movement (see Reform)
Tennessee 160, 173, 184, 185, 186, 187, 188, 192
Texas 173, 174, 175, 176, 177, 178, 179, 182, 184, 185, 187, 188, 189, 192, 195
Textile industry (see industrialization)
Trade 13, 14, 15, 19, 20, 21, 22, 23, 28, 37, 38, 41, 42, 44, 47, 54, 55, 75, 77, 103, 153, 155, 156, 158, 164, 184
  Triangle trade 21, 54, 55, 59
Tradition 69, 73, 76, 77, 79, 85, 91, 92, 93, 94, 95, 96,
Trimble, Hannah Mary **110,** 112, 114, 115
Trousseau (see Marriage)
Tuscany (see Italy)

University of South Carolina 38
University of Rhode Island 37, 38, 44, 48, 53, 58, 59, 61, 63, 66

Venice (see Italy)
Vermilionville Historic Village 76
Vermont 160
Virginia 20, 131, 146, 156, 160

Wadsworth Atheneum Museum of Art 25, 26, 62, 63
Wales 23
War of 1812 103, 131, 132, 164
Washington, George 103, 148
Washington, Martha 148
Washington State
  Spokane 7, 8, 18

Watts, Isaac 127
Webster, Marie 146
Wesley, John 126
West Indies 41, 53, 54, 59, 155
West Virginia 192
Williams, Maria Bond Wehner 110, 114, 117
Women's Rights 103, 135
World War I 57
World War II 183

# In Appreciation

The American Quilt Study Group expresses sincere appreciation to the following for their substantial support of Seminar presentations and underwriting of papers presented in this volume.

Anonymous

Kathryn & Larry Bernstein

Theodore H. and Lynda Salter Chenoweth

Eastern Shore Quilt Study Group and Antique Quilt & Vintage Dating Club in memory of Cinda Cawley

Marianne Fons

Friends of Gail Hand in memory of Gail Hand

The Robert & Ardis James Foundation

Lone Star Quilt Study Group

Midwest Fabric Study Group in honor of Sharon Pinka

Professional Association of Appraisers-Quilted Textiles (PAAQT)

Washington Quilt Study Group

Jill Wilson

# Color Plates

Color plate 1. Quilt top #1, Hexagon Mosaic, "Planned and sewn by Dr. and Mrs. Hasell Crouch." Cotton. 84" x 83" Historic Textile and Costume Collection, University of Rhode Island, gift of Franklin R. Cushman 1952.63.124.

Color plate 2. Quilt top #2, constructed in part by Franklin R. Cushman. Cotton. 98" x 60". Historic Textile and Costume Collection, University of Rhode Island, gift of Franklin R. Cushman, 1952.63.125.

Color plate 3. Acadian cotonnade quilt made by Eve Vidrine Thompson (Laf Sci Thompson in the appendices), c. 1930, 88 x 58 inches, Lafayette Science Museum 1985.3c.1950. Photograph courtesy of Lafayette Science Museum.

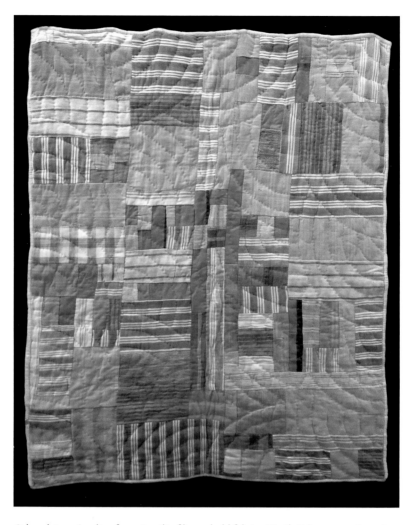

Color plate 4. Acadian format quilt of household fabrics (Erath #1), c. 1970, 62 x 46 inches, Acadian Museum, Erath, Louisiana. Photograph by the author.

Color plate 5. Early Designer I blocks, one dated 1846. Many motifs are composed of multiple pieces in several layers. Cotton, 86 x 84 inches, Daughters of the American Revolution Museum 98.31.

Color plate 6. Baltimore Presentation quilt, c. 1849. Cotton, 106 ¼ x 103 ¾ inches. Metropolitan Museum of Art, NY, 1974.24.

Color plate 7. Baltimore Album quilt made for Rev. Elias Heiner by women of his First German Reformed congregation in 1848. Four elaborate blocks are Designer I early style, the cornucopia in mature style. Cotton, 106 x 106 inches. Courtesy of Elly Sienkiewicz.

Color plate 8. Botanical Album Quilt, made by Cinthia Arsworth, Baltimore, Maryland, 1840–1845. Philadelphia Museum of Art, Gift of Mr. and Mrs. Percival Armitage, 1942-4-1.

Color plate 9. Mariner's Compass quilt, probably American, circa 1840–1860.
International Quilt Study Center & Museum, University of Nebraska-Lincoln,
2008.040.0193.

Color plate 10. Sunburst quilt by Sally Beaird Lewellin, Elkins Community, Brown County, Texas, c. 1885, 62 x 78 inches, private collection. Photograph by Matthew Lawrence McCoy.